THE PRACTICAL PROPHET

Pastoral Writings

Reflection on Ministry[*]

It helps, now and then, to step back and take a long view.

The Kingdom of God is not only beyond our efforts,
it is even beyond our vision.

We accomplish in our lifetime only a tiny fraction
of the magnificent enterprise that is God's work.
Nothing we do is complete, which is a way of saying
that the Kingdom always lies beyond us.
No statement says all that could be said.
No prayer fully expresses our faith.
No confession brings perfection.
No pastoral visit brings wholeness.
No program accomplishes the Church's mission.
No set of goals and objectives includes everything.

This is what we are about:
We plant the seeds that one day will grow.
We water seeds already planted, knowing that they hold future
   promise.

We lay foundations that will need further development.
We provide yeast that produces effects far beyond our capabilities.

We cannot do everything,
and there is a sense of liberation in realizing that.
This enables us to do something, and to do it very well.
It may be incomplete, but it is a beginning, a step along the way,
an opportunity for the Lord's grace to enter and do the rest.
We may never see the end results,
but that is the difference between the master builder and the
   worker.

We are workers, not master builders; ministers not messiahs.
We are prophets of a future not our own.

---

[*]Often called the "Archbishop Romero Prayer" and later thought to be by Cardinal John Dearden, this was actually authored by Ken Untener when he worked with Cardinal Dearden in Detroit.

THE PRACTICAL PROPHET

Pastoral Writings

Bishop Ken Untener

INTRODUCED BY
Elizabeth Picken, CJ,
Jeffrey Donner, and
Walter L. Farrell, SJ

FOREWORD BY
the Most Reverend Joseph L. Imesch

Paulist Press
New York/Mahwah, NJ

Cover design by Stefan Killen
Book design by Lynn Else

Library of Congress Cataloging-in-Publication Data

Untener, Ken, 1937–
    The practical prophet : pastoral writings / Bishop Ken Untener ; introduced by Elizabeth Picken, Jeffrey Donner, and Walter L. Farrell.
        p.   cm.
    ISBN 0-8091-4429-8 (alk. paper)
    1. Pastoral theology—Catholic Church. I. Title.
BX1913.U58 2007
253—dc22

                                                        2006034092

Published by Paulist Press
997 Macarthur Boulevard
Mahwah, New Jersey 07430

www.paulistpress.com

Printed and bound in the
United States of America

Contents

Acknowledgments

"Local Church and Universal Church," *America*, October 13, 1984. © 1984.

"If a Pope Resigns," *America*, March 25, 2000. © 2000.

"Cardinal Dearden: A Gentleman of the Church," *America*, November 26, 1988. © 1988.

"How Bishops Talk," *America*, October 19, 1996. © 1996.

All rights reserved. Reprinted with permission of America Press. For subscription information, visit www.americamagazine.org.

"Forum: The Ordination of Women," *Worship*, January 1991. Reprinted with permission.

"Is the Church in Decline: An Optimistic Bishop Says 'No.'" Copyright Summer 1999, CHURCH Magazine. Published by the National Pastoral Life Center, 18 Bleecker Street, New York, NY 10012. Used with permission. Subscription: $33 a year. Web: www.nlpc.org.

"'Humanae Vitae': What Has It Done to Us? And What Is to Be Done Now?" © 1993 Commonweal Foundation, reprinted with permission. For subscriptions: www.commonwealmagazine.org.

"The Lord Hears the Cry of the Poor," *Millenium Monthly*, September 1999.

"What Catholics Believe about the End of the World," *Catholic Update*, September 1993.

Reprinted with permission of St. Anthony Messenger Press.

List of Abbreviations

Documents

CCC   *Catechism of the Catholic Church:* 2nd edition, corrected by John Paul II for the English translation, September 8, 1997 (first published in English, 1995)

CD   *Christus Dominus:* Decree on the Pastoral Office of Bishops in the Church, October 28, 1965

CDF   Congregation for the Doctrine of the Faith, reorganized by Paul VI, December 7, 1965

CIC   *Codex Juris Canonici:* The Code of Canon Law, 1983 (revision of 1917 Code)

Denz.   *Enchiridion Symbolorum,* H. Denzinger (collection of church documents), 32nd edition, 1963

ES   *Ecclesiam Suam:* Encyclical of Paul VI, August 6, 1964

GIRM   *General Instruction on the Roman Missal,* Paul VI, 1975, 4th edition; new revised edition 2003

GS   *Gaudium et Spes:* Pastoral Constitution on the Church in the Modern World, December 7, 1965

HV   *Humanae Vitae:* Encyclical of Pope Paul VI on the Regulation of Birth, July 25, 1968

LG   *Lumen Gentium:* Dogmatic Constitution on the Church, November 21, 1964

MD   *Mediator Dei:* Encyclical of Pius XII, November 20, 1947

PO   *Presbyterorum Ordinis:* Decree on the Life and Ministry of Priests, December 7, 1965

SC *Sacrosanctum Concilium:* Constitution on the Sacred Liturgy, December 4, 1963

UUS *Ut Unum Sint:* Encyclical "That They May Be One" by John Paul II, 1995

Organizations

ARCIC Anglican-Roman Catholic International Commission (sponsored by Pope Paul VI and Dr. Michael Ramsey, Archbishop of Canterbury, in 1970)

NCCB/USCC National Conference of Catholic Bishops and United States Catholic Conference (organizational names prior to combining the two organizations into a reorganized USCCB, July 1, 2001)

USCCB United States Conference of Catholic Bishops

Preface

Bishop Kenneth Untener served the diocese of Saginaw, Michigan, for nearly twenty-five years until his death from complications of leukemia on March 27, 2004. Shortly afterward, Father Tom Sutton, then the administrator of the diocese, called Untener's "theology squad" together and proposed that a book be published of his writings that would reflect his creative pastoral theology, his understanding of the mission of the church, and how he viewed his role as a diocesan bishop.

The idea was not hard to sell to the group. This "theology squad," as Untener called it, was a group of seven theologians—religious women and priests, most of them also pastors—whom he called together four or five times a year throughout his ministry to advise him and comment on a wide range of topics of interest to him: liturgy, preaching, social justice, youth and lay ministry, scripture, ecclesiology, and so on. Nearly always, these meetings were occasioned by an article he was working on for *America* magazine or *U.S. Catholic*, a retreat for priests or series of talks he was preparing, or a pastoral letter to the diocese he wanted to compose.

The meetings were not hard to attend. After nearly a quarter century of them, the group members knew they were in for a treat, a lively and incisive discussion (always including dinner) with one of the most thoughtful, creative, and distinguished bishops ever to come from the church in the United States.

Besides his doctoral dissertation on Yves Congar, Untener only wrote two other full-length books, one on improving Sunday liturgy and the other on preaching. Nonetheless, he was a prolific writer of articles, talks, entire commentaries on the gospels, homilies, and so on. The reason was simple: He was one of the most sought-after speakers in the country. All of his published writing is now archived at the library of the University of Notre Dame.

People all over the United States and other countries have become avid readers of Untener's "little books," prayerful reflections on the scriptures of the liturgical seasons, which, even after his death, continue to sell more than 2.5 million copies a year. Yet, what most have not been exposed to is the depth and range of his thought and reflection. This first collection of his writing is a small step in helping to fill that need.

By its nature, a collection of different writings lacks the focus and synthesis of a single, longer work. Nonetheless, the reader will find here the consistency of view and the unity of theme and vision that were the hallmark of Untener's work. No matter what topic he addressed, he was always relating it to and seeing its implications for many others. His was, without a doubt, one of the finest systematic minds at work in the church today, concerned solely for the spread of the gospel and the revitalization of the church he so loved.

This pastoral concern was the origin of Untener's work. It led him to his single, perhaps most important insight: The rich tradition of the church was not a dead letter, a collection of doctrines, rituals, and practices simply to be repeated. It was, rather, a storehouse of wisdom, a chest of treasures to be opened and used to help the healing of a broken yet hopeful world. He saw his own work through the same lens: He was, simply, a minister of the church in service to the reign of God.

In time, a proper biography of this extraordinary servant will need to be written. For now, we have this collection of his words. They have been grouped in individual chapters related to their overall themes. For context, each chapter begins with a short introduction by Sister Elizabeth Picken, CJ, a member of Untener's "theology squad." A good friend of Untener's, Bishop Joseph L. Imesch of Joliet, Illinois, has graciously written a Foreword to the collection.

Bishop Untener left the "theology squad" no instructions or expressed hopes for the publication of this book. Yet, we know he would have liked nothing more than that his own published reflections would continue to inspire equal reflections in the church for the sake of its mission and ministry. May this collection serve this good purpose.

Jeffrey Donner, Pastor of St. Mary Parish, Midland, Michigan
May 13, 2005, Eve of the Feast of St. Matthias, Apostle*

---

*Fr. Jeffrey Donner wrote this preface in 2004, while he was pastor of St. Mary University Parish, Mount Pleasant, Michigan. On March 4, 2006, while celebrating the Saturday evening Mass for Sacred Heart Parish, Gladwin, where he had been serving as pastor since the summer of 2005, Jeff suffered a massive heart attack. He died the same evening. The diocese mourned the loss of this faith-filled and gifted pastor, musician, writer, theologian, and teacher.

Foreword

When I was invited to write the foreword to this compilation of writings of Bishop Ken Untener, I was honored and pleased. Ken and I had been close friends for more than forty years, and I thought that this would be an easy thing to do and a great way to remember a dear friend.

I was wrong. This is not an easy thing to do, not because it is difficult to find things to say about him, but because there are too many things to say, a number of which are probably best saved for a late-evening reminiscing session. The difficult thing is to try to capture the spirit of a person who was an innovative leader, a profound thinker, a thought-provoking homilist, an intense competitor, a theologian who could speak not only to fellow theologians but also to the average person, a prankster, a chocolate maker, a contest organizer, a challenging opponent, a clerical Victor Borge, a man of humor and quick wit, a compassionate shepherd, a constant friend, and so much more, known to his family, his friends, and his God.

Writing about Ken is like reading the instructions on the carton of a child's Christmas toy: "some assembly required." Those words indicate that this is not going to be an easy task, and so it is with writing about Ken.

He grew up in a family of nine, the seventh child, the fourth boy, and lived on an island in the Detroit River, Belle Isle. It was a recreational area on the lower east side of Detroit. His father was in charge of the canoe shelter. Growing up in a family of four sisters and four brothers helps to keep one humble. Ken learned that lesson early on and lived it throughout his life. He never forgot from whence he came.

Ken was involved in athletics from early on, though his activity was limited to sports that did not require a great deal of distance running. From birth his right leg was shorter than his left, requiring him to wear a built-up shoe. Later, while in the seminary, he broke his leg while playing handball, a sport in which he was especially proficient.

The doctor recommended that the leg be amputated, and so it was, just below the knee. The prosthesis soon became a part of him. He rarely talked about it, but never tried to hide it either. When people saw him playing hockey or golf, and, yes, even skiing, they were amazed to learn of his handicap. I think that is the wrong word to use when talking about Ken. For him, it was never a handicap; it was more of an advantage. If you felt sorry for him in a competition, it was all over—for you.

People still smile remembering the hockey game when, after a particularly hard check, he came off the ice with his leg dangling. Spectators gasped, but were even more astonished when he returned to the ice a few minutes later, skating as if nothing had happened.

I recall the time we were playing golf in northern Michigan. He hit his drive in a stand of pine trees on the right side of the fairway, something that he did not infrequently. While searching for his ball, he was stung by a bee. That is when he learned that he was allergic to bee stings. Within a few minutes he needed to leave and be taken to the hospital. When he came back later that evening, his comment was, "How in the world did that bee know what leg to sting?" Sand traps were a bonus for him, because he said he only had to shake the sand out of one shoe! His athletic activity was not limited to his younger years. In his fifties and sixties he continued to play hockey, racquetball, and handball.

Ken attended the local parish elementary and high school, St. Charles. After eight years in the seminary, he was ordained a priest. He spent two years as a parochial vicar before serving as assistant vicar for clergy for five years. In 1969 he was sent to Rome and attended the Gregorian University, from which he received a doctorate in sacred theology. His four-hundred-plus-page thesis was entitled *The Church–World Relationship According to the Writings of Yves Congar, OP*. His moderator was René Latourelle, SJ. Both of these men had a significant influence on Ken's priestly life and, later, in his episcopal ministry.

When Ken returned to Detroit, he was named rector of St. John Provincial Seminary in Plymouth, Michigan. During that time he also served as teacher of homiletics. In November 1980 he was ordained diocesan bishop of Saginaw, but not until after a number of doubtful days and two trips to Rome to clarify some concerns.

He set the theme for his episcopal ministry at his Mass of Ordination, when he introduced himself to the people of Saginaw with, "Hi, I'm Ken. I'm here to be your waiter." To him, ministry was service, especially his episcopal ministry.

Shortly after his arrival as bishop, he sold the episcopal residence and began living in rectories, three months at a time, more than sixty of them over the next twenty-four years. This dizzying sequence of domiciles found him sometimes waking up not knowing where he was.

The people of Saginaw soon found that their bishop was different in a number of ways. The Sunday gospels were delivered from memory, thus becoming a true narrative. He did it, he said, because he was a poor reader! His homilies were memorable, not only because of their brevity—something indeed unusual for a bishop—but for their content. He had the knack of using examples that everyone could relate to because they themselves had had a similar experience. When people left the church, they knew what point he was trying to make and could remember the examples he used, even years later.

Ken was in great demand as a preacher and retreat master for priests, so much so that he had to limit his retreats to three a year. In addition, he was a frequent speaker at various conferences, seminars, and convocations. He would often play the piano at some of these events, but never just for entertainment, always to teach a lesson. He often used the style of a concert pianist performing for the audience. This was followed by a sing-along, in which people participated. He used these as examples of what Mass ought to be, not a solo performance by the priest, but a prayer by all of the people.

He wrote numerous articles for various church periodicals, always thought-provoking, frequently challenging or questioning, but always respectful.

Many people came to know Ken through reading one of his "little books." They were written for the seasons of Advent, Lent, and Easter, along with two reflection books on stewardship. Word about the "little books" soon spread, and more than a million copies were being sold for each season. They were perfect examples of his homiletic style. The scriptures were unfolded, examples from daily life were frequently given, and finally a challenge or an encouragement was presented to make that day a memorable one.

While he did not often speak at the bishops' meetings, Ken was one of the people to whom the bishops listened intently when he did. There were many areas of church life that he questioned, with the intent not of bringing about a change, but rather of finding a better way to clarify a teaching or a practice.

His contributions in this book are just a small sample of his writings on any number of topics. It was not just the depth of his writings, it was also the breadth. In reading them you will become aware of his crisp style of writing, his judicious choice of words, and his brevity. He does not put you to sleep with long-winded passages, but keeps you awake with unexpected questions.

Ken was a deeply spiritual man without being overly pious, both a teacher and a student, a man of learning, a pastor who was a theologian and a theologian who was a pastor, a man of reflection, a scholar. He used understandable language and examples, a teacher who taught by making the reader think, one who taught by asking questions, not answering them.

At the outset I said this would be a difficult task. Even if I wrote more, words would not begin to describe Ken adequately. A song that keeps running through my mind is "Maria" from *The Sound of Music*. Among the phrases describing Maria are two: "How do you keep a wave upon the sand?" and "How do you hold a moonbeam in your hand?" How do you describe a Ken Untener? Perhaps he himself summed it up best: "Hi, I'm Ken, your waiter."

The Most Reverend Joseph L. Imesch
Bishop of Joliet, Illinois

1

Vision and Creative Imagination

Introduction

"There was a time when I wanted to be the master builder, the architect. But more and more I have come to realize that my task is to craft something small, something good, that the master builder will use."[1]

Ken Untener was bishop of Saginaw for twenty-four years. A quarter of a century is a long time to be a bishop. The gospel of the Mass for his ordination to the priesthood in 1963 was Christ's commission to Peter, "feed my sheep." Ordained a bishop in 1980, his vision of church and a leadership role in it had remained essentially unchanged. He selected again the gospel text of Christ's commission to Peter, "feed my sheep." His crest as bishop bore the motto "that they may have life" from John's Gospel.

Bishop Ken's vision of a shepherd as one that "leads sheep out to pasture rather than bringing them into the fold" gradually focused on, through circumstances and events that affected the Diocese of Saginaw, the church in the United States and in the world at large. His vision of church centered on the well-being and growth in discipleship of the whole people of God. Some bishops focus on the first half of St. Augustine's famous statement: "For you I am a bishop; with you I am a Christian." Ken focused on the second half.

A creative mind, keen insights, a way with words, and a gentle, persuasive voice made Bishop Ken a popular speaker and visionary leader within and beyond the church of Saginaw.

Bishop Ken discovered early in ministry that he had a lot to learn about shepherding the church of Saginaw. At his second diocesan priests' assembly, an outside facilitator led the assembly of priests to assess the diocese and the leadership of its bishop. They openly told him where he was lacking in communication and leadership. They had already benefited from a good bishop in Francis

Reh, who preceded Bishop Ken. They were accustomed to frankness. Ken was humble. He could grow, and he treasured the difficult experience. Afterward, he remarked that CEOs in the business world pay thousands for such frank assessments in order to succeed in less important endeavors. The priests learned, too, from Bishop Ken's freer style of leadership.

Prior to becoming bishop, Ken had written a book, *The Sunday Liturgy Can Be Better!*, that set forth principles and practical suggestions for ministers and planners of Sunday liturgy. He now set about putting vision into practice with Mass and the sacraments in the Diocese of Saginaw, critiquing with pastors and ministers the celebration of parish Mass and sacraments, especially sacraments of initiation, through videos, tapes, and teachings in varied settings. His goal was greater participation from laity as decreed in the Vatican II Constitution on the Sacred Liturgy No. 14.

During later years Bishop Ken's emphasis shifted to the Word as the primary task of the bishop. It was in this later period that he appointed an administrator of the diocese so that he could spend more time on the essential task of a bishop, to teach and preach the Word. In that period he wrote, together with a number of published articles, his book *Preaching Better*, a practical theology of preaching gained through interaction with small groups of those engaged in preaching. He also began to write the "little books," which followed the liturgical seasons and encouraged the whole diocese to pray the scriptures daily in harmony with the seasons. The "little books" spread far beyond the diocese to reach a distribution of 2.8 million copies. He also introduced four-minute teachings, given before or at the end of Mass, to introduce Sunday assemblies to "painless" and gradual catechesis for adults. We pick these topics up in later chapters.

Bishop Untener did not enjoy confrontation. Still, he became the object of national and local controversy at times because of his positions on explosive church issues such as ordination of married men, the role of women in the church, birth control, liturgical practices, and an innovative practice of educating seminarians at national universities together with local diocesan formation. He expanded education and formation of laity to include advanced degrees for pastoral ministry. He understood profoundly that *all* of the faithful are the church, not the hierarchy.

In civic and ecumenical communities he was a leader: for the advancement of ethics and values for Dow Chemical, Midland, and the Bay Medical Association. He participated in Habitat for Humanity and Ezekiel ecumenical projects, and met frequently with the leaders of other church groups of the area.

Optimistic by nature and grace, Ken often imaged the church as a young sapling in the history of the world and universe, not old or even in the prime of its life, but very young. This evolutionary view prevented Ken from getting too discouraged when he perceived the church retreat from insights of the Second Vatican Council rather than move forward. He believed that the inevitable swing of the pendulum would bring the church once again to develop those richer insights of the council.

Note

1. "What a Prophet Does and Does Not Do," *Origins* 21/2 (May 23, 1991), 39.

The Differing Visions of Camelot and the Magnificat

Origins 16/13 (September 11, 1986)

The church has related to the world differently in past ages. Thus, the newness of the way outlined in the Second Vatican Council's Constitution on the Church in the Modern World should not be underestimated, said Bishop Kenneth Untener of Saginaw, Michigan, in an address to the August 10 to 14 convention in St Louis, Missouri, of the Conference of Major Superiors of Men. "The church has never attempted to relate to the world as we are today.... I think we have to come to terms with the newness of this," Untener told his audience. "The shaping of this world is part of the process of shaping the kingdom," Untener added. Thus, he said, "those who tell us to leave history alone and deal only with 'church matters' miss the whole point of the incarnation and fail to understand the very nature of the church itself." But, he said, "people are puzzled by what the church is doing....People such as you and I have journeyed through this new understanding of the relationship of the church to the world, but many, many people have not.... When we present them with conclusions and not the journey, they are baffled. We need to help them make the same journey, for it cuts through new territory." The convention's theme was "Discipleship: Mission for the Reign of God."

I will be approaching this talk from the point of view of ecclesiology. I will point out some aspects of the church—ecclesiological

6

principles, if you wish to call them that—and then offer some reflections in the light of the theme of this assembly.

I will call to mind the fact that the practical implications vary somewhat for different people within the church. While all church members share the basic calling to live faith, hope, and love, the specific purpose of each way of life differs. Laity (I use that term to distinguish them not only from the ordained, but from religious as well) would describe the purpose of their Christian life differently than priests or religious.

Furthermore, I think that we need to distinguish more than we have the way of life and the spirituality of diocesan priests as contrasted with religious. Further still, religious would distinguish the purposes of their ways of life among themselves. You even use different Latin expressions to capture the distinctive purpose of your life: *Solus Deus, Ora et Labora, Contemplata Aliis Tradere,* or *Contemplativus in Actione.* When you speak of the relationship of a particular Christian life to preparing for the kingdom of God and when you speak of practical implications, you must take into account the different "ways of life" within the church.

In setting forth my pastoral reflections I will not attempt to explain how these might differ for a contemplative, a Benedictine monk, a Dominican, a Jesuit, a diocesan priest, or a layperson, but you must keep those in mind. And as I speak, I have religious particularly in mind.

Relationship of the Pilgrim Church to the Kingdom

One of the most popular descriptions of the church since Vatican II is "pilgrim church." It has a nice ring to it and presents a good image of disciples journeying in the footsteps of the Lord. The story of how that became part of *Lumen Gentium* is an interesting one.

A chapter on the eschatological character of the church was not part of the original outline of the Constitution on the Church.

In the course of the development of the document, John XXIII asked that something about the veneration of the saints be included. This introduced an awareness of the eschatological dynamism of the church and set in motion a chain of events that resulted in chapter 7 of *Lumen Gentium*, titled "The Eschatological Nature of the Pilgrim Church and Her Union with the Heavenly Church." This represents one of the significant shifts in the way we view the church today—as something not yet "finished," but moving toward and pointing toward the kingdom of God.

At first, the title of the chapter spoke of the "Eschatological Nature of Our Calling..." and thus introduced the concept of the incompleteness and sinfulness of church members rather than of the church itself. This individualistic tone was criticized, and it was changed to read "The Eschatological Nature of the Pilgrim Church...." It is a short chapter, with two articles about eschatology as such and two articles about the saints. Nonetheless, it has had far-reaching effects. Listen to this paragraph from that chapter:

> Already the final age of the world is with us (cf. 1 Cor. 10:11) and the renewal of the world is irrevocably under way; it is even now anticipated in a certain real way; for the church on earth is endowed already with a sanctity that is real though imperfect. However, until there be realized new heavens and a new earth in which justice dwells (cf. 2 Pt. 3:13) the pilgrim church, in its sacraments and institutions, which belong to this present age, carries the mark of this world which will pass, and she herself takes her place among the creatures which groan and travail yet and await the revelation of sons of God (cf. Rom. 8:19–22) (no. 48).

That is not new, but the emphasis is, also the approach. We used to speak of it when we described the church militant, the church suffering, and the church triumphant. Somehow that did not capture, as this chapter does, the fact that the redemptive grace of Christ, which is rooted in the church, engulfs every dimension of human existence and destines the cosmos toward the kingdom. We are moving toward something that has not arrived, not been completed, and the church is part of that movement. The church is part of what will "pass away" and become transfigured, incorporated into the kingdom.

Avery Dulles, in the seventh chapter of his book *Models of the Church*, points out that this does not quite mean that the church is something temporary, but at the end of time it will "truly come into its own." He then goes on to say:

> The final coming of the kingdom, I believe, will be the work of God, dependent on his initiative. But it seems likely that, as Rahner suggests, the parousia will not occur until human effort "has gone to its very limits and so is burst open by salvation from above by developing its own powers." The coming of the kingdom will not be the destruction but the fulfillment of the church. More than this, it will be the future of the world, insofar as God's gracious power is at work far beyond the horizons of the institutional church. The final consummation will transcend the dichotomy between church and world. The glorious, triumphant church will be indivisibly united with the renewed cosmos, "the new heavens and the new earth" foreseen by the prophets. And the triumph will not be that of a church resting on its own laurels, but that of Christ who triumphs in his church in spite of our weakness and sinfulness.

What are some of the pastoral implications of all this? I will offer several.

1. We must not claim too confidently to have answers. As sort of an aside, I would like to point out that this applies to things with the church as well as to things that have to do with the world. The church that we read about in the Acts of the Apostles was a church journeying through history under the leadership of the risen Christ, with many "gaps" in its understanding. The church of today is no different. Consider some of the things within the church that we face today with uncertainty—basic sacramental practices such as the appropriate age for confirmation, the frequency and way of celebrating the sacrament of reconciliation. There are other fundamental questions ranging from the ordination of women to the union of Christians to christology itself.

The church would be much more credible if it acknowledged the gaps and was willing to speak with less certainty. This does not mean that we lie dead in the water, unable to manage until we have the final answer. As with any family, we have to "make do" as we journey along. But our credibility would be enhanced by less certainty. I remember Cardinal Richard Cushing, during the hubbub of those days just after *Humanae Vitae*, who found his own way of applying this pastoral principle by making use of—of all the things for him—a Latin phrase. He said something like, "Now look, '*Roma locuta, causa finita*'—at least for the time being!"

The same must be true of the way we deal with those things that have to do with our mission to the world. I believe that the U.S. bishops have recently modeled this approach in their pastoral letter on peace and in the one being drafted on economics. We don't claim to have definitive answers to peace in a sinful world or the distribution of our resources as we journey toward the kingdom. Despite this, there are values that must be honored and lived, and these we preach.

Sometimes, I am afraid, we imply that if people lived by gospel values, everything would fit together in perfect harmony. That is not true, and eschatology teaches us that this is not true. We must tell people to hold to the values even when they do not make life easier or provide solutions. While preaching against abortion, we must not imply that the pregnant high-school sophomore who does not have an abortion will have a rosy path. While preaching against capital punishment, we must not give the impression that we will solve the problem of crime. Instead, we must openly declare that, short of the kingdom, things do not and will not always fit together. We are not giving solutions to complex problems. We are giving values to be lived along the way in the belief that if we live them, the kingdom comes closer. If you follow the gospel, everything will not work out—we will have to find a way to make do for the time being. We have to live with the fact that the gospel does not fully fit in this "time between." We have to live with ambiguity and incompleteness, and we have to be honest about this when we preach.

2. We have to be able to go "beyond the categories" that exist as we journey along.

You'd have to know Clem Kern. He was a beloved—legendary—priest of inner-city Detroit who would be a saint by acclamation today, made so by the rich and the poor, liberals and conservatives, Catholics and non-Catholics. You'd have to know him, so I won't try to describe him. But one of Clem's greatest gifts was the ability to go beyond the categories. There are a lot of categories—statements of right and wrong, personality types, laws, distinctions between men and women, rich and poor, worthy and unworthy, saint and sinner.

Some reject such categories or don't even understand them—and that is no way to live. It is the "unexamined life" that Socrates describes. Some, perhaps most, try to live their lives within them. Some very few go beyond them. Clem Kern was one of those very few.

Of course, he learned it from the Lord. When the pagan Syro-Phoenician woman asked for the Lord's help, there was this category of Jew and Gentile, of which Jesus reminded her. But she persisted, and Jesus went beyond that category.

I remember the day when Jimmy Hoffa was going to jail, and Clem Kern said a special Mass for him and a lot of his friends at his parish. When outraged citizens asked how he could do that for a notorious criminal, Clem simply said: "Jimmy needs prayers, and the best thing we know how to do is pray." I remember the time he picketed with the bunnies in front of the Playboy Club in Detroit when they were asking for higher wages. Television cameras were there, and a newsman asked Clem how he could join with these immodestly dressed women, and Clem said, "Oh, I'm for modesty. But these women aren't being treated properly."

St. Paul spoke of such things. "May Christ dwell in your hearts through faith, and may charity be the root and foundation of your life. Thus you will be able to grasp fully, with all the holy ones, the breadth and length and height and depth of Christ's life, which surpasses all knowledge." When you do that, then "there does not exist among you Jew or Greek, slave or freeman, male or female. All are one in Christ Jesus."

Monika Hellwig has talked and written about this. We are to live the kingdom now, as if it were here, even though it isn't and doesn't fit. And that is how you work for the kingdom.

I can't tell you exactly how to do that. Your life must be extraordinarily in tune with God's love, whose sun rises on the just and unjust, whose rain falls on the good and the bad. If you learn to love that way, you will find yourself in the strangest places, with the strangest people, who, because of you, know for sure that the Lord loves them.

Relationship of the Church to the World

I would like to present, in oversimplified fashion, four ways in which the church has related to the world.

1. For the first four centuries, the church lived more or less on the periphery of the world. It did not regard the world as evil, as the Manichaeans did, but saw it as more or less neutral. Christians lived in the expectation of the kingdom that was coming soon. They did not see the coming of the kingdom as a historical enterprise. It was to be given by God, from above, and the complex questions of the world had little to do with it. The Christian simply lived in this world, waiting for a new world and preaching the sure hope that this new world would come.

2. With the peace of Constantine this radically changed. The church was no longer on the periphery, but enjoyed a privileged place at the center of the world. The task now was to transform this world into a here-and-now kingdom, which was closely identified with the church. The church took over the world, and by the time of Charlemagne we had "Christendom." Church and state were to share a common goal. It would be something like trying to turn the whole world into a Benedictine monastery. Everything is supposed to become church and work directly and immediately for the same goals. Holy days are holidays, military forces are to work for the church; this world's economic resources are under the direction of the hierarchy. It was, as Yves Congar put it, the "confiscation of the world." The church saw its mission in terms of regulating the entire framework of life in order to Christianize or "churchify" the people. It was an attempt to make people Christian through institutions, rather than making institutions Christian through people. This didn't work well. You had popes leading armies, and emperors resolving heresies.

3. In the eleventh century, Pope Gregory VII, a religious monk, instituted his great reform. It was designed to extract the

church from its symbiotic relationship with the world and establish it as a spiritual society that could stand on its own in rivalry with secular society. The church no longer was to depend on secular laws. It would have its own law, which became our canon law. It was to have all the components proper to a society, but it would be a spiritual society distinct from secular society and, eventually, in rivalry with it. Among other things, reason and faith were clearly distinguished. There were two domains: church and world. One was led by the pope and the hierarchy. The other was led by the emperor and secular leaders.

From this there developed a view of the world that was very negative. It easily spoke of "the world, the flesh and the devil." There developed a Christian spirituality that was heavily monastic.

As this progressed, the world continued on its way. It took over, without knowing it, the eschatology of the kingdom of God and fitted it into the framework of a purely cosmic and anthropocentric history. It responded to a religion without a historical-cosmic vision without God. We called it the "myth of progress," "rationalism," "modernism." This church-world relationship continued right down to our own day.

4. With Vatican II, a radically new vision was introduced. No longer was the church seen as a "perfect society" in opposition to the world, but "the church *in* the modern world." The trajectory begun with Constantine and modified by Gregory VII had ended. The church no longer sought to exercise a jurisdiction over society, but rather to exert an influence through the consciences of the faithful. The church was to be salt, light, leaven to the world...the sacrament of salvation oriented toward the world. A new age had dawned for the church and for the world.

What are the pastoral implications? We are still trying to figure them out. Perhaps I should not say "still," because it has only been twenty years, which is not very long in the perspective of history.

1. For one thing, it is very new. The church has never attempted to relate to the world as we are today. One cannot overestimate this. It truly boggles the mind and we should allow ourselves to be boggled and admit it. People are puzzled by what the church is doing. What does relating to the world have to do with being Roman Catholic? Why don't we just go back to teaching the commandments?

I think we have to come to terms with the newness of this. People such as you and I have journeyed through this new understanding of the relationship of the church to the world, but many, many people have not. We understand the organic relationship of our political involvements with the gospel, but many people do not. When we present them with conclusions and not the journey, they are baffled. We need to help them make the same journey, for it cuts through new territory.

When one adds to this all the forces that have been exploding in our world during these past twenty years, one appreciates the difficulty. I use the word *exploding* very consciously. We recently had a convocation of all the priests of Saginaw, and one of the things we did was brainstorm together a time line of all that has happened in the church and in the world since 1960. We put it up on newsprint—Vatican II, the Vietnam War, the exodus of priests and religious, the hot 1960s, Watergate, the space program, black rebellions from coast to coast, women's liberation, four popes, the assassinations of John Kennedy, Robert Kennedy, and Martin Luther King, Jr., *Humanae Vitae*, the drug culture, and so many other things. It became a vortex of forces leading right up to our own day, like a new birth. We must not underestimate the newness of it all.

2. We are a servant church, a band of footwashers, waiters. There is something of Charlemagne in all of us. We feel that if we could only take over, we could set things right. To tell the truth, it has been the temptation of the church since Constantine. We must resist the temptation to use power. We must be gentle, loving, powerless, as salt, light, leaven, the mustard seed, in our approach. Our style is not that of Constantine, Charlemagne, or Gregory VII, but more like that of John XXIII, who never claimed to understand perfectly all the forces that came in through his open window, but was kind and loving to all of them.

Tension between Church and World

Earlier I told the story of how the chapter on the pilgrim church was born. There is also an interesting story related to the entire document titled *Gaudium et Spes*, which was not planned as part of the council's work. No commission had been set up to prepare a text on this topic. However, as work on the document on the church progressed, there emerged a growing awareness of the need to develop something about the involvement of the church in the great enterprise of history. Having described the church beautifully, one might then ask, what is it for? This is the impetus that gave rise to one of the great documents of Vatican II, *Gaudium et Spes*. It went through many drafts. There were long and sometimes heated debates, and even toward the end of the council many bishops did not think it would see the light of day. But it did, and it has had a remarkable impact. I have no way of proving it, but I suspect it is the most quoted document of the council.

The way in which this document was born—in a sense, from *Lumen Gentium*—and the struggles surrounding its final acceptance express in their own way the tension between the church *ad intra* and *ad extra*. We need to be true to our nature as church, healthy, vibrant, before we can go outward with our distinctive mission to the world. On the other hand, we cannot wait until we are entirely healthy and vibrant before reaching outward—the tasks continue simultaneously. It is not easy to work out a formula balancing the two. There is a tension between them, and the tension simply has to be lived. Some reflections on this follow.

1. The further the church reaches outward, the more it must be true to its center, who is Christ. And the more it is true to its center, the more it reaches outward. The liturgy commission wants to raise money for a much needed new organ, and the Christian service commission wants to raise money to organize a soup kitchen in the poverty-stricken section of town. Liturgy commission members ask how the parish can carry out its mission if it doesn't have good liturgies. The Christian service commission members ask what good are liturgies if they don't have any effect after Mass is over.

I think we have to do a better job of integrating concerns of social justice with the Eucharist. If we were given a test and were told to rank in importance the activities in a parish, we would all know enough to put the Eucharist at the top. What is not as well known is that when Vatican II spoke of the eucharistic liturgy in this way, it meant not simply that it is number one in ranking, but that it is the integrating source for all the activities of a parish. We recognize its importance; I'm not sure if we recognize its integrating role. It was at the Eucharist that early Christians learned what to do with their material goods. It was at the Eucharist that they learned of concern for the poor. It was at the Eucharist that they faced the struggle to be inclusive.

Everything we do must be brought into and flow out of the Eucharist. I don't think we have done that very well. For example, while the general intercessions very often speak of peace for troubled spots in the world, the sick, the poor, and so forth, I do not sense an awareness of the very basic economic struggles that most people are facing. We're moving in the right direction, but we have some distance to go.

We have buildings and we live our own way of life, but we ourselves are not part of the basic economic struggles of the people of the world. It is difficult for us to find ways to insert ourselves into their lives. We come first as religious persons, and from there we might become brother or sister Christians and then perhaps even neighbors. The worker-priests tried to do it from the other end, and that has many advantages. There is a tension between being church and being for the world.

2. We need the courage to keep going outward once we have started. A priest friend of mine who is one of the best I have ever seen in this area of social justice recently told me a story that is sort of a parable on this. He told about a fellow student in his theology days. Whenever the big exams came near, this student would always start cleaning his room. The furniture would be out in the hall, and you could hear him cleaning the floor. It was as though the frightening task of facing exams caused him to turn inward to something he could control. My priest friend then commented: "The church does that. We get into the struggles the people are facing—jobs, housing, racial conflicts—and we do some good things, and then we pull back. We decide that some internal things need tending to—restructuring, remodeling, new policies and guidelines." I think there is some truth in that. We get "out there" and feel out on a limb because we don't have the answers, and it is something we cannot control, and we pull back. We need the courage to keep going.

Conclusion

What a difference between the lyrics of the song "Camelot" and the lyrics of the Magnificat. "Camelot" speaks of an imaginary place where July and August cannot be too hot...where winter is forbidden until December and exits March the second on the dot...where the rain may never fall until after sundown and by eight the morning fog must disappear. In a repeated refrain the song tells us: "In short, there's simply not a more congenial spot for happy ever-aftering than here in Camelot!"

The Magnificat, on the other hand, speaks not of "ever-aftering" but of a God who has become flesh and blood, who helps the lowly here and now, a God of mercy and might who helps the hungry.

Luke further emphasizes this in his majestic beginning to the gospel proper: "In the fifteenth year of the rule of Tiberius Caesar, when Pontius Pilate was procurator of Judea, Herod tetrarch of Galilee, Philip his brother tetrarch of the region of Ituraea and Trachonitis, and Lysanias tetrarch of Abilene, during the high priesthood of Annas and Caiaphas, the word of God was spoken to John, son of Zechariah in the desert."

The purpose of this is not to tell us the exact date of the public life of Jesus (we wish he had), but to make it clear that what is taking place is the coming of God into world history. This is not a vignette about something that happened in a distant corner of the world. It is the turning point of history, the decisive entry of the kingdom within world history.

It would seem so much easier if God had never done this and instead had maintained his kingdom of somewhere else, like Camelot, and promised us a place in it after the world was destroyed, if only we passed the test. But God did not do that. The shaping of this world is part of the process of shaping the kingdom. *Gaudium et Spes* tells us: "The word of God...entered world history, taking that history into himself and recapitulating it. He reveals to us that 'God is love' (1 John 4:8) and at the same time teaches that the transformation of the world is the new commandment of love" (No. 18).

It is a strong kind of kingdom. *Gaudium et Spes* describes it in terms of "a new earth in which righteousness dwells, whose happiness will fill and surpass all the desires of peace.... Then with death conquered the children of God will be raised in Christ and what was sown in weakness and dishonor will put on the imperishable. Charity and its works will remain and all of creation, which God made for us, will be set free from its bondage" (No. 39). It is a kingdom that does not fit this world. Our king is Jesus, and he stands in sharp contrast to the cast of worldly leaders Luke gives us—Caesar, Pilate, Herod, and the others.

Yet we must live this kingdom now, as though it were fully here even though it doesn't fit. We are to challenge others to do so even though it may seem foolish. Those who tell us to leave history alone and deal only with "church matters" miss the whole point of the incarnation and fail to understand the very nature of the church itself.

To tell the truth, I don't know if a whole country or a whole world can live by the values of this kingdom and build these values into its structures. But individuals can. More important, the church can. The church must. We are summoned by Christ to be a community of footwashers, waiters, misfits in a world that God loves very much. May the Lord, who has begun this good work in us, sustain us and bring about its completion.

A Vision of Future Ministry

Origins 13:552 (January 26, 1984)

*Images of the priesthood in the twenty-first century were con-
trasted with present and past images of the priesthood in an
address to the annual National Conference of Diocesan
Vocation Directors' convention in Seattle by Bishop Kenneth
Untener of Saginaw, Michigan. In the popular mind the
church has the image of being old, said Untener. But, he
stressed, in light of the history of the world and the human
race, the church is young—but "a few seconds old." He said,
"Ministers are leaders of a pioneering young church cutting a
new edge at the early frontiers of Christianity." Their task is
one of "leadership in an adventuresome journey." The bishop
said that he was arbitrarily picking four historical dates about
which he would ask four questions concerning priesthood:
What kind of leadership did priesthood involve at that time?
What ministry of the word was exercised? What cultic ministry was exercised? How much witness of life was involved? In
his discussion, Untener also examined the relationships
between priests and bishops and between priests and other
church ministers.*

I would like first to offer three reflections in the light of the
theme of this gathering, "Behold, we are doing something new."
The frontier pioneering spirit of a place like Seattle is also included
in your theme. I was delighted to see this approach because it represents a spirit that needs more emphasis in the church.

The Church Is Young

In the popular mind the church has the image of being old, even stodgy. For example, in workshops on ecclesiology I occasionally ask people to draw an image of the church and then talk about it. Many draw a tree, but it is always an old tree. This expresses our conscious or unconscious image of the church as old, fully developed, fixed, like a big, old, sturdy oak tree.

Reexamine that image for a moment. It may have been understandable not so long ago when we thought that the world was only five or six thousand years old. Today we're told that the universe is perhaps eight to ten billion years old, and the human race is between three and four million years old. This means that Christianity has existed for only a tiny fraction of history. We are, comparatively speaking, just a few seconds old. We've only just begun. If I were to draw a tree to represent the church, I would draw a tiny sapling—with strong roots, but still very much in a formative stage. Someday far into the future they will look back at us as the "early church."

The pioneering, refreshing theme of this convention needs to be injected into ministry. We have to get rid of the caricature of the minister as bland, colorless, safe, secure, and withdrawn. Ministers are leaders of a pioneering young church cutting a new edge at the early frontiers of Christianity. Theirs is not a task of maintenance; it is leadership in an adventuresome journey. Ministers have to be vibrant, full of zest, risk-takers, spirit-filled.

Sense of Mystery

Another reflection has to do with our need to recapture a sense of mystery. As you know, *mystery* is a very old term in our tradition, and it does not mean a dark secret or something distant or aloof in the way that Howard Hughes was a mystery. Rather, it conveys a sense of richness, depth, and breadth. A mystery is like a little child. You can't capture a child in a word or a paragraph. A child is touched by eternity, with nearly infinite possibilities, with a value that cannot be measured. Our beliefs as Christians are mysteries in the same sense. We celebrate them in symbol and ritual, and our words are incomplete and inadequate attempts to express them.

I have been very struck by the words of the sacramental prayer said by the bishop at confirmation: "Give them the spirit of wisdom and understanding.... The spirit of right judgment and courage.... The spirit of knowledge and reverence.... And fill them with the spirit of wonder and awe in your presence." We need more of that wonder and awe. People filled with wonder and awe could never limit themselves to maintenance. Instead they are celebrating, enjoying, searching, moving on, because the mysteries they touch are so vast and so beautiful. There is always the possibility of a new insight, a new perspective. There are always more colors and shades to be added to the landscape.

Jesus, in his opening words in Mark's Gospel, tells the people that the mystery of the kingdom of God is near, and they must have a *metanoia*. That word means something like a change of mind, rethinking, getting a new slant, expanding horizons. His life and message were going to require a lot of this, and the ability to do it was the bottom-line difference between the Pharisees and the disciples. The Pharisees wanted to stay entirely within the categories and thought patterns they knew. The disciples, on the other hand, were able to walk in the footsteps of someone who was always turning a new corner, changing their outlook, moving on. The Pharisees couldn't accept mysteries beyond their grasp and control; the disciples could.

Capacity for Growth

Given the above, one of the most important qualities for anyone in the ministry of leadership is the capacity to grow, learn, adapt. I recently told a group of seminarians that if I were the rector of a seminary, I would be most concerned about three human problems in any candidate: underdeveloped intellect, undeveloped affect, and rigidity—and the worst of these is rigidity. It doesn't matter whether you are liberal or conservative. If you are rigid in your approach, you cannot be a good leader in a young, pilgrim church.

My concern about fundamentalistic tendencies in Christianity today has more to do with attitude than content. Fundamentalists leave no room for wonder and awe. They rigidly cling to narrow formulations and practices as though they were the last word. They do this, it seems to me, not for reasons of theological principle, but for reasons of personal survival, and that is precisely the problem. Every disagreement, every possible change, is perceived as a personal threat and dealt with accordingly. Such an attitude is as inappropriate for a leader in our pilgrim church as a fear of heights would be for a mountain man.

I would now like to talk about the priesthood—yesterday, today, and tomorrow. I am going to pick arbitrarily four dates in our Judeo-Christian history and then ask four questions of the priesthood as it existed in each of those periods. The four dates are: 663 BC, AD 163, AD 1963, and AD 2063. (I was ordained a priest in 1963 and that explains something about my choice of dates.) The questions are (1) What kind of leadership did the priesthood involve at the time? (2) What ministry was exercised? (3) What cultic ministry was exercised? (4) How much witness of life was involved?

I will give a brief and somewhat oversimplified description of the priesthood at each of these periods and then pose our four questions.

663 BC

The Israelite priesthood of 663 BC was the product of an evolutionary process begun way back in the patriarchal era. Originally, families celebrated their own priesthood. As time went on, larger local sanctuaries developed and with them some specialists—priests—who tended the sanctuary. They were more along the lines of tradesmen. Their task was to take care of the sanctuary and also to discern the will of God at certain times. The discernment process was an interesting one. They used the *Urim* and *Thummin* dice to discover whether it was favorable to plant seed at this time, go to battle, or things like that.

In the settlement period, the Tribe of Levi for some reason didn't get any land. As a result, many of them were drawn toward this role of professional priesthood, and that is why priesthood became identified with the Levites. Again, it was more a craft than a divine call.

All of this is background to the priesthood that existed at our arbitrary date of 663 BC. By now, centralized sanctuaries had developed with a staff of priests, most of them Levites. They offered sacrifices and were responsible for anything that had to do with contact with the altar. These priests also had a limited teaching role, but it had more to do with knowing, safeguarding and passing on the fixed laws. It was not what we would normally mean by prophetic proclamation.

1. LEADERSHIP

Leadership was not part of the "job description" of the priest of 663 BC. He was in charge of those people involved with the sanctuary, but there was no role of leadership of the larger community. He would hardly be described as a shepherd.

2. MINISTRY OF THE WORD

While there was a responsibility for safeguarding and passing on the legal tradition, it was not a ministry of preaching and teaching. It was more static, a job of maintenance. Furthermore, it was very much secondary to the cultic task. The prophetic role had been taken over by others.

3. CULTIC MINISTRY

The cultic ministry was paramount. This is the skill that was the trademark of the priests. They knew how to take care of and jealously guarded anything that had to do with the altar and the sanctuary.

4. WITNESS OF LIFE

The priest of 663 BC was not expected to have a special role of witness. He was expected to be a respectable person and keep the law like anyone else, but his lifestyle was not in itself part of his preaching. He was not a prophetic leader; he was a religious tradesman.

We might speculate about the qualities one might seek in a candidate for this form of priesthood. The question, however, is somewhat artificial inasmuch as this priesthood was the result of inheritance, not vocational discernment. The priest simply had to be a Levite, learn his craft, live a respectable life, and get a position.

At this point I would like to make an aside. The Levitical priests got their vocation more or less by default. Their tribe did not get any land, and they were left looking for some other source of livelihood. By analogy, we might reflect upon a concern I have today.

Back in the days when we got vocations by going into elementary schools and inspiring young boys to consider dedicating their lives to a great cause, we would get more or less a cross section of boys who showed promise. They had not yet had a chance to test their social skills or their talents, to succeed or fail.

Today we are tending to recruit young men at a later age, many of them during or after college. The pool of candidates is likely to be much different. We no longer have a cross section of untested, dedicated boys. We have young men who, unlike many of their peers, have for one reason or another not chosen a profession or a woman they intend to marry. There may be many reasons for this, but a higher percentage is more likely to be available by default, something like the Levites who were left without land. I do not intend to criticize all the young men who come forward. Many would not fit this category. It is simply more likely that some of them will have failed to make it in the early testing process of socializing or choosing a profession. If you took a cross section of high-school freshmen who might be drawn to the priesthood and one of twenty-three-year-old men who also feel drawn to the priesthood, you are going to have a different pool of candidates. Some will be in the latter group by default.

I don't know what to do about this. I'm not suggesting that we go back to sending eighth-graders to a high school seminary. I am simply acknowledging a situation that I sense is factual (although I have not researched it scientifically) and submitting it for your consideration as vocational directors. There are, after all, many bad reasons for wanting to become a priest.

AD 163

In the years immediately following the death and resurrection of Jesus, Christianity was not perceived as a "new religion." It seemed more like a movement within Judaism, a movement whose trademark was belief that Jesus was the Messiah. Its distinctive ritual was simple, its structure relatively underdeveloped.

As Christianity drew apart from Judaism, particularly with the destruction of Jerusalem in AD 70, its structures, rituals, and distinctive identity developed more fully. By the time we reach our chosen date of 163, we find the kind of church and ministry reflected in the pastoral epistles. There were bishop-elders serving as leaders of the local churches, with a group of elders surrounding them as sort of a college. There were a wide variety of other ministries, varying from place to place according to particular needs. We also have the early Christian use of priestly terminology to describe the chief leaders of the church.

1. LEADERSHIP

In terms of leadership we have a significant shift from the Old Testament priest centuries earlier. Back then, the priest had no particular role of community leadership. In the year 163 this is one of the main tasks of the priest. It is precisely why he was chosen to serve in this capacity. The people of a particular church wanted to have an identity as a community. They wanted unity, support, nurturing, and leadership. They chose someone who had the gift of drawing them together and leading them as they walked in the way of the Lord. Leadership was one of the primary tasks of the priest. He was clearly a shepherd.

2. MINISTRY OF THE WORD

Here again we have a significant shift from the Old Testament priest. In the Epistle to Timothy, the author refers to "taking care of the Gospels that were entrusted to you." The "ordination ceremony" seemed to have as one of its highlights the reading of the substance of the gospel and the promise on the part of the elder that he would authentically preach this message. This was their biggest concern—just as we today might be concerned about "Who is going to hand on the true message of the Lord?" After all, they had lost the firsthand witnesses, and they had experienced the rise of heresies and splinter groups. More than anything else they wanted to be sure that they had a leader who had imbibed and understood the true message and who would guarantee that they were on the right path. It was not a question of simply handing down fixed laws. It was a question of understanding the depths of the "way" so that they could apply it to the new frontiers of Christian experience.

3. CULTIC MINISTRY

Actually, we don't know a lot about the cultic role of the priest in 163. The Eucharist was celebrated under the auspices of the bishop-elder. But when you consider the other six sacraments we have today, it is very hard to say how they existed at the time and what the role of the priest was. These cultic celebrations didn't just happen "all anyhow." Yet cultic ministry does not seem to be as central to the role of the priest as it was in the Old Testament priesthood or, as we shall see, in the priesthood into which I was ordained in 1963.

4. WITNESS OF LIFE

We have here, as in the above three questions, another significant shift. Witness of life was central to the role of the priest of 163. The very term *elder* indicates that this was a major concern. It did not simply mean someone who was old in years. Rather, it meant wisdom, understanding, right judgment, courage, knowledge, reverence, wonder, and awe. It designated someone who had shared the struggle of living and gospel in the thick of real life, a role model. His life was in itself understood to be a proclamation of the message.

Given this "job description," we might speculate about the qualities sought in a candidate. Happily, we have a description as set forth in the Epistle to Timothy. He must be

> irreproachable, married only once, of even temper, self-controlled, modest and hospitable. He should be a good

teacher. He must not be addicted to drink. He ought not to be contentious but, rather, gentle, a man of peace. Nor can he be someone who loves money. He must be a good manager of his own household, keeping his children under control without sacrificing dignity; for if a man does not know how to manage in his own house, how can he take care of the church of God? (1 Tim 3:2–5)

Note the emphasis on leadership, a "people person," who was experienced in leading a family, servants…the whole household—not the affective, relational ties and ability to teach. These are traits far different from the criteria for the Old Testament priest of 663 BC.

AD 1963

I won't attempt to describe the evolution of the priesthood from the second century to 1963. Nor will I spend much time describing the priesthood of 1963. Most of you have actually experienced the style of priestly ministry that had developed by the twentieth century. I simply ask you to think back to how it was as it applies to our four questions.

1. LEADERSHIP

There was a book of meditations we all used in the seminary titled *The Priest's Way to God*. At the beginning of the meditation of the priestly ordination ceremony the author says:

Very fittingly, the bishop starts out with a reference to the *rector navis* (captain of a ship). The idea that the church is a ship and that the bishop is the captain, the priest the crew and the faithful the passengers undoubtedly goes back to the day when the Savior selected Peter and the other fisherman to apostolate on the banks of the Sea of Galilee. For, as Noah's ark was destined to save eight souls from the deluge, so is the ship of the church destined to convey the souls of the faithful over the stormy waters of this world into a safe harbor. The priest is an officer of the ship. To him the passengers must render implicit and absolute obedience.

The leadership that priests were called upon to exercise in 1963 was more along the lines of helmsmanship—guiding people by using fixed charts and a sure compass. It was not the sort of thing we generally mean when we speak of the gift of leadership. The latter refers to the ability to inspire people, work closely with them, unify them, take risks, generate ideas, know when to move fast and when to move slow. Back in 1963 we didn't have too much of that, except perhaps with youth. When it came to adults, we simply acted as more or less "chaplains" to various groups—the ushers, the altar society, the Holy Name Society. Often the greatest single adult enterprise requiring leadership was the parish festival, and this was a very directive kind of leadership. As for leadership of diverse ministries, there weren't any. They had all been effectively absorbed into the priesthood.

Thus leadership was not a prominent part of the priesthood in 1963. A pastor was sent to administer a parish, as compared to the pastor back in the year 163 who was called forth to lead people.

2. MINISTRY OF THE WORD

I went back and read the ordination ceremony as it was in 1963. I was astounded to find no ceremony dealing with the ministry of the word. Even when I was ordained a deacon there was simply the bestowal of the power to read the gospel. Today, by contrast, the ceremony is quite different in this regard. The deacon ceremony reads: "Receive the Gospel of Christ, whose herald you now are. Believe what you read, teach what you believe, and practice what you teach." The priesthood ordination today also includes this question by the bishop: "Are you resolved to exercise the ministry of the word worthily and wisely, preaching the Gospel and explaining the Catholic faith?" These words were not in my ordination ceremony.

The preaching and teaching back in 1963 involved more or less the communication of fixed truths. There were manuals of dogma and morals, and sermon outlines from the chancery. Ministry of the word, as we would understand it today, did not have a high priority in the training of seminarians in the ordination ceremony or in the exercise of priesthood.

3. CULTIC MINISTRY

Let us return again to the ordination ceremony as it existed in 1963. If you attended such a ceremony you walked away with one overriding impression: This person has now been given the power to say Mass. Secondary impressions would also have to do with cultic aspects of ministry—the power to forgive sins and the power to bestow blessings. The ceremony reflected reality, for cultic ministry was the trademark of the priesthood.

4. WITNESS OF LIFE

While the priest of 1963 was expected to live a very special kind of life, I'm not sure how much "life witness" was involved. It was more a pedestal kind of witness—set apart, consecrated, above. It was not quite the same as the life witness of the elder, who was looked upon as someone who had "been there," who had struggled through problems of life, whose prayer and holiness was a role in the thick of life. The 1963 priest was more like the guru on the mountaintop.

What particular qualities would be important for a candidate to the 1963 priesthood? Most of all, he was to be trustworthy, much in the sense of a bond clerk. There were many other qualities, of course, but trustworthiness to transmit doctrine, fulfill sacramental ritual, and administer a parish was paramount. It strikes me that in many ways the ministry of 1963 has more external similarities with 663 BC than with AD 163.

AD 2063

We are twenty years past 1963 and on our way to the next millennium. The priesthood has changed more in these past twenty years than perhaps in any brief period since the second century. It is still changing. What will it look like in the year 2063?

1. LEADERSHIP

Leadership is an increasing expectation of the priest. Ask any parish what they want in their new pastor, and they will describe many things that would fit under the heading of leadership. They want someone who can unify them, organize them, inspire them, supervise personnel, make collegial decisions, and move them ahead. They want a good shepherd. The role of the priest is less and less that of carrying out prescribed rituals and procedures, and more and more that of creative leadership. It is less and less exercised from above or from the outside, and more and more from within the common struggle to make sense of life. I expect this to increase rather than decrease in the years ahead.

There is one area of leadership that we might give special consideration. This has to do with the leadership of diverse ministries within the parish. I see the pastor of the future fulfilling the kind of "overseeing" role that was characteristic of the bishop in earlier times. Our parishes today are much like the cathedrals of times past. The pastor oversees the whole enterprise, but he does so in collaboration with a large number of ministering people. A great deal of his ministry has to do with calling forth, nurturing, and coordinating the ministry of others. He is now an orchestra leader rather than a one-man band.

To tell the truth, we aren't there yet. Right now, the other ministers appear to function as his substitute because he is too busy or because there is a shortage of priests. This means that the addition of ministers actually increases rather than decreases his "work load." If he has ministers of the Eucharist who bring communion to the sick, they are supposed to function only when he cannot do so. They are "extraordinary" ministers of the Eucharist, because he is the ordinary minister. This means that besides training them and ministering to them (which is very much his responsibility), he should also do their ministry whenever he can. As a result, besides continuing to minister communion to the sick, he now has the additional burden of ministering to the ministers of communion to the sick.

The same is true of other ministries, at least as they are perceived by the people. If there are ministers to lead prayer services—wakes for example—the priest is still expected to take wakes when he can. This means that he has double responsibility: training and organizing prayer leaders and taking wakes or other prayer services whenever he can.

The same holds true for those who catechize youngsters and adults, or do marriage preparation or home visits. Such ministers are looked upon as substitutes for the priest, not ministers in their own right. Besides ministering to these ministers, he should do their ministries whenever he possibly can.

We have to turn a corner on this. Two things have to happen. First of all, the people have to be helped to understand that these "nonpriestly" ministers are full-fledged ministers. They are not substitutes for a busy priest. Second, these ministers have to be good at what they do—teaching, preparing people for the sacraments, leading prayers, giving spiritual direction. We aren't there yet and this means that we do not yet have a good parish model of what I'm talking about. We've only just begun to move in that direction.

In the future I see parish ministers serving not as substitutes for the priest, but as ministers in their own right. The role of the priest will be to call them forth and minister to them. He will be a minister to the ministers, much like a bishop.

2. MINISTRY OF THE WORD

There is no doubt in my mind that the importance of the ministry of the word will increase. Far and away the most frequent comment I hear about priests concerns the way they preach. If they are good, little else matters. If they're not so good, all else seems to be in vain. In a way, it is a return to the earliest expectation of the elders who were chosen—someone who has struggled to live the gospel in his own life and who can make it come alive for them and for their children. I recently heard a layperson comment on the way in which the church helps him live his faith in real-life situations, and he put it this way: "You do your job, and I'll do mine." He was referring most of all to the proclamation of the gospel message.

People do not feel as much need for specific directives on the details of their life in the world or in marriage or single life. They want basic truths that give meaning to life. They want to have a deeper faith, to be in touch with the mysteries that make life worthwhile. They want effective ministers of the word.

3. CULTIC MINISTRY

The cultic ministry of the priest will, in one sense, decrease. This does not mean that it will decrease in parish life. It simply means that the priest will not be the exclusive minister of liturgy and prayer. We already have the beginnings of this with permanent deacons celebrating baptisms and marriages. Other parishioners are effectively ministering the Eucharist to the sick and shut-ins. Still others lead morning and evening prayer and wake services. The development of a ministry of healing will have effects on the sacrament of the sick. An increase in lay spiritual directors will affect the sacrament of reconciliation.

The priest will be the overseer of these cultic ministries. His day-to-day schedule and his identity, however, will be less bound up with their actual celebration.

4. WITNESS OF LIFE

The "prophetic" expectations of the priest are on the increase. There is a growing awareness among parishioners that their membership in the church involves being countercultural. The Lord's teachings and way of life are quite radical. So are to forgive seventy times seven, to love our enemies, cherish the poor and the "losers" in society, be peacemakers, give things away, seek treasures that are not deposited in banks, be gentle in the face of violence, have hope in the face of pessimism. None of this can adequately be preached in words. It can only be lived, and priests are expected to serve as role models.

Personal witness is also expected in less dramatic ways. People want their priest to be a warm, understanding human person. Next to the way priests preach, I hear people talk most about these qualities—"he's friendly...he seems to understand...he's patient...he's good with young people...he truly believes what he preaches and celebrates...he acknowledges his own weaknesses and struggles." Priesthood is becoming more a way of life and less a state in life.

We might speculate about the kinds of qualities that we would seek in candidates for the priesthood of the future. I will leave that to your own reflection and discussion as vocation directors. I believe that it is a kind of priesthood that is more attractive rather than less attractive. About a year ago in a tape played in all the parishes of the Diocese of Saginaw, I expressed my thoughts in this way:

> Most priests could tell you a happy story about their life as a priest. Oh, there are tough times, and we are not afraid to talk about them. A few weeks back, all the priests of this diocese gathered for two and a half days and talked about what it is like to be a priest today. We talked about being pulled in so many directions—to be there when people are dying…and then to baptize little babies…to reach out to young people and old people…to visit homes…to prepare people for marriage, to preach week in and week out, to help the poor to speak out on issues that aren't so popular, to take a stand, to read and think and study about the great issues of the world, to comfort the sick and the suffering.
>
> But do you know what? We wouldn't trade it for anything. Because there is nothing greater than to be in the thick of life. I can think of no better place to be than where there is life and death—and struggles and dreams and the search for meaning, and a crowd of people, lonely individuals, little children…and song and celebration and sometimes weeping.…If my vocation were taken away from me, do you know what I would miss most of all? Being in the thick of things where the Lord is at work.

The Rich Abundance within an Earthen Vessel

Origins 14:60–61 (June 7, 1984)
May 4th Sisters' Jubilee Celebration in Saginaw

It is interesting that today's readings fall on the day we celebrate Sisters' jubilees here in the Diocese of Saginaw. I think they have something to say to women religious.

The early Christians were very confident of the richness that lay within the earthen vessel called church. The Gospel account of the feeding of the five thousand helped remind them of this abundance. They remembered other stories too: the plentiful wine at Cana, the countless cures and healings, the victory of life over death. The same Lord who did all this was still with them, and they were rich in blessings. All they asked for was the freedom and space to grow.

Which brings us to the first reading from the Acts of the Apostles. When the apostles were brought before the Sanhedrin in those early days of opposition, a very dramatic thing happened. A Pharisee named Gamaliel stood up and reminded the Jews that there had been popular movements like this in the past, but once their leaders died, they soon faded away. Gamaliel's advice, therefore, regarding these followers of Jesus was: "Let them alone. If their purpose or activity is human in its origins, it will destroy itself. If, on the other hand, it comes from God, you will not be able to destroy them without fighting God himself" (Acts 5:38–39).

It is safe to say that there is a good deal of Luke's own hand in Gamaliel's speech as it is told in Acts. It is Luke and the early church who are pleading: "Let us alone. Give us space to grow and develop, and you will see that this is something truly from God." They were confident of the riches that lay within this earthen vessel called church. All they asked was the freedom and the space to blossom.

I can sense many women religious saying somewhat the same thing to the church today: "Give us space. Let us find creative ways to express the charism of religious life in today's world. If these efforts are not from God, they will fail. But if, on the other hand, they are truly from him, then they will produce much fruit."

My own experience of religious women today is that they have a certain self-confidence regarding what they are about. They are not groping aimlessly or tentatively. They are convinced that they are moving in the right direction. They don't have all the answers, but there is a certain assurance that they are on the way to something that is from God. They are much like the early Christians who didn't have all the structures and forms worked out, but who had not the slightest doubt of the rich abundance within an earthen vessel. Many religious women ask only that we give them some freedom, space, and support.

I think we ought to do that. We ought to take more interest than we have in the past, but our concern and our support should not stifle their creativity. They need space, and they need freedom. After all, this is how they have flourished over the centuries.

I've learned a lot lately about the history of women religious. It is a topic very much on the mind of the bishops these days, and I've done some reading I might otherwise not have done. Across the centuries, religious women have shown remarkable adaptability and creativity. I would venture to say that this comes as news to most Catholics. We tend to think that the forms of religious life familiar to us as we were growing up were forms that more or less fell from heaven early in the church. Nothing could be further from the truth. The history of the forms and structures of religious life for women has been one of change, adaptation, modification, permutation, and innovation. It has been a history of success and failure, growth and decline. That which is from God continues. That which is not passes away.

We ought to become more familiar with the history of women religious. Some excellent things are being written these days. I would especially urge that anyone who is critical of their contemporary creative efforts study the past. It is an eye-opener. I never realized the evolutionary development of this charism. Certain strains develop, then others branch off (usually in response to some particular need in the church and/or in the world), some of these endure and some pass away, then new shoots spring up, and so on and so forth. The forms of religious life with which we grew up were relatively recent innovations. To fix and freeze these forms is to deprive women religious of the dynamism that has been the key to their success throughout the centuries.

Women religious have had the inner conviction and confidence that this charism has a richness that is not exhausted in any one particular form. They ask only the space and the freedom to allow it to flourish. Every effort may not be successful, but these pass away. Some will be successful, and the church has always been the richer for having allowed the freedom for new forms to flourish.

I pray that the church today will give women religious the space and the support to continue their adventuresome journey through history. The Holy Father has called upon bishops to take more interest and become more involved in developments in religious life today. That can be a very positive thing. What we have to be careful of is the kind of involvement that we often characterize in our country as "government interference." When the government gets involved, we almost expect creativity and freedom to get stifled, bogged down with regulations, paperwork, and so forth. We bishops have to be careful not to let our pastoral supervision become patriarchal suffocation.

I would like to raise one last point. If you do not receive the space, freedom, and support to develop as you feel called to develop, how will we know that whatever emerges is "from God"? By what signs will we be able to discern your success or your failure?

I don't think the sign will be numbers—a sudden geometric increase in your membership. In themselves, numbers don't prove anything. The speech of the Pharisee Gamaliel pointed out that the earlier movements attracted great numbers, but in the end they came to nothing.

What should we look for? I think we should look for the impact of your lives upon others. The difference today is that your lives have more of an individual impact. In the past, women religious provided a group witness to poverty, chastity, and obedience. You dressed the same; you lived in the same house; you ate the same food; you prayed the same; you carried out a common apostolate. Your presence as religious was very much felt in a parish or community, but it was the presence of a group.

Today your witness is more individual. Today we notice how each of you prays. Today we notice how each of you finds ways to live out the vow of poverty. We notice how celibate commitment is expressed through your own person. We notice your attempts to be obedient to the Lord's call, to the work of your community, to the needs of the church. Your response unfolds in many different ways before our eyes.

You are aware, I'm sure, that this places different demands upon you. It is one thing to be a member of a community whose collective life makes an impact. It is quite another thing to make an impact through your own individual life. The church needs both. Some religious women today are developing forms of religious life that call upon members to give powerful witness through their individual lives to the gifts of poverty, chastity, and obedience. The measure of success will be the measure to which this has an impact on the rest of us. To do so, it must be striking, even prophetic. Most of all, it must be genuine, for there is really nothing to fall back upon except the witness of your own life.

But if it is good, if it is "from God," then it will have great effects. The rest of us will not be able to live our own lives without taking into account the implications of yours. Your creative efforts to live the gospel will make us creative in the circumstances of our own lives. Your prayer will affect our prayer. Your poverty will affect our temptation to consumerism. Your celibacy will affect our attitude toward relationships in our own lives. Your obedience will affect our commitment to people and things beyond ourselves.

I pray that the church will give you the space to make these creative efforts. I call upon all of us here in the church of Saginaw to support you and challenge you as you go about this. Finally, I thank you women religious—especially those celebrating their jubilees—for all that you have done to help shape the church more in the image of Jesus Christ.

Is the Church in Decline? An Optimistic Bishop Says "No"

Church (Summer 1999), 5–10

Among many Catholics these days there is a worried feeling about their church. They feel it not necessarily about their own parish, but about the church in general. It's an impression that's in the air, a taken-for-granted feeling that the church is in decline.

Is it? Yes and no. Feeling and fact. There is a "church" whose sun is setting, in decline, and the glow of the sunset brings nostalgia and sad feelings. It is a church whose heyday some of us remember and all of us have at least heard about—a regal, orderly church that didn't preach *about* the kingdom of God. It *was* the kingdom of God. We were used to it, at home in it, and to watch it decline is like seeing your old school building torn down.

The fact is, however, that the church itself is not in decline. This may sound strange because the feelings cloud the facts. When people rue the decline of their church, I ask them for specifics. They say, "It's obvious. Just look around you." And they talk about this and that, mostly general impressions, mostly inaccurate.

What follows are eight things often cited, which we'll look at in the light of the facts.

1. DECLINE IN MEMBERSHIP?

This is usually at the top of the list: "We're losing members at a terrible rate." Get ready for this one. Our membership has gone up.

A short while back I attended a two-and-a-half-day ecumenical gathering of leaders who were what we would call "bishops."

Our purpose was to discuss common problems. At one point the presenter (of another faith) was talking about the general decline in church membership and said as an aside, "Of course, the only main-line church whose membership has been going up is the Catholic Church." I was in the back row, which was good, because not many saw me jerk my head. Like most other Catholics, I had assumed that our numbers are going down. They are not. In the United States, membership in the Catholic Church has been increasing every year for the past forty years.

Most of us have failed to distinguish between membership in the church and weekly participation in the Sunday Eucharist. The latter *has* declined.* But people who do not go to Mass every week, or even every other week, still count themselves as full members of the church and are proud to say so.

Now, the drop in weekly eucharistic participation is serious. There are many reasons behind it, the main one being that we don't have the same incentive (or the common expectation) we used to have. When I grew up you had two choices: go to Mass…or go to hell. Most of us chose Mass. We don't present it quite that way nowadays, but we shouldn't make light of the expectation (and obligation) of weekly participation in Eucharist. But that is another article.

For the moment I wish only to point out that we have to distinguish between decline in membership and decline in Sunday eucharistic participation. If a large percentage of "practicing" Catholics considers three out of four Sundays "good attendance," that in itself is a significant drop in weekly attendance among people who do not intend to distance themselves from the church.

Keep in mind also that in terms of Sunday participation, the U.S. church has a far better percentage than most other countries in the world. Not long ago, when I was talking to a cardinal in the

---

*The October count is a method used annually in every parish of the Saginaw Diocese to record the actual number of people attending each Mass throughout the first four Sundays of October, then calculates the average Mass attendance, as opposed to a count of those who call themselves Catholics and who remain "on the books" but practice their Catholicism irregularly. For example, in 1999, at the time this article was written, the total average October count was 61,786, and the estimated number of Catholics in 1999 was 149,009. In 2005 the actual October count was 50,328, and the estimated number of Catholics in 2005 was 131,937.

Curia about the overall percentage of Mass attendance in the Diocese of Saginaw, he was astounded to find it so high.

When I returned from the ecumenical conference mentioned earlier, besides checking the statistics on U.S. Catholic membership, I checked the gross operating income of the 110 parishes of the Diocese of Saginaw (we are not an area of population growth). In 1991 to 1992, it was $30.5 million. In 1997 to 1998, it was $44.1 million. Other dioceses are experiencing a similar trend. This is not a sign of a church in decline.

2. THE SHORTAGE OF PRIESTS?

Unlike the first symptom, this one is real and getting worse. It is the biggest problem I face as a bishop. It is helpful to point out that the priest shortage is a worldwide problem, and the United States is better off in this area than almost any other country in the world. Still, the situation is serious.

The shortage of priests is a cross we have to bear and, as Archbishop Rembert Weakland pointed out to the people of his archdiocese, if we bear a cross well, it brings many graces. It's up to God to get us through this, and it's up to us to go where God is taking us.

This cross has already brought us some new life. Lay ministry is not meant to exist only when there are not enough priests, but the truth is, if it weren't for the shortage of priests, lay ministry would not have blossomed so quickly. Because of it, we are discovering what it is like to have gifted laywomen and laymen preach,** conduct some of our rites (e.g., funeral vigil services), administer parish communities,

---

**Bishop Untener wrote this article nearly six years *before* the Prefect of the Vatican Congregation for Divine Worship and the Discipline of the Sacraments, Francis Cardinal Arinze, published an instruction entitled *Redemptionis Sacramentum*. This instruction, issued in April 2005, declared, among other things, that preaching may not be delegated to laity (nos. 64–66). The text is available on the Vatican website at http://www.vatican.va/roman_curia/congregations/ccdds/documents/rc_con_ccdds_doc_20040423_redemptionis-sacramentum_en.html. The English translation of the *General Instruction of the Roman Missal* (G.I.R.M.), 3rd ed., with adaptation for dioceses of the USA, issued by the USCCB Committee on Liturgy 2003, states that preaching may not be delegated to laity. (See no. 66 of G.I.R.M. as well as canon 767.)

provide pastoral counsel (e.g., befrienders). This will have incalcula-ble effects on the church of the next millennium.

The shortage of priests is real, but is not a sign of a dying church. As families do, we'll manage and we'll trust in the Lord. We'll find a way…and learn some things along the way.

3. THE WHOLESALE CLOSING OF PARISHES?

The truth is, this one is largely a myth. There have been much-publicized closings of parishes, but not because of a decline in church membership.

In most major and middle-sized cities, there are the "old sec-tions." This is where the city began and where the immigrants came and founded parishes based on nationality. Parishes, and neighborhoods, were French, German, Polish, Italian, Lithuanian, and some of them were only blocks apart. As the second, third, and fourth generations moved outward and mixed with each other, these parishes no longer fulfilled the needs of their founders. Parishes were still needed in those areas, but not within a few blocks of each other. There is an old axiom, "For something to have been good, it doesn't have to continue." Besides, the ethnic roots of a parish can work against its ministry to the new ethnic groups that move into the neighborhood.

In Saginaw, there were eleven parishes in the older part of town, and we eventually merged five of them into one parish. There are still seven parishes in this area (including our cathedral) and that part of the city still has the largest concentration of parishes per square mile (with far fewer Catholics) than any place in the city or diocese. But the shift made for media attention—as larger mergers did in larger dioceses—and gave the general impres-sion that this is an enterprise gradually going under as it closes one branch after another. Not true.

The Catholic Church in this country is not closing parishes because of a lack of membership. Rather, it is because of population shifts and an effort to serve better the area in which multiple parishes were attempting to sustain an identity rooted in the past.

The shortage of priests is now driving us to look at all of this, and it is painful and controversial. But it is not a symptom of a church in decline.

4. THE GRADUAL DEATH OF CATHOLIC SCHOOLS?

The decline in Catholic schools is sad to see. I am the product of twelve years at a parish school, and I am unabashedly biased in their favor.

What I appreciate most is the close connection the school gave me with the church. From the first grade on, I was connected with my parish in a way that would otherwise not have been. For twelve formative years, I "swam" in those waters. The church building became a second home to me, and I grew up with its sights and sounds and smells. The church year became part of the rhythm of my life. Feast days, holy days, Advent, Lent, and Holy Week were part of what I breathed. Church symbols surrounded me, not protectively but expansively. My Catholic school opened up to me a world where God was present.

Then why have so many Catholic schools closed? Money. The cost of education has increased geometrically. We can all identify with skyrocketing costs in every area of our lives. Education is no different.

Catholics have not lost their belief in Catholic schools. They're glad we have them and wish we had more. They have the illusion that someone else should (and can) pay for them—the parish to which they're attached, or the parents of the schoolchildren, or the diocese, or the Vatican. All of the above are impossible. It's simple mathematics, but Catholics are only gradually coming to understand the economics of their church. (Not their fault, by the way. Financial reports are relatively new.) Once Catholics discover that everyone has to pitch in to support Catholic schools, they will.

We've already started endowment funds for schools (we're latecomers to this form of funding, but it holds great promise), and there is a gradual move toward more public funds. We're laying the foundations for more and better Catholic schools in the next millennium.

5. THE GRADUAL DEATH OF RELIGIOUS LIFE?

"The handwriting is on the wall," some would say. "Religious communities can't come close to staffing our schools and hospitals the way they used to. Nuns and brothers and monks will soon be a thing of the past. Some communities have already died. As for the larger ones, their members have been leaving, left and right, for over twenty years. They're getting only a trickle of new members, and some haven't had a candidate in years."

The first thing to say is that religious communities blossom because of a gift of the Spirit. You can't plan and build them like you plan and build a house. They spring up like wildflowers, and you don't know where or when they will grow. And, like wildflowers, they come and go. Religious communities aren't meant to last forever. Some have relatively short lives. Hundreds and hundreds of religious communities had come and gone before the twentieth century began.

Our mistake has been to see religious as a labor force in the church. Not that they shouldn't labor. But they are not *our* labor force, that is, meant to staff positions we've created in parishes, schools, and institutions. For the last few centuries we've looked upon them that way and now it is changing. We are having to raise up and train a wide variety of ministers in the church to fill the positions previously filled by religious. That is all to the good—both for lay ministry and for religious life. And it is a sign of life, not death.

Actually, the last thing we need to worry about in the church is the future of religious life. Religious need the freedom to grow where they will. And it is God through the Spirit, who gives the growth. We are witnessing not the death of religious life, but the end of religious life as a labor force to perform the regular tasks that we create for them. What we need to do is let them emerge in new ways to give their unusual witness and do the unusual good works that they have always done since the church began.

6. PUBLIC AND COSTLY SCANDALS, ESPECIALLY AMONG THE CLERGY?

In recent years Catholics have suffered the embarrassment of national coverage of scandals involving the clergy.

Because of the high publicity given to some of the priests involved, many people have the mistaken notion that there is a higher percentage of such problems among priests. The fact is, the media pay more attention when such things occur among Catholic priests. This isn't because the media are anti-Catholic. It is because in the eyes of most everyone there is a certain mystique about Catholic priests. Thus, when a Catholic priest is involved (in anything), the media know that it is a bigger story than if ministers of other faiths were involved. Leaders of other faiths tell me that one of the problems that consumes a major part of their time is sexual misconduct.

There are three things worth keeping in mind. First, priests are part of the normal human population. When you are dealing with a sickness (e.g., cancer, alcoholism, pedophilia), whatever percentage is found in the normal human population will probably be found among priests. These are things you can't catch in advance by careful screening.

Second, sometimes the church is judged by today's standards for something that occurred before today's standards existed. Not too many years ago the word *pedophilia* was not even in a psychologist's vocabulary. Such behavior wasn't considered a disease. Nor did anyone realize the effects it had on the victim. It was simply inexcusable conduct, a moral failure, and it was handled accordingly—the same way parents handled it when they discovered that a relative or family friend had abused one of their children. Now, we know differently.

Third, the huge financial penalties assessed against Catholic dioceses can be misleading, giving the impression that the Catholic Church is guiltier than others. The truth is, we are more vulnerable to such lawsuits. As a lawyer friend of mine explained to me, in any lawsuit you look at three things: culpability, liability, and collectability. Culpability: Did the person do what is alleged? Liability: Is this person (or someone beyond this person) exposed to penalty, expense for what was done? Collectability: Can those liable come up with the money?

Most cases of pedophilia involve a relative or family friend. You may be able to establish culpability, even liability, but the collectability of a penalty in six or seven figures isn't there. When it comes to a Catholic priest, as my lawyer friend put it: "You folks are sitting ducks—the liability and collectability are there for the asking. The diocese or religious community is considered liable because a priest is perceived as in its service twenty-four hours a day, seven days a week. As for collectability, the diocese may not be rich, but (unlike a family acquaintance) it can probably find some way to come up with the money."

My purpose here is not to minimize these diseases and moral failures or their possible effects. I simply want to dispel the false notion that the Catholic clergy has had a higher percentage of offenders, or that church leadership is lax in dealing with it. Now that the social sciences have recognized and diagnosed the dimensions of this problem, I know of no bishop who fails to deal with it swiftly and seriously.

7. SEVERE POLARIZATION IN THE CHURCH?

In dealing with news stories (as distinct from feature stories) the media try to find people on opposing sides of the issue. Thus, when a church leader makes a decision, the media look for people who disagree...and some are always available. Among other things, this makes for good copy. Readers and viewers see this over and over, and quite understandably picture the church as fragmented.

So do reporters. They ask me about polarization all the time. For many years I answered by talking about the changes of Vatican II, the time it will take to adjust, the usual stuff. Then it occurred to me: This isn't a polarized church. A *pole* is an extremity of an axis or sphere. A polarized church would mean that its members are clustered at different extremities.

I go from parish to parish, give talks and retreats around the country, and have a chance to converse with many people. This is not a fragmented, polarized church. Catholics have differing opinions, sometimes strong opinions, but that is not divisiveness. You have the same thing in a normal, healthy family.

I know, I know...the old bromide of the "silent majority" or blame it on the media. I'm not suggesting that the church is one large silent majority, accepting and happy about everything. For one thing, they are definitely not silent. They have differing opinions, and they're quite willing to express them. But a split church we are not. As for the media, they're simply reporting what's there through the lens of controversy, which is normal fare. What we need to do is put it in perspective. A good way to start is to look around you at Sunday Eucharist.

8. RUMORS OF SINISTER PLOTS WITHIN THE CHURCH?

Not long ago I gave a presentation during which I talked about how unscrupulous salespeople prey on the fears of others (especially the elderly), telling them that if they don't get this or that repair done to their furnace or their car, something terrible will happen. I pointed out that this goes on in the church too. Unscrupulous publications and/or suspicious individuals make unfounded and sweeping charges that generate rumors in all directions.

Here is a sample of three rumors I've heard over and over: (1) Mafiosi, Communists, and Masons have infiltrated the church at the highest levels and some are now cardinals in the Vatican; (2) some U.S. "liberal" bishops are trying to separate from Rome and make us an "American church"; (3) Bishop Ken Untener refuses to ordain another priest until he can ordain a woman.

It's the old story; start big rumors (not small ones) because they're more believable. And if you keep repeating them, people will at least begin to wonder if they aren't partly true. I'll deal very briefly with this trio.

This first rumor (cardinals who are Mafiosi, Communists, Masons) is too far-fetched to rate more than a sentence. This pope, who as a young man fought to keep his faith alive despite a repressive materialistic government, who stood as a bulwark against Communism, who has had the courage to speak out against the Italian Mafia—this pope is going to appoint such people cardinals. Right.

The second rumor (liberal bishops trying to create an "American church") is promoted by several arch-conservative publications. When people see the rumor in print they think it has more substance, which it doesn't. I've been a bishop for over eighteen years and I have never, ever heard a bishop suggest even indirectly or in a whisper…that we should think about the possibility…that perhaps someday we should give some theoretical consideration to the chance that some of us might one day step back just a little bit from full communion with the Holy Father. Not on your life.

To disagree with the successor of Peter is one thing. (St. Paul did it with Peter himself.) To break communion with him is another. I would never consider it, and I have never known or ever heard of any bishop who would remotely think of it.

The third rumor (that I won't ordain another priest until I can ordain a woman) has been circulating for at least ten years, and I've heard it all over the country. This, despite the fact that during these ten years I have been regularly ordaining priests. Strange how rumors have a life of their own.

A CLOSING THOUGHT

We don't know how much time is left in history. There's no compelling reason to think we're near the end. Our solar system has millions of years left in it. If we think in those terms, then the church is very young.

Strange how we generally think of it as old. When people use the image of a tree for the church, they usually draw a large, old, fully developed tree. I would rather think of it as a young tree, whose final shape we don't yet know.

Whatever its age, the tree is strong and full of life. There are some broken branches, some twists in its trunk. But none of these problems are life-threatening. The vital signs are very good. It is a strong, healthy tree.

We've got some major things to deal with, and I believe the biggest one is the role of women in the church. But we've got the inner strength to face this and other major issues, despite a minority opposition even to look at them. We are a strong church; our strength is rooted in the church as it exists in parish after parish, diocese after diocese. The *sensus fidelium* (sense of the faithful) is strong and robust. We face challenges, but the body is hale and hearty and is up to them.

There is some sort of major shift going on in the world, and when you're in the middle of it you don't know exactly what it is. This tree has already gone through several great shifts and many storms. By God's providence, Pope John XXIII called a council thirty-five years ago. It was a council that took us back to our roots, restored them, and did some needed pruning. It couldn't have come at a better time, although its effects are only gradually emerging.

I have my own feelings of frustration with this church that I love. I have a whole list of things that I would like to see changed, as do many of you. But, am I optimistic about the church? You bet I am. Our hope does not rest on the abilities of bishops or popes, or the sinlessness of all of us, or a good public relations department. Our hope rests on the Spirit, promised always to the church by Jesus, who never breaks his promise.

The words of St. Augustine sixteen centuries ago ring true today: "People look upon [the church] and say, 'She is about to die. Soon her very name will disappear. There will be no more Christians; they have had their day.' While they are thus speaking, I see these very people die themselves, day by day, but the church lives on."

What Catholics Believe about the End of the World

Catholic Update (September 1993)

In January of 1843, a preacher named William Miller—the founder of the American Adventist movement—announced that the end of the world would take place between March 21, 1843, and March 21, 1844. He had combed the Bible for clues and figured it all out.

Thousands from all denominations believed him, and tension mounted as the yearlong vigil began, heightened by the appearance of a comet. Alas, the fateful year came to an end, and the world didn't. Neither did the speculation. There had been a miscalculation, Miller pointed out. He and his followers found a passage in the prophet Habakkuk about a "delay," and a verse in the Book of Leviticus about seven days and ten months. Neither passage, of course, had anything to do with the end of the world, but never mind that. A new date was announced: October 22, 1844. Tension mounted once again. You know the outcome.

Similar scenarios have taken place in every age and continue at this moment. Such prophets never fail to find believers. Elvis lives. The hype increases as we approach the year 2000. Some take it seriously, even fanatically, as did the Branch Davidian sect in Waco, Tex., in 1993. One radio church lists twenty-four signs from the Bible that the end is near. Crop rotation in Israel, for example, fulfills a prophecy in Amos about the plowman overtaking the reaper. And on and on it goes.

Some Key Questions

The problem with all this is that it creates a doomsday mood, and causes people to treat this world like a throwaway ballpoint pen. These past weeks I made it a point to converse with various parishioners about this topic, and I'll treat here the things that came up most frequently. I do so from a Roman Catholic perspective, based on the work of recognized scripture scholars and theologians of various denominations. Let's look first at some commonly asked questions.

What is Armageddon? There is a road running through the middle of Israel to the sea. About fifteen miles before it reaches the sea lie the ruins of a city called Megiddo. Its strategic location made it the scene of colossal battles going back six-thousand years. When speaking of any great conflict, people often spoke of it as Megiddo or Armageddon, Hebrew words referring to the area around this city. Some go to great lengths in speculating about a final battle of Armageddon between the forces of good and evil preceding the end of the world (see Rev 16:14–16).

There is no reason to believe that the city or plain of Armageddon has any connection with the end of the world. It is simply an image, not unlike saying, "Well, next Tuesday is D day." If someone overheard this and started watching for something to happen next Tuesday on the beaches of Normandy (where the Allies began the invasion of France in World War II), we would think it strange.

What is the significance of the millennium and "The Thousand-Year Reign of Christ"? A passage in Revelation reads: "Then I saw an angel come down from heaven, holding in his hand the key to the abyss and a heavy chain. He seized the dragon, the ancient serpent, which is the Devil or Satan, and tied it up for a thousand years..." (Rev 20:1–2).

The thousand years simply means a long time, just as we might say, "You won't guess this in a thousand years." We are now in the long period between Christ's victory (symbolically expressed by tying up Satan) and his coming in glory. It could last millions of years.

There are people (*millenarians*) who take this passage literally and search for signs of some thousand-year period on earth. When you start thinking in terms of a millennium, the approach of the year 2000 can get exciting. The same thing happened as the year 1000 approached. It's the old problem of taking symbolic language literally.

Should we be preoccupied about the year 2000? We number things for convenience. The pages in a book, for example, are numbered for easy reference. The page numbered one hundred really isn't the one-hundredth page, since the first few pages either aren't numbered or have Roman numerals. The numbers simply help us find the right page.

We have done the same with our years, and there have been different numbering systems—the Jewish calendar, the Chinese calendar and others. The Gregorian calendar, now in common use, was introduced some four-hundred years ago and took the birth of Christ as its reference point.

The year 2000 is not really the two-thousandth year. For one thing, the Gregorian calendar has no year *zero*—which means we are already one year off. For another thing, there was a miscalculation on the date of Christ's birth, which took place between 7 and 4 BC. In other words, the year 2000 is not the two-thousandth year after Christ's birth. Calendar dates are just numbers for common reference, with no particular scriptural or theological significance.

What about the "rapture"? We normally use rapture to signify spiritual or emotional ecstasy. However, the more basic meaning of the word is "to seize, to transport." End-of-the-world prophets use it in this latter sense. Matthew's Gospel speaks of two women grinding meal; one is "taken" and the other is left (see 24:41). Literalists do not accept this as symbolic language, and they expect that at the end of time the just will be plucked from the earth by God (see 1 Thess 4:17). Bumper stickers read, "Are you ready for the rapture?" It is another example of taking symbolic language literally.

How should we understand the Antichrist? The term *Antichrist* appears only in the first and second epistles of John. It is clearly a term symbolic of the forces working against Christ in all periods of history, not a clue about a specific individual. If someone observed, "Every family has skeletons in the closet," you would miss the point if you started searching the hallway closet!

Doomsday Passages in Scripture

We now take a closer look at how the Bible treats the end of the world. We are familiar with various kinds of literature: poetry, science fiction, history, satire. Most people are not familiar with a kind of literature called *apocalyptic*. It was very popular from about 200 BC to AD 200, a time of great crisis in Israel.

The Greek word *apocalypse* (in English, *revelation*) literally means "to draw back the veil." When times were tough, writers tried to bring comfort by putting things into a wider perspective. Baseball managers try to do the same when their team is in a slump: "We were riding high at the beginning of the season, but now the sky has fallen in. Well, we've been through tough times before. It's a long season and we've got the horses."

Apocalyptic literature attempts to give assurance that, however bad things may be, one need only draw back the veil and see things in perspective of the great battle against evil, and appreciate the length and breadth and depth of God's victorious power at work among us.

To paint this larger picture, writers drew from a storehouse of stock apocalyptic images that dwarfed the immediate crisis. Among the standard images were: stars falling from the sky, the sun and moon darkened, lightning, thunder, dragons, creatures with many eyes, four horsemen, trumpet blasts, water turning to blood, plagues. It's a way of saying that the present order of things is not the whole picture and will be giving way to something new and much larger.

Strange pictures are conjured up when people take these apocalyptic images literally. Imagine what would happen if people in future epochs took literally images we use today: raining cats and dogs, hit the roof, money coming out of his ears, two-faced, forked tongue, on cloud nine, and so on.

Don't Look for Coded Messages

Biblical writers addressed the problems of their day. These past events have parallels in every age, and we can learn from them.

But there is not the slightest indication that the authors were giving secret coded messages about distant future events. The Bible is not a coded message for a select few. It is the basic story of human life for all people in every age.

But people continue to look for coded messages. For example, the Book of Revelation, using apocalyptic language, speaks of a beast with "feet like a bear's." Some people in modern times have actually thought this was a secret message about Russia. Never mind that the Book of Revelation was written for an audience of the first century! This is the sort of thing that happens when scripture is treated like a word game.

And then there are numbers. A thousand years simply means a long time, and a certain number of months means a short time. Those who take these numbers literally become the William Millers of every age. One of the favorites is the passage in the Book of Revelation that assigns the number 666 to one of the beasts. The author, using the numerical value of letters, was probably referring to the Roman emperor Nero. Since then, people have applied it to world leaders in every age, including Hitler, Mussolini, Stalin, and many others. Popes have been fairly regular targets.

Sayings of Jesus about the End of the World

When the disciples marveled at the beauty of the Temple, Jesus told them that some day it would all be destroyed. He uses apocalyptic language: "There will be powerful earthquakes, famines, and plagues from place to place; and awesome sights and mighty signs will come from the sky....Woe to pregnant women and nursing mothers in those days, for a terrible calamity will come upon the earth and a wrathful judgment upon this people" (Luke 21:11, 23). Taken literally, this sounds like a dreadful end to the whole world, but it actually refers to the destruction of Jerusalem in AD 70. Because he uses apocalyptic language, many of the sayings of Jesus about the end of Jerusalem are wrongly applied to the end of the world.

Still there are times when Jesus does talk about the end of the world, and here too he uses apocalyptic language: "the sun will be darkened, and the moon will not give its light, and the stars will fall from the sky, and the powers of the heavens will be shaken" (Matt 24:29). We find the same stock images in the thirteenth chapter of Isaiah, referring to the fall of Babylon six centuries before Christ: "The stars and constellations of the heavens send forth no light; the sun is dark when it rises and the light of the moon does not shine…the heavens tremble and the earth shall be shaken from its place."

There will be an end to history as we know it, and the fads and fashions of this world are passing. When it will come is irrelevant—it will come for each of us at death. And how it will come is unknown, because apocalyptic language is symbolic and cannot be plumbed for secret clues that simply aren't there. The basic message of these passages is a clear one: If we live as though the finite horizons of this life were the whole of reality, we are fools indeed.

The Second Coming of Christ

There was a time when it was customary on ascension Thursday, after reading the gospel, to extinguish the paschal candle—as though Jesus were gone and we were left to await his second coming at the end of time.

Scripture doesn't use the phrase second coming, but speaks of various comings of the Lord, often using the Greek word *parousia* ("presence, coming"). Jesus promised his disciples that he would come back to them, and he did come back after the resurrection, breathing the Spirit upon them and fulfilling the promise that the Father and he would make their dwelling with them (and with us). In Matthew's Gospel, his last words are, "And behold, I am with you always, until the end of the age" (Matt 28:20).

We believe that his presence will be manifest in a much fuller way at the end of the age, which will be the Parousia. We shouldn't picture this as an arrival from outer space, as though he had to come "from a distance." The image of Jesus "seated at the right hand of the Father" expresses honor, not geographic place. The image of Jesus coming on a cloud is an apocalyptic expression, taken straight from the Book of Daniel—"I saw one like a son of man coming on the clouds of heaven" (7:13)—and should not be taken literally.

The Eucharistic Prayer for Children III expresses all this quite well: "Jesus now lives with you (Father) in glory, but he is also here on earth among us....One day he will come in glory." We don't really know what it will be like when Jesus, already present among us, fully manifests himself in glory at the end of the age. It will probably be as different from our expectations as was every other parousia, including the incarnation.

Is the end of the world near? No one has any idea. It could be forty million years away (the sun has at least that much fuel), or it could happen a week from Tuesday.

A Frightening End or a New Birth?

Perhaps the best way to describe the end of the world is to see it as history coming to term. This is a birth image, which is one of the images Jesus used. We are within history, which is like being in the confines of the womb, and what a mistake it would be to think there is not a wider reality ahead of us. It would be equally a mistake to think that what we are about now is unimportant. Just as in a pregnancy, what is being formed is very important to what shall be, so in the process of history, what is taking shape will be very much related to what is born into the reign of God. We are not throwaways, and this is not a throwaway world.

While the end of this stage might be frightening, as birth can be, it need not be seen as catastrophic. It is a passing over into something not fully known. When a child is born, almost all its points of reference are changed, and that can be traumatic. But it is a beautiful event.

We have a wide picture of salvation. We really believe in the saving of this world, the one we're living in. In his miracles Jesus gave us a taste of the kingdom emerging into this world, and the world into the kingdom. We don't take this world or history lightly.

Catholics generally are not preoccupied with prophecies of impending doom. They have an optimistic view of the world and see the end as the gradual (not sudden) passing of creation into

God's realm. They give value to the things of earth by incorporating them into their journey to God. Perhaps this is related to our rather "earthy" tradition of using material things—palms, ashes, water, bread, wine, oil, fire, incense, vestments, colors, icons, symbols—in our worship.

But on the other hand, we don't have the illusion that this is the whole of reality. What a tragedy it would be if a person were to gain the whole of this world and destroy oneself in the process. Apocalyptic imagery can be used badly to make it seem as though "the end" were simply a matter of the just being plucked from the deck of a sinking ship (the universe) and transported to a new ship unrelated to this one. It can trivialize the significance of Jesus becoming part of our world in the incarnation. In so doing, it can trivialize the length and breadth of salvation.

When Will It All Happen?

When will history come to term? When will the "birth" happen? We don't know. There is no indication that it is near, and there is no assurance that it is far. What is important is not when it will happen, but that it will happen. History is short when put in perspective. The Second Epistle of Peter reminds us, "But do not ignore this one fact, beloved, that with the Lord one day is like a thousand years and a thousand years like one day" (3:8).

What is also important is that our own end is relatively near. By the insurance mortality charts, I have twenty-three years left. Only God knows the actual count. In the parable of the rich fool, Jesus presents this perspective in language we can all understand. After a bountiful harvest, the rich man plans to store his grain in bigger barns, believing he can now rest, eat, drink, be merry. God says to him, "You fool, this night your life will be demanded of you; and the things you have prepared, to whom will they belong?" (Luke 12:20).

When we see ourselves and this world in the perspective of history coming to term, we see with different eyes. Things that seem so important within the limited horizon of the womb of history become not so important. Things that seem not so important in this world's eyes become very important. It changes one's whole attitude about what you want to do with your life.

Instead of fretting about the question of "when," therefore, we are wiser to focus on the question of "who"—namely, upon a loving God who promises to walk with us to the end, whenever that occurs. Our understanding of the "end" flows from a real-life conviction about the here-and-now meaning of our lives and our universe. In short, we believe with St. Paul that the same God "who began a good work in you will continue to complete it until the day of Christ Jesus" (Phil 1:6).

Resource, Not Source:
The Role of Central Offices
in the Diocesan Church

Talk to Diocesan Employees
August 17, 1981

I remember vividly an incident that occurred a couple of months ago when the air controllers strike was supposed to go into effect at midnight. It was Sunday evening, and I was on a DC-10 from out west going to Chicago. Everyone was hurrying to make it back home. The flight went routinely enough for a couple of hours, and then the captain came on the speaker and said that there was a back-up of air traffic in Chicago, and we didn't have enough fuel to circle for the amount of time necessary, so we would have to go to Kansas City for refueling. This meant going quite a bit out of our way and also a long delay that would cause most of us to miss our connections at Chicago. With the imminent strike, many of us expected to be marooned. As if that weren't enough, once we landed and arrived at the gate, the stewardess came on the speaker and said that there weren't enough personnel in the airport, so we would not be allowed to get off the airplane. This really caused a stir, because a large number of people wanted to phone their families to say that they would be missing their connections. The mood inside the plane grew surly, and then all kinds of rumors started. People were saying that large planes like this could fly the Pacific Ocean, so why couldn't they make it to Chicago. Others said that they didn't see any fuel trucks out there, so they didn't believe this business about refueling. A number of people were crowding around the exit and arguing with the stewardess. I happened to be in that area and, although I had no reason to have to call anyone, I entered the discussion. I asked her why we couldn't get off, even though there weren't enough gate personnel, and she said that it would be too difficult to round the people up when it was time for the plane to leave. I asked what would happen if we took it as our own responsibility and left the plane only with the understanding that we did so at our own risk. She didn't have much to say to that, and that was all it took for the group to storm the jetway and head for the terminal. I felt like I had led a mutiny.

As I was standing there, enjoying a soft drink, the pilot came by and I began to chat with him. I asked him some of the questions that I had heard asked—why a plane like this wouldn't have enough fuel, and so forth. He explained that it was a very hot day and that the temperatures on the runway when we took off were probably around 110 or 120 degrees. Since a jet engine is made to function at 30 or 40 degrees below zero, it does not run very effectively at high temperatures. Furthermore, the plane was very full because of everyone's anxiety about the strike. For that reason, he took on less fuel than he normally would, to reduce the weight on takeoff. He had checked with Chicago and the weather seemed fine, and there were no apparent tie-ups. However, as the day wore on (and after we were already in flight) the air controllers apparently started to space out the traffic a little more, and when you do that at the busiest airport in the world, you very quickly have a backlog of planes that will have to circle for 40 or 50 minutes. As soon as he got word about that, he realized that we would have to take on more fuel, so he diverted the flight to Kansas City.

It made perfectly good sense, and now I understood. I said to myself, "why didn't he just tell the people?" *Information builds trust; lack of information breeds suspicion and rumors.* It convinced me of something I already believed in, namely, that it is best to tell people everything—the good news and the bad news. I want you to know from the outset that that is one of my operating principles. It is one of the reasons why I started a newsletter. And, the purpose of this meeting is to help put that principle in effect.

Since my coming here to Saginaw, almost nine months ago, some of you, no doubt, are wondering about my view of a chancery office or of central offices in general. You probably wonder what changes I have in mind, and what may be lurking around the corner. The following reflections, I hope, will help to answer questions like that.

I Used to Work in a Chancery Office

In 1965 I was assigned to the chancery office of the Archdiocese of Detroit as assistant chancellor. There was a chancellor, a vice-chancellor, another assistant chancellor, and I was about as low on the totem pole as you could get. I worked in those central offices for about ten years. At different times, I remember we used to complain a little bit that those in charge had probably never worked in a chancery office, and didn't know a lot of what we went through. They had been in parishes, or in seminary work, but never in a chancery office.

Well, for whatever it's worth, I want you to know that I have been there. I know what it's like to try to work on a limited budget, to be subject to review, to set goals and objectives, to deal with a public that sometimes seems so unreasonable or impatient, to be told that office people don't know what it's like "out there" in the parishes, and so on. I have experienced that, as you have, and I want you to know that we have this in common. I hope it helps me to understand you better.

The Role of Central Offices

I remember talking to Bishop Dozier a couple of years ago. He had put on a city-wide celebration of the sacrament of reconciliation. It was done very carefully and it involved a year-long preparation. However, since general absolution was involved, it got a lot of notoriety and there was some misunderstanding about it in Rome. Various offices of the Curia (Rome's central offices) sent him inquiries about it and there was a bit of a flap. My conversation with Bishop Dozier took place after all this was over, and I asked him how he handled inquiries like that and how it affected him. He looked at me and said, "Well, first thing you have to understand is that the people in those offices are *my* staff."

Theologically, of course, he is absolutely correct. The church is not made of a central office in Rome, with branch offices called *dioceses* around the world. *The church is made up of individual "churches" called dioceses, and these are in communion with one another. Each diocese is fully "church" and exists in its own right.* They are linked with one another in a communion, but they are not branch offices. Thus, Bishop Dozier was correct. He does not work for those office people in the Curia. They work for him, and for all the bishops of the world.

Now to some extent, the same thing is true of a diocese. Pastors and ministerial leaders around this diocese could look to these offices and say, "That's my staff." *We do not constitute a headquarters with a lot of branch offices called parishes. Wherever people gather around the eucharistic table, there you have the local church.* These are not meant to be *isolated from one another in a diocese—they are in very close communion. But, they are not branch offices whose source is general headquarters.*

Those of us who work in central offices have to keep reminding ourselves of that. Quite easily and unconsciously we adopt the more normal model of business or government, with a central staff that is in charge of branch offices.

When you stop and think about it, there is no reason for any of us to have the illusion that we are the source of all that is happening out there. When you go from parish to parish you see thousands of things going on that are creative and unique to that place. There are things we never could have thought of. *Our task* is to be supportive of what *they are doing,* to *stoke the fires of their creativity,* provide services that make *the task* easier, and *respond to their needs.* In a sense, *we are like a good library* at a university, *a resource center* that tries to provide high quality services and also tries to stimulate good *academic* work.

The best way of describing why and how central offices came into being is to describe them as a pooling of resources and services. Religious education is an example. Every parish runs some kind of religious education program. It makes sense to have an office that obtains and reviews the mass of materials on the market, and makes them available, rather than having each parish do this on its own. The deposit and loan program is another example. Parishes with excess funds put them on deposit and make them available to those that have to borrow, and it becomes a family affair. You need a central office to coordinate that. There are other obvious examples—the tribunal, Catholic family services, the Latin American affairs department, and so forth.

There are also times when it makes sense to adopt a common diocesan policy. Such policies are not set by us, but with the participation of the parishes and ministerial leaders themselves, primarily through the Senate/DPC. Our marriage preparation guidelines are an example of this. Requiring a six-month preparation was felt to be an excellent approach, but it would only work if we get together on it. So, we have a diocesan policy. A number of such common approaches have been developed over the years. Coordinating them and providing supportive services is one of the other reasons for central offices.

There are times, of course, when we are more than people standing by. There are times when we have to take a good look at some local situations that seem to be out of step with things we have agreed to do together or must do together. But the spirit behind such interventions must be that of service offices, not of general headquarters. Each pastor out there is entrusted with the main responsibility of leading that local community. He can truly look to us and say, "That's my staff." If there is a problem with pastoral leadership, then it is my responsibility to try to do something about it. This is part of my basic responsibility as bishop, not as "manager" of central offices.

We Are "Waiters"—but Not Drones

While I was installed as bishop of Saginaw, I told the people that I had come to be their waiter. I did not create that analogy. I took it from the gospels, where we read that Jesus said to his disciples: "For who is the greater: the one at table or the one who serves? The one at table, surely? Yet here am I among you as one who serves!" (Luke 22:27). Jesus also used the example of a foot washer, and he expressed it in deeds, not just in words, by washing the feet of his disciples at the Last Supper. This is the normative model for anyone in ministry, and that includes all of us.

This spirit has to characterize everything we do. But, we must not lose sight of the fact that what we do calls for a very high degree of skill. As waiters, we want to serve the very best. We have to have expertise in each of our areas and provide the highest quality of resources. We have to have extraordinary human skills so that we can deal helpfully with people, whether on the telephone, or through a letter, or in a personnel meeting. This includes everyone from a receptionist to the head of a department.

We should not underestimate the importance and the far-reaching effects that this kind of service can have. I remember, for example, the person who ran the library at St. John's, Sister Claudia Carlan. She is retired now, but she built that library into one of the finest theological libraries around. She was a gentle person in the very best sense of that term. She was highly competent, and you always knew that the books and resources were of the finest quality. She also had personal skills that created an atmosphere in the entire library, and when you came there you could feel it. Her work had effects that went beyond the library and affected the entire institution of St. John's. It lifted the academic excellence and spirit of the entire place. You see, this was not an operation that fostered such excellence by mandating it. She didn't give out assignments in class and she didn't flunk anybody. She simply provided a service that helped to draw the best out of everyone, including the teachers. The library was not the "headquarters" of the seminary. It provided a service, but the way that service was provided had powerful and profound effects.

I have seen other libraries (we all have seen them) where this was not so. The materials were often second rate or hard to get. In some libraries there are signs all over the place giving directives—no food, no drink, certain dress requirements, limited hours, silence—with certain things underlined, exclamation points, and the rest. All these things seem like restrictions or demands, and you feel like an outsider in someone else's kingdom. Furthermore, when you approach one of the staff in such a library, it's as though you're interrupting *their* schedule. And sometimes they make you feel small, or even dumb, because you don't know where certain information is.

Now, Sister Claudia certainly ran a good library, and you knew that there was to be a spirit of peace and quiet. You knew also that books were to be returned on time, because, after all, they are meant to be available to everyone. And, the place was well organized because she was a highly competent professional. But all of this was achieved in a way that made you feel that the resources of the library and the entire staff were there for *you*. And that is the spirit we must have, a spirit of excellence and service that affects the whole diocese and draws the best out of everyone, not so much through mandate as through example and service.

Role of the Chancellor-Moderator

Given all that I've said, you can see that the overall leadership of the complex and valuable activities of the diocesan center and the diocesan agencies is an important responsibility. But we can't lose sight of the fact that the overall leadership of any of our parishes, whether it be St. Stephen's Parish in Saginaw or St. Roch's in Caseville, or St. Athanasius in Harrison, is also a complex and important responsibility.

I have often referred to my role as "ministering to the ministers," and you are included among those ministers. If I devoted myself to the actual management of any one of our operations such as the diocesan center, or one of the parishes, I would become almost totally consumed in that and have little time to go around ministering to the ministers. For that reason, I have opted not to take even the nominal role of the direct management of diocesan offices and agencies. I have delegated this responsibility to the chancellor-moderator, and I have distributed to you his revised job description and the revised flow chart incorporating this change. The chancellor-moderator carries out his responsibility, *not only in my absence*, or *when I am too busy*, but as part of his normal responsibility just as, for example, a pastor does in a parish.

This is not because I consider what you are doing unimportant or not deserving of my time. Rather, it's because if I give my time to

the direct management of any one of the many important operations in the diocese, I no longer would be able to minister in other
ways to *all* of them. *I do recognize the fact that I am accountable for all*
that is happening in the diocese (including what is happening at the
diocesan center), but the director management is handled by various individuals, primarily pastors, and in your case the chancellor-
moderator.

I might say that, so far, I don't think I've done much about
ministering to the ministers in your regard. Most of my efforts have
been directed to visiting parishes and groups of people "out there."
This is the first time we've all come together in this way, and I
assure you that it marks the beginning of more ministry in your
direction.

Quality of Work, Salaries, and Such

People who have done national studies and try to assist personnel in reaching their full potential say that most employees
work at 40 to 50 percent of their effectiveness. The reason is not
general laziness. Rather, it is usually the fault of the organization
itself. Employees have the feeling that if they work at full capacity,
they will run out of things to do on a given day, and people truly
want to have something to do. Or, if they finish their work, they
know from experience that their supervisor will give them unimportant things to do, and people don't want simply to be given
"busy work" to keep them occupied.

From my observations, we have a much higher rate of personnel effectiveness in our diocesan offices. For one thing, we have
a more close-knit organization and we can work together better.
Also, people tend to come to work here out of some sense of dedication, which means that they come with very high motivation.

However, I am also aware that we can expect to have a certain
degree of the problems common to any organization. We are not
exempt from that. My goal is to find ways to help all of us operate
at our full effectiveness. You do not accomplish this by being a slave
driver or operating a sweat shop. You accomplish it by building
trust, by listening to the suggestions of people, because people truly

want to do their jobs well. You do it by subsidiarity, that is, allowing each person as much freedom and responsibility as possible.

If we can achieve a higher percentage of effectiveness, it will certainly add more meaning to each of your lives. It will also help the diocese, because we cannot afford to carry all the extra employees that would be needed to take up the slack if we were generally operating at 50 percent effectiveness.

When it comes to salaries, I would like to make an important distinction between pay for priests and religious, and pay for lay employees. Priests and religious do not really receive a salary. They are given basic financial support in order to free them up to do the things that they are about. Normally, a salary is an attempt to pay someone proportionately to the value of their services. The more important your responsibilities and the better you perform, the more money you receive. This is not true for priests and religious. They are given room and board and some financial support to relieve them of worrying about such things while they are doing the other things, some of which no one could ever pay for. The money they receive is not intended to reflect the value of their services. And the level of financial support given to priests and sisters is generally far less than would be expected for professional people of their caliber.

Now a person might conclude that this should be true for all church employees. In other words, when people work for the church they should, out of a sense of dedication, work for much less. I do not believe this. You cannot mix together the very different situation of priest and religious on the one hand and lay employees on the other. (On the other hand, I would not want to exclude the possibility of some people freely deciding to take less pay out of a sense of ministry, because I consider your work a ministry. However, this is an area that needs further exploration.)

We can't compete at the top of the salary scale of lay corporations. But we shouldn't be at the bottom either. We shouldn't try to squeeze as much work out of you as we can for the lowest salary you can tolerate, and then claim that you should just do this because you work for the church. Some might call this responsible stewardship, since we are using monies placed in our trust by the people of the diocese. That is not stewardship; it is injustice. Besides, that is not how you get the very finest people to work with you and stay with you, and we want the very finest people.

We can't give you the top salary, but we don't want to be at the bottom either. I'd like to see us somewhere in the middle, paying a wage that is just and that also helps to give you a sense of self-worth, a sense that what you are doing is very valuable and very much appreciated. I also want to see that we provide the other things that far exceed what the very best corporations can offer, things such as a climate of working together, a sense of doing things that are worthwhile, flexibility, and so forth. We have an extraordinary opportunity here in the Diocese of Saginaw to provide for our employees a very high degree of job satisfaction and achieve a very high degree of personnel effectiveness. If we do that, we exercise good leadership in helping you to live up to your potential and sense your own self-worth.

Sense of "Community" among Us

There was a time when I felt that, because we are involved in work for the church, and because we share a common faith, those who work in a diocesan center such as this, or in a diocesan agency, should be very close-knit. We should socialize and pray together a lot.

Then, someone pointed out to me that this is not necessarily everyone's "primary community." You have religious women, for example, who live in a small community that is close-knit and that does pray together every day. You have priests who are assigned to a parish, and the parish is really their primary community. You have people who have their own families, and this is their center of gravity.

I guess I had never thought of it that way, and it was a real eye-opener for me. Now that I have rethought it, I think we should certainly make provision for those who want a close social contact and prayer life, but we shouldn't force it on everyone or make it one of those unspoken expectations. There are special events when we come together, of course, and that is part of our responsibility to each other. But in day-to-day relations, people should be free to be part of the "community" in varying degrees.

Having said that, I think there are some expectations that are higher for us because we are part of the church and because we share the same gospel. We may have options about our degree of community, but we don't have options about caring about and for one another. I think we should go out of our way to find out what one another is doing. It means a great deal when other people consider what you are doing important enough to be interested in it. It also helps us do a better job when the right hand knows that the left hand is doing. Beyond that, a personal level of concern also ought to be there. Sometimes, you just know that someone else is having a bad day, or a bad week, or is just plain going through some tough times. There are lots of ways to help a person at a time like this— just to stop by the office to say hello, or to do something kind for them and restore their faith in human nature (and in themselves), or simply let them know that someone cares. We have the flexibility to do that. There aren't people peering over your shoulder, marking down every time you leave your desk. We have the freedom to minister to one another and that is not optional. It runs through the gospel from beginning to end.

Where I Stand on Theologies of the Priesthood

Priests' Assembly, 1998

You asked me some months back to do something specific for this assembly. You asked for current ecclesiologies and theologies of priesthood, and where do I stand?

I'm going to answer that, and ask a further question: Where do you stand?

The presbyterate, in the teaching of Vatican II, shares in the fullness of the orders of the bishop of the diocese.

The first office of the bishop according to the Vatican documents (LG, CD) is the office to teach. You share in that.

We have in the past few years concentrated on the Word in our diocese, in its many dimensions. These are a few of them: preaching groups, Liturgy of the Word preparation of readers, introductions for the scripture readings, particularly the Old Testament, and Lent 95–99.

Second, the bishop, by office, is responsible for the means of sanctification: for eucharistic worship, the sacraments, the general spiritual health of the diocese. We do these well, and together have made real strides in meaningful celebration of baptisms, funerals, weddings, confirmations, the care for the bereaved, and so forth. The opportunities for spiritual growth in the diocese are numerous and varied.

Third, the bishop, by office, is responsible for the good governing of the universal or great church as part of a college, and, of the diocese to which he is assigned. Although governing is not the same as good leadership, good leadership and good government are complementary. You share in that responsibility by representing the bishop in your parishes with leadership and with authority.

You share in and extend the threefold office of the bishop wherever you are throughout the diocese. Now. How can the unity and diversity of this mission be enhanced?

We have a lot going for us in the Diocese of Saginaw, a lot of pluses, a lot for which to be thankful. We're small. We are small enough to know one another, and to be aware of things that happen to one another on a personal level—sickness, anniversaries, family deaths. That is a real plus. We can look south to Detroit to see the difference this makes when our presbyterates get together for an assembly, a golf outing, priests' jubilee, or death, as well as other occasions. I can tell you the difference from personal experience. We have a camaraderie among priests that others envy.

We preach well. Our liturgies in general are very good. Parishioners compliment us with, "I missed the Saginaw liturgies when I moved out of the diocese." They mention missing them when they are somewhere else for summer vacations. We do the sacraments well: baptisms, confirmations, funerals, weddings. [Bishop Ken gave an example from St. Mary's, Bay City, where Father Jim Heller has turned his parish around: a baptism where the community truly enjoyed the ninety-five-year-old woman meeting the newborn member.] Liturgical music, the Liturgy of the Word, and the eucharistic prayer are done very well and prayerfully. We have priests and others who try to improve their preaching by gathering in small groups to critique each other. I'm part of each group. We've made major efforts in the diocese to improve the Liturgy of the Word and Eucharist.

We have a lot going in ministries across the diocese, on diocesan levels, and in the parishes. We have educated laity in programs of scripture, liturgy, theology, and pastoral ministry. We have successful diocesan-wide programs like Lent 95–99.

There are a lot of pluses in the diocese. About the good things we say, "Just keep doing them."

We have another plus. Imagine for a moment a priestless parish, and then a priestless diocese. We are ourselves the major resource of the Diocese of Saginaw. What would it mean if we were not here at all?

Without us, the churches would be empty of eucharistic worship, the sacraments would not happen, preaching the word of God as "good news" would take a radical dip, and a purpose for parish life would need radical regrouping.

Consider the image of a priestless diocese. Well, it would no longer be a diocese, would it? Consider your own parish or parishes, without you. We are the major resource for the diocese.

We have minuses too, and we have to deal with these. The shortage of priests is a tough problem. That in turn causes overwork and discouragement among priests. Across the diocese we are working on it in an ongoing effort that involves all of us on parish and vicariate levels. We need to be creative. Some things we can do within parishes to make the burdens lighter, like the rescheduling of weekend masses. We are working toward solutions on the vicariate level and with a diocesan task force. Another task force is working on priesthood vocations. We've made numerous efforts for vocations during the past years.

We can dwell on negatives together and lament them. It's better to come up with constructive solutions as best we can. Part of our time together we can talk more about these if you like.

Right now I'd like to talk about the mission of the diocese, to teach, provide means for sanctification, and to govern by leading. We all share this office—mission? I want to relate this to ecclesiology and a theology of the priesthood.

This is more practical than we may sometimes think. Scratch a ministry and you will find an ecclesiology, either explicit or implicit, but always operative. At the end, I'll mention briefly some current ecclesiologies and theologies of priesthood. We might discuss where we are with these.

All of us need to go back to Vatican II documents regularly. We ought to reread the documents about once a year. Seriously. The reason is that interpretations are inevitable and over the years, interpretations of these interpretations gradually skew the meaning. It happens all the time in lots of ways for nearly everything we do. It happens to us in the parishes.

Vatican II ecclesiology emphasized the church as mystery (LG, chapter 1) and as the people of God (LG, chapter 2). Other relationships in the church flow from this. One way to describe the church since Vatican II is a communion or a community of the disciples of Christ. In that community, the relationship among bishops is fraternal and collegial. The pope is first among brother bishops (LG chapter 3). Communion among these bishops, which includes the pope, is more than just the collective number of the bishops who gather. The bishops collegially are a body responsible together with the pope as head of the body for teaching and governing of the church.

A simple and practical example of this is a question I've been asked more than once, "Would I ordain a woman to priesthood, even though that was illicit?" No. That's a decision for the whole church to make, and I wouldn't even consider it. It would be more than illicit; it would be invalid. Unlike Anglicans, for example, we don't make that kind of decision on a local or regional level, only as a whole church. Might I ask that the bishops and the whole church talk about the issue? Sure, and I have. That's a collegial responsibility as a member of a collegial body in the church to ask to discuss issues that affect the church.

Communion within the great church is a communion that transcends individuality. But without a "church of the churches" the great church would not even exist. The great church is a communion of the particular churches. The mystery of church extends beyond the communion of particular churches, however. It is a communion across time and space. It includes Charlie O'Neill and Jack Gentner. This is a communion worth thinking about.

Vatican II also said something (not enough) about the theology of priesthood (*Presbyterium Ordinis* [PO]). For one thing, the PO changed the language about priesthood, from the term *priest* to *presbyter*, and from an emphasis on the word and concept *sacerdotal* to ministers in the church. That's a very significant shift. Since the council, there has unfortunately been a reinterpretation and shift back again to the former images, the priest as *sacerdos*.

The council did not talk about the presbyterate in the same way that it talked about the episcopacy. Rather than the collegial relationship among bishops, the presbyters participate in the mission of teaching, sanctifying, and governing with the bishop.

The bishop, according to Vatican II, has the fullness of the priesthood, and the pope can have no more of priesthood than any other bishop. The presbyterate, according to the council, participates in the fullness of priesthood of the bishop. It isn't a matter of two different levels of the same collegiality: collegiality among bishops in the church, and among presbyters and bishop in a diocese. It is a difference of collegiality and participation in mission. A presbyterate participates in the teaching, sanctifying, governing, and leadership office of the bishop.

One practical consequence is that a priest represents the bishop on the parish level. He does not function then as a priest outside his own diocese without some arrangement real or tacit with the bishop.

On a practical level, we could ask a number of questions. I think we can and should ask what makes for unity for our Diocese of Saginaw? What "makes" the Diocese of Saginaw? One question is whether one can be outside communion with the bishop of the diocese and claim to be part of the Catholic diocese of the church of Saginaw. The answer is "no."

Diversity of opinion among the presbyterate and with the bishop isn't the issue here. There's room for lots of diversity of opinion, action, and approach to the church from within the presbyterate. We have our disagreements. The question is the unity of a diocese—whether, to give an example, a parish church can erect itself in the diocese and claim to be part of the diocese, even though it is not in communion with the other parishes of the diocese, the presbyterate, or the bishop of the diocese. It can't, according to the ecclesiology in Vatican II. It can't, according to the tradition of the church. The parish priest represents the bishop in this parish, and a self-erected parish with a nonappointed priest/presbyter is not in communion with the bishop or other parishes and priests of the presbyterate. The presider of that self-erected parish does not represent the bishop.

A practical example in the Saginaw diocese: Emmanuel Church on Jefferson is not in communion with the presbyterate of the church of Saginaw, and therefore has no claim to status as a Catholic church in the diocese. If it wishes to try to relate to Rome directly, that's an option (but not one that will be successful). No one who presides in that assembly is appointed by me, the bishop, to represent myself, nor is this group in communion with the parishes and presbyterate of the church of Saginaw.

What about parishes that have begun through the efforts of communities that are without a resident priest and who borrowed one when and where they could, until they finally had a more stable arrangement? That's laudable. But there is a certain point at which they became parishes.

LeFebvre, for example, was excommunicated because he was not in communion with the bishops of the church, not because he disagreed with the pope on this or that issue, for example, whether there should be altar girls or not. No, he rejected an ecumenical council and the authentic tradition in the church, and fell out of the "communion of the churches."

The priests participate in the priesthood of the bishop and represent the bishop in their parishes. A diocese is hierarchical in structure even when the internal processes have many elements of democracy.

That's a negative example of unity in the diocese, not of great moment perhaps. Sharing the common ministry of teaching, sanctifying, governing, and leading, the church as the body of Christ is in positive communion with the bishop of a diocese. The ways that we shepherd this flock of Christ should exhibit the greatest diversity and creativity possible, together with unity of purpose. Unity concerns the common good for the body of Christ, the church of Saginaw. Diversity and creativity concern the "how" of achieving the common good.

It is with the common mission, and where we deal with the minus side of our mission, that unity is really important. Teamwork is found in sports and war, to name two (unrelated?) fields. Teamwork in either of these is most important when the odds are against you and the team is behind. This is not the time to go it alone and be the virtuoso, but it is the time to function selflessly as a team.

It is important that we work together when we deal with difficult issues and not be at cross purposes with one another. Otherwise we tear ourselves apart from the inside out. John Paul II, in his encyclical *Ut Unum Sint*, said something very important to religious leaders of the world: "Won't you please help me? I cannot do this job alone." I, too, say that as your bishop. And none of us can do it at all, without the Spirit working in and through us collectively as a body.

The Diocese of Saginaw is responsible to its people, the community of the followers of Christ of Saginaw diocese, that they have the word of God and sacramental life, "in abundance" (LG, chapter 4). If they do not (the same says) "they are to make representation to their pastors." That abundance of the Word and sacramental life is what, to the best of our ability, we must provide—simple and good, necessary fare.

You have asked, what do I see as the ecclesiologies, pre– and post–Vatican II, operative in the church today, and where do I personally stand? And what are theologies of priesthood, pre– and post–Vatican II, operative in the church, and where do I stand? I can line them up and present them briefly here.

Pre–Vatican II Ecclesiology	Post–Vatican II Ecclesiology
hierarchical model	people of God model
communio as universal mystical communion	*communio* as "communion of the churches"
church as mystical body, sacrament of Christ	church as body of Christ, community of disciples in the Spirit

Pre–Vatican II Theology of Priesthood	Post–Vatican II Theology of Priesthood
priesthood as *in persona Christi caput*, another Christ	priesthood as representative of the church in worship
sacramental imagery	Trinitarian imagery
preaching morality and doctrines (priestly exhortation)	preaching God's word (prophetic word)

Where I Stand

faithful to the tradition	faithful to the tradition and Vatican II
hierarchy	scriptures
authority	liturgy renewal
teachings	personal prayer and spirituality
sacramental life	laity, ministries
	sense of hierarchy of truths

Memo to Myself as Bishop

I remind myself to resist mightily the temptation to introduce too many diocesan-wide programs that require or suggest strongly the participation of all parishes. I will remember how little eager I have been to follow through on such initiatives to involve the whole church in a single project, when these have come out centrally from Rome. No matter how good they are (Jubilee 2000, for example) I will remind myself that for others as well as myself such initiatives can stifle creativity on local levels.

2

Liturgy and the Word

Introduction

"We're worried about the holy days. We should be worried about the Sundays and basic liturgical calendar. Especially the Triduum."[1]

"We...craft a jewel rather than trying to seize the whole event with our preaching. If we approach it this way, we are more apt to preach well, and preach from the heart."[2]

Good liturgical prayer held a high priority with Bishop Ken. One of the first areas of church life that he focused on was that of liturgy, especially the Liturgy of the Eucharist. In talks he sometimes reflected, "We pray well in the Saginaw diocese. When I'm away I can't wait to get back to it. But we could do better." Every Mass was the paschal mystery remembered and reenacted within its particular community. He wanted the diocese to recognize that together at liturgy we are most truly the church. Without losing a sense of the great trinitarian mystery (*Lumen Gentium*, no. 1), he could make good liturgical prayer also an intimate experience— whether for a large community at the Easter Vigil or the residents at St. Francis Home.

It bothered Bishop Ken that the national bishops' conference centered conversations on which holy days to keep mandatory or what wording and translation we should use for liturgical prayer or the recipe for altar bread, rather than attending foremost to the central mysteries and how we pray as church these central mysteries of our faith. Consequently, he emphasized the triduum, in practice and directive, as the most important three-day feast of the year for the whole diocese and for every parish. (The Easter Vigil, the holiest night of the year, was not to be celebrated before sundown, for example.)

Sacraments and symbols took on a larger expression through-out the diocese during his time as bishop. He used oils lavishly for confirmation, ordination, and the sick. For the dedication of an altar, he spread the oil so generously over the whole altar that signs of the event remained indelibly in the vestment he wore. As bishop he reestablished the original order of the early church for the sacra-ments of initiation—baptism, confirmation, Eucharist—and directed that, when possible, baptism be celebrated during the Easter Vigil by immersion. Church renovations throughout the diocese included baptismal fonts large enough to allow for immer-sion. Bishop Ken encouraged pastors to celebrate not only bap-tisms, but also weddings at the Sunday liturgy when this was feasible, so that a whole community might welcome the couple into its midst in a new sacramental relationship.

Everyone in the diocese must be welcomed and able to par-ticipate fully in the Eucharist (*Sacrosanctum Concilium*, no. 14). For the Hispanic communities, Bishop Ken promised on his arrival as bishop that he would learn Spanish and celebrate the first Mass of Our Lady of Guadalupe in Spanish. And he did. Later he went to Mexico and lived with a Hispanic parish priest in a poor parish where the only language spoken was Spanish, both for the experi-ence and to learn the language firsthand. He wanted everyone to know that they are included in the family and to be able easily to participate in the liturgical prayer of the church.

Every year Bishop Ken presided at Mass for the physically and mentally challenged with a presence that combined simplicity, compassion, and humor. The community of the hearing-impaired loved Bishop Ken because he made an effort to learn their signs and to ensure that they had access to interpreters. Because divorced couples who remarried found themselves in such painful situations in the church, he dramatically speeded up the process toward dec-larations of annulment by directing that lay ministers be trained to help, and he eliminated fees for the process.

From 1990 onward, Bishop Ken began to focus more on com-munication of the word of God through proclamation, preaching, and catechizing. He realized that at Mass the assembly could pray only a few words that were truly their own; that they listened pas-sively, often distractedly, during the eucharistic prayer and indeed during much of the Mass. To remedy this, he introduced responses throughout the eucharistic prayer as permitted in the Mass for children. Recognizing that liturgy needs some catechesis, he celebrated "teaching" masses at parishes around the diocese. He also gave a seven-part series of four-minute teachings on the Mass that could be used by pastors of the diocese. With a diocesan scripture scholar he wrote short introductions to the Sunday readings, so that the people could more easily understand what they heard.

In 1991 Bishop Ken started gathering those who preach into small groups to critique one another's homilies. They gathered five at a time with the bishop and a resident theologian, for four consecutive sessions. Ken submitted his own homilies for critique along with the rest. A communications journalist edited one or two homilies in each session. Ken's book, *Preaching Better,* grew in part from his interaction with these groups. All of the pastors had attended such sessions, and a second round of them had just begun at the time of his death.

Bishop Ken knew he couldn't do all that he envisioned, whether through better understanding of the Sunday scriptures for the faithful, or well-crafted homilies, or four-minute teachings, but he became a master at presenting small windows that open up great vistas and single pearls that present the vastness of the kingdom of God.

Notes

1. "We're Losing the Triduum," *Hosanna* (February–March 1993), 10.

2. "The Fundamental Mistakes of Preaching," *New Theology Review* (February 2001), 13.

"We're Losing the Triduum"

Hosanna (February–March 1993)

In the chapel at St. John's Seminary just outside Detroit (opened in 1949, and closed in 1988), stained-glass windows pictured young men portraying each of the minor orders. When those windows were being planned, Cardinal Mooney cautioned the artist to make the design of the shoes generic so they wouldn't go out of style as time passed. Years later a faculty member liked to say, "He was worried about the shoes. He should have worried about the minor orders."

One wonders in the same vein about NCCB discussions on the holy days of obligation. We're worried about the holy days. We should be worried about the Sundays and basic liturgical calendar—especially the triduum.

Everything rests on the triduum. The holy days of obligation couldn't hold a candle to the triduum. What are the feasts of the Immaculate Conception, the Assumption, All Saints, apart from the triduum? What is the feast celebrated on New Year's without the triduum? (Well, actually, what *is* the feast celebrated on New Year's?) Even Christmas loses its significance without the triduum. Our logo is not the manger. Our logo is the cross.

We're losing the triduum, and we're worried about the shoes.

What's the Big Deal?

I can hear friends of mine asking, "What's so important about this remembrance?" The story of what happened to Jesus in those last days of his life is interesting, but why get so worked up about going to church to hear it, or expect me to take time off from work, or waste a long weekend? What happened two-thousand years ago doesn't have much to do with my life today.

I would tell them to think of those times in their lives when they ask themselves, or the nearest priest, or ask the sky, or ask no one at all but simply let the question cry inside—why does a little child die, why does my father have terminal cancer, why does my daughter have to be the victim of such abuse by her husband, why does my cousin have AIDS, why is there so much crime in our city, why does God let these things happen, why should I try so hard to do what is right?

Come and join us for these great three days. This is when we wrestle with the great questions—your great questions. Come and join us as we pray together with the Lord who addressed the problem of evil and put his own life on the line for our sake. This is not past history. This is our story.

These are questions that can't be faced alone or in an isolated moment of crisis. Come and be with the whole church as we struggle together and find light in darkness. Come and connect with others who put their faith on the line. Come and connect with our roots, our great traditions. Come and settle in, and listen, pray, sing, take in the symbols, sit quietly, and "let be."

This is what we are about in the triduum, and this is why it is such a big deal. It's everything. (All this, of course, assumes that the triduum is celebrated in a way that engages the community in all this, which is something that deserves considerable attention.)

We Hold These Truths

When it comes to the importance of days that are holy, the church puts the triduum at the top of the list. In 1969, Pope Paul VI solemnly promulgated the General Norms for the Liturgical Year. The triduum is described this way:

> Christ redeemed humankind and gave perfect glory to God principally through His paschal mystery. By dying He destroyed our death and by rising He restored our life. The Easter Triduum of the passion and resurrection

of Christ is thus the culmination of the entire liturgical year (no. 18).

The Easter Vigil, in the night when Christ rose from the dead, is considered the mother of all vigils. During it the church keeps watch, awaiting the resurrection of Christ and celebrating it in the sacraments (no. 21).

Finally, the liturgical days are listed in order of importance:

- Easter Triduum
- Christmas, Epiphany, Ascension, Pentecost
- Sundays of Advent, Lent, and the Easter Season
- Ash Wednesday
- Weekdays of Holy Week (Monday to Thursday)

There are more on the list, but note that we haven't even gotten to the holy days of obligation yet, except for Christmas, and the feast of the ascension, which is really part of what we celebrate in the triduum.

We're worried about the shoes. We should be worried about the triduum.

In our society we tend to be very practical. We try to make things all alike and interchangeable. We sift out things that are singular because they do not easily fit into our lives. Our national holidays are an example—we put most of them on Mondays. They no longer break into our weekday schedule as singular events. They are flattened out to become long weekends, one just like the other. Labor Day, which began with a parade in New York City on Tuesday, September 5, 1882, for example, has lost its meaning.

When a religious feast becomes a holiday, the original significance goes the way of Labor Day. The original meaning of the event recedes into the background, and other things take priority; religious rituals are pushed aside because they get in the way. The last days of Holy Week become simply a good time to get away for a brief spring break.

We need to get serious about the triduum, and recover the tradition whereby Christians break stride on those three days, interrupt their routines, turn things upside down, and make these days like no other days in the year.

This is not unthinkable. We do it for other things—for example, an out-of-town family wedding. The preparations (showers, parties, fittings, shopping) start months in advance, but the event itself begins on Thursday evening, because you have to travel to get there. Friday is filled with last-minute errands, visiting friends and relatives, then the wedding rehearsal, followed by the rehearsal dinner. Saturday is a day like no other day, beginning with a morning full of prewedding preparations, then the wedding ceremony in the afternoon, the pictures afterward, the wedding reception that goes far into the night, and a postreception gathering of family and close friends that ends about 2:00 a.m.

It is that important to us.

There are other things that interrupt our usual pattern of life and keep us up half the night or get us up early in the morning— poker games, deer-hunting trips, fishing trips, the birth of a child, a college graduation out of town, and, of course, a death in the family.

We need somehow to get it across that Holy Thursday evening to Easter morning is an event like that.

We've Gone Backward

Actually, we have gone backward. Not so long ago, even though the Easter Vigil was virtually nonexistent, there were some interruptions in our schedule on those days that made them very different. We stayed up late on Holy Thursday night (or got up in the middle of the night) to be part of the all-night adoration. On Good Friday, we spent from noon to 3:00 p.m. at church or in silence at home.

For an increasing number of Catholics today, Holy Thursday is virtually nonexistent, there is no religious practice on Good Friday, and the "Saturday evening Mass" is too late and too long.

We bishops have talked plenty about the holy days. We've argued about having to maintain them so as to give people a "wake-up call," and to be countercultural. That's interesting because Holy

Thursday, Good Friday, and Holy Saturday are not holy days of obligation. And we haven't said a word about them.

Writing about the spirituality of the future, Karl Rahner said that it will have to concentrate more on what is most essential. Until several centuries ago, the core and decisive truths of our faith were more or less taken for granted and undisputed in our Western culture. So, we assumed those and concentrated our energies on varied types of piety—devotion to the precious blood, to the child Jesus, to Mary's seven sorrows, a complicated pattern of indulgences. Today, it is different.

> But, in a bleak age of world-wide secularism and atheism, it may be presumed that far fewer individual flowers of Christian spirituality will be able to bloom....The spirituality of the future will be concentrated on the ultimate data of revelation: That God is, that we can speak to God...that we can live and die with Jesus and properly with Him alone in an incomprehensible cross that is set up above our life and that this scandal reveals the true, liberating and beautiful significance of our life (*Concern for the Church*, pp. 146–48).

We need uncommon schedules at times to remind us that we believe and celebrate uncommon truths. It is a heritage we must pass on to future generations, and we're not doing it.

We bishops should harness all the energy we've spent on the holy days of obligation, and turn them toward finding ways to revive the triduum—not just in theory, but in practice. We do need to be countercultural. We do need a wake-up call. But we've been worried about the shoes. We should be worried about the triduum.

Do This in Memory of Me, But Do It Well

U.S. Catholic (September 1999)
The editors interview Bishop Kenneth
Untener (excerpts)

In the nearly two decades since Detroit native Bishop Kenneth Untener was named to head the Diocese of Saginaw, Michigan, he has earned a reputation as one of this country's most innovative episcopal leaders. His required homily evaluation program for parish preachers and instructional "four-minute teachings" before the final blessing have resulted in higher-than-average Mass attendance in his diocese. A longtime advocate of a more collegial and collaborative style of leadership in the church, Untener is constantly gathering input from everyday Catholics in the pews as well as from a lively group of scholars he affectionately calls his "theological squad."

In recent years, Untener has turned his attention to improving Sunday liturgy, arguing that the weekend eucharistic celebration is the most important work parishes do. He has written two books, both touching on liturgical issues: *Sunday Liturgy Can Be Better* (St. Anthony Messenger Press, 1980) and, more recently, *Preaching Better* (Paulist Press, 1999). Whether he's talking about liturgy or leadership, Untener always keeps his focus on what he believes is the primary purpose of the church: to bring people closer to God.

You've written about the busyness in parishes these days. How is that a problem?

The problem isn't that people are necessarily working too hard, but in too many directions. Parishioners are becoming consumers, and parishes are marketing wares. So you have all these programs to meet all human needs, but there are problems: One, we don't have the answer to every need, and two, the church was never meant to be the sole agent of goodness out there.

We ought to focus on what we're about, and the most important thing a parish does is liturgy and prayer. But in practice, that isn't happening. I always want to ask priests, "What do you think about when you're driving?" Pastors are not thinking about how they can make the weekend liturgy come alive. They're thinking about personnel; they're thinking about planning.

The question we ought to be asking as pastors is: "How can I help people get closer to God?" That sounds pious, but I think that's the real question that ought to preoccupy me when I drive— not all of the organizational things.

How are you trying to improve liturgy and help people get closer to God?

One thing we have been emphasizing in the Saginaw diocese is preaching. We have a required program for all those who preach, including priests and deacons, pastoral administrators and pastoral associates.*

I gather a group of four priests and another person who preaches and ask them to audiotape their homilies in battle conditions: in church with babies crying and ushers in the back reading the bulletin. We get tapes of their homilies, too—including mine— and then get together to give each other feedback.

We do what golfers do after a match; golfers are dead honest. We talk for about two hours about one another's homilies, and then we go out and tape another one the next week. We do this for four weeks. I've been doing it for five years, and it has just really lifted up the realization of how important a homily is.

I also have liturgies videotaped. Here the purpose is not just to look at the presider, it's also to look at the whole liturgy. One

---

*Regarding references here and throughout this article to preachers other than the ordained—Bishop Untener wrote this article in 1999, before the current legislation in G.I.R.M. and nearly six years before the instruction *Redemptionis Sacramentum*, issued in April 2005, which states that the homily is reserved to the priest or deacon during Mass (nos. 64–66).

time I asked one of the camera people to keep the camera on the congregation during the whole Mass. It was total inaction; the poor people never get to do anything.

These efforts have elevated the awareness of the importance of liturgy—that you've got to spend creative effort. The objective of good liturgy is not good manners, it's prayer. You can feel it in the air if we're praying. But too often the presider is not praying; he's performing. It doesn't look like he's talking to God at all. He's reciting.

Another thing some parishes in our diocese do is the "four-minute teaching" before the final blessing. We introduced that for two reasons. One is to stop priests from teaching during the homily. What should make the homily come alive is the illumination of the power of God's word. Let God do it, not the brilliance of the homilist. And the second reason is that many Catholics are, through no fault of their own, relatively illiterate about our traditions and thirsty to know.

So I said, give me four minutes before the last blessing—four minutes because when you say five minutes, it's a euphemism for anywhere from ten to twenty minutes. By the way, the presider doesn't have to be the one to do it. There may be somebody else more skilled in this.

What topics do you cover in these "four-minute teachings"?

In the three or four parishes that are doing it fairly consistently, one is walking through the sacraments, another one is walking through the Creed, and another one is just taking whatever the people last week said they'd like to hear more about.

It might be "Did Jesus on the cross suffer more than anyone else, because I think my grandmother suffered more when she died of cancer?" or it might be "What is the difference between a cardinal and an archbishop?"

Why spend time on that? Because Catholics want to be literate. In one parish, I recently noticed how few people drank from the cup. So last week I spent four minutes talking about why we do it. You could hear a pin drop.

You said the most important thing we do in church is worship. Some people might disagree and say that the most important thing we do is when we leave liturgy and then go out into the world.

Well, first of all, I'd modify what I said: The most important thing we do is help people get in touch with God. We have the symbols that are meant to open us up to God, but we get stuck arguing over the symbol or the ritual.

This awareness changes the way we see the world. Spirituality is a way of looking at God, at myself, and at people in the world that changes the way I think and act. I'd say that the most important thing is for a parish to do that well so that people can be nurtured to make sense out of their week.

What are the key characteristics of a liturgy that feeds people's spirits? And what are the biggest mistakes that prevent that from happening?

The biggest thing that is not generally understood is that this is liturgical prayer. Liturgical prayer is the Catholic trademark, but it's been absent for a millennium because the Mass became an individual experience.

My nephew in Saginaw drove himself down to the Joe Louis Arena in Detroit to watch the Red Wings hockey team on television against Philadelphia for the finals of the Stanley Cup. He could have watched it at home, so why did he go all that way? Because the crowd puts something in the air. There's something about doing this together. That's a close cousin to liturgical prayer.

The most evident liturgical prayer that I'm aware of is the veneration of the cross on Good Friday. You just sit there and watch people come to the cross. You watch the little kid go up and touch it, and this old person kisses it, and somebody else just stands there and looks at it.

If I'm attending Mass, I sit there at communion and just watch the people and think, "God, they believe the same thing I do." That's liturgical prayer.

It's something you feel in the air, like my nephew did, and you can't accomplish that by terrific liturgical planning. It's got to be more than that. It certainly helps to have good music—and if the homily's not an irritation—but you could overcome that. I gave a talk once on how to pray well at a Mass that's not celebrated well.

So, how do you pray well at a lousy Mass?

Squint for a few minutes; take in the whole thing that is going on. Use the message; use the stained-glass windows. The Mass is a grand buffet of God's presence. Watch for a word in a song or in the homily or in a reading or in a prayer that catches you. Maybe that's how God wanted to catch you today.

The other thing is: When you pray, pray. Most people don't know that the song is a prayer, for example. I try to tell people to always think of whom they're singing to. Sometimes they're singing to each other, and sometimes they're singing to God, and sometimes they're singing to themselves. But you should know which it is, because you're praying.

On those videos of the liturgy that I mentioned earlier, I can always tell when the presider is really praying. Sometimes, for example, at the end of Mass the priest will wing a little blessing for a holiday or something, and it'll be obvious that he is really praying. Then I rewind to the eucharistic prayer, where his tone of voice and style are totally different. I'll ask him, "Whom are you talking to here?" I can tell when you're praying.

I can't tell you how to do it because everybody does it differently. It's really hard when you're the celebrant and trying to pray because really talking to God is like baring your soul in front of people. But real prayer is catching, and you can't fake it. That's why the most important preparation for liturgical ministers and preachers is getting close to God.

What about the "consumer mentality" of Mass-goers—that if they're not entertained properly, then they'll go somewhere else, that there's really no sense of belonging to this community?

Yes, like spectators. No wonder they feel like spectators, because in many ways that's exactly what they are. They get to speak for 126 seconds in a one-hour Mass, and over half of that is the Creed. You add up every word they say—I timed it with a stopwatch with a video of a Mass—and in a one-hour Mass, 126 seconds is all parishioners have to speak. Except to stand and sit, the first movement they had was the sign of peace, forty-eight minutes into the Mass. And the only other movement they had was communion.

The simplest way to explain the Mass is to see the whole Liturgy of the Word as God moving toward us. That's when we are receptive to how God is acting upon us. But after the Liturgy of the Word, you begin the reverse—us moving toward the altar, toward God. What we're all doing is putting our lives, our joys and our sorrows, our fears, broken relationships—everything on the altar and joining with the Lord just as he took all his joys and sorrows and entrusted them to God. That notion of the congregation moving toward God, though, is often lost. It really is two separate motions; one is God toward us and the other is us toward God. Unless people feel that, they think the flow is all from God to us.

In the Saginaw diocese, one year we emphasized this movement toward God during Lent through almsgiving. Every week, parishioners were asked to bring something. I didn't want them putting things at the door. I wanted them to come forward during the Mass, not in a line but from all directions. They bring food, clothes, or sometimes a card saying they're going to work for justice.

One week I asked people to think of the one thing that stands between them and God, and then to decide to give it up. I had a week to think about that and I wrote something down for myself. That Sunday, I walked up and put my card on the altar. As a result of doing that, I was faithful to the pledge I made.

The ritual made all the difference. You don't just walk up to the altar and put something in and say, "I was just kidding." When people walk up with their alms, then their money isn't paying their dues; it comes out of their work, out of their lives, out of their homes. But when we pass the basket like people are paying their dues, the wrong people are moving.

Sunday Liturgy Can Be Better

Paulist Press, 1980

Bishop Ken began his ministry as bishop of Saginaw with some definite thoughts on the liturgy, as the following excerpts show, and he went about implementing these ideas throughout his twenty-four years as bishop of Saginaw.

Introductory Thoughts
It Is Never Enough to Be Correct

Liturgy is supposed to communicate to real people. If it doesn't—no matter how "correct" it may be—it is a failure.

My feeling is that we occasionally grow righteous about liturgical celebrations. We read the best books, use the best materials, and stage a ceremony we think is wonderful—except that the people don't like it. Saying, "But they *should!*" doesn't help. It is never enough just to be correct. Liturgy is communication, which means that it has to be more than correct. It has to do what it is meant to do: help people to pray.

A Question of Reverence

The conversation went pretty much as countless others had on the same topic, the changes in the Mass. Reference to "the changes" was vague, but there was nothing vague about the people's feelings. They were definite, and they were negative.

What caused such feelings? The conversation touched upon individual changes, such as standing for communion, guitars, lectors, lay ministers of the Eucharist, and many others. The discontented speakers could agree with logical explanations of individual changes; they could accept this or that innovation. But when the changes were all lumped together, they had problems.

There was something mysteriously wrong with those changes. Within these people there was sort of a sixth sense telling them that something was amiss. What was causing these good and reasonable people to react so negatively?

It's hard to say how the subject came up, but when it did we all knew that we had the answer. It was something very simple: reverence. Or, rather, it was the lack of reverence. Those people could accept change. What they could not accept was less reverence.

When you think about it, it's very understandable. Reverence is terribly important. It is defined as "a feeling of profound respect often mingled with awe and affection." What it comes down to is our recognition that we are not God, that he is infinitely greater, beyond what eye has seen or ear has heard. It would be hard to overestimate the importance of this belief. It is absolutely fundamental to everything believers do, especially their worship. And this is the belief we convey through reverence.

The danger of irreverence is always with us. St. Paul chided the people of Corinth for their lack of reverence. Every generation since has needed a reminder or two.

Our generation is no exception. Unintentionally, we have conveyed the wrong message to people. We have seemed to say, "You don't have to be reverent anymore." That is something we can never say. Vatican II did not discover that the pearl of great price was really costume jewelry. Nor has God been devalued along with the dollar.

Creating and maintaining a sense of reverence is the first responsibility of all who plan liturgies and of all who minister in public roles. This assumption lies beneath everything I have to say. I hope to offer some practical suggestions for achieving that atmosphere.

Don't Surprise Us

The liturgy is…a time for basics, not surprises. Planners of liturgy sometimes feel that they have to create dramatic scenes to capture the people's attention or to make the appropriate impact. Well, it captures their attention all right and it makes an impact, but I'm not so sure the overall effect is good.

Generally speaking, the liturgy is not the time for surprises. Planners keep forgetting that we're already dealing with very powerful words and actions. They don't need tricks to come alive.

I don't mean that liturgy has to be dull routine. Creative efforts are needed constantly. It's just that they shouldn't come as a *surprise*. People should be told beforehand what to expect rather than deliberately caught off guard.

The Pleasure of Predictability

Another way of putting all this is that the congregation should be treated to the "pleasure of predictability." There is a certain pleasure in predictability.

Why is it that people so often say, "When are the changes going to settle down so that things aren't different from parish to parish, or even from Mass to Mass in our own parish?" Are they saying this because they want to return to rigid uniformity in every detail?

I don't think so. I think they are simply asking for the pleasure of predictability. And they are doing it for good reasons, not bad ones.

The Mass is meant to be an experience in which we can all share. To put ourselves into it, we have to know what is going to take place. We can't be on the edge of our seats trying to follow a series of unexpected prayers and actions.

On the other hand, if there is a structured ritual expressing very basic mysteries, there is room for everyone to fit in no matter what their mood.

Those who plan and lead liturgies should have a deep appreciation of this fact. It is not *their* prayer. It is the prayer of the church. The people—the church—have a right to that.

Let the Mass Be Very Incomplete

One of the problems with the Mass is that it is often cluttered. We try to include comments along the way on the theme, all three readings, the feast, and the parish programs going on that week.

There will be other masses. We have to leave many things for other celebrations and allow each Mass to be very incomplete.

We should try to do only a little bit, realizing that it is actually a great deal and leave the rest in the Lord's hands. If we could only do that, we would discover a rich simplicity that is very powerful.

A Space for Silence

Silence is beautiful. It can be improved upon with the right combination of sounds, but that is not an easy thing to do. Silence has a lot going for it all on its own.

Which brings up the whole question of silence in the liturgy. The first prerequisite for anyone who leads or plans liturgy should be a deep appreciation of the value of silence. Sound is not an end in itself. It should always be an improvement on silence. And that is not easy.

We need space for prayer, for reflecting, for readiness to listen or speak; silence gives us space. I do not necessarily mean a complete lack of sound. I mean freedom from unpleasant sounds, or from sounds to which we are supposed to pay close attention—sounds that intrude themselves upon us. Background music—instrumental or sung by a choir—can give us space, as long as we are not supposed to listen to every word or every note.

The new liturgy calls for such spaces at various points in the Mass. The congregation has a right to moments of silence, but is often deprived of them. One of the best contributions we can make toward the spirituality of our people is to provide some quiet spaces for them in the Mass.

The "Amen" Makes All the Difference

Eucharistic Minister (September 1994)

It happened while I was ministering communion in a parish alongside the pastor. I sensed that something different was happening next to me—not dramatic, just different. I noticed it without intending to.

Something was going on between the pastor and each communicant. There was this momentary engagement, connection, intersomething-or-other. What he was doing was placing the consecrated bread in their hand, leaving his own hand for a moment to rest there, looking them in the eye as he said, "The body of Christ," then attentively receiving their "Amen."

So I tried it myself. It took about a second longer, but it made all the difference in the world. One didn't need a degree in liturgy to catch that something good was happening.

For weeks I tried to figure out why it made such a difference. Then one day while I was driving, the light bulb flashed and I understood. At least I think I did. I'll do my best to explain, and you see if you agree.

To What Do We Say "Amen?"

It all has to do with what the "Amen" means to the communicant. To what does the person receiving communion say "Amen?" Here lies the difference. The focus of the "Amen" is not the real presence. That is a given. The communicant is saying "Amen" to *receiving* the Risen Lord into their lives. In that brief moment, and in that one word, they are saying in effect: "I'm not perfect, but I really do believe in Jesus Christ, and in all that he taught, and in all that he stood for. I don't claim to understand it all and have all the answers. But I do believe in this way of life, and from the soles of my feet to the top of my head I commit myself to walk in his footsteps. I accept the Lord and all that he stands for into my own life."

This is the difference—inviting the communicants to say "Amen" to *receiving* Jesus Christ into their lives, rather than simply affirming their correct faith in the real presence. The gesture evokes this—if I hold up the consecrated bread before them and say "The body of Christ," it can seem as though I am primarily asking them to affirm their belief in the real presence. If I place it in their hand and, still with my hand resting there, look them in the eye and say "the body of Christ," the whole scenario is changed. They are saying "Amen, yes, I do accept the Lord into my own life, with all that this implies."

Remember that the Liturgy of the Word has preceded this and flows into it. Perhaps even more, one has to keep in mind that the eucharistic prayer has preceded this and has called forth not only our consciousness of the real presence, but also our willingness to join with the Lord Jesus Christ in giving over everything in trust to God. Now, at communion, in a moment of intense personal faith, in the face of the tangible reality of the Risen Christ, we are called upon to receive into ourselves the whole event. (This, incidentally, is the problem with taking hosts from the tabernacle for communion. The flow of everything leading up to communion— the word, the procession of these gifts, giving over of ourselves, and our world in the eucharistic prayer—is broken.)

Someone recently commented to me about the number of Catholics who come forward at a Billy Graham crusade to declare their acceptance of Jesus as their personal Savior. "I guess it's okay that they do that," he said, "and the leaders try to refer them to their own church for follow-up. But if Catholics only realized what they do each time they come to communion, they would have the same experience magnified a thousand times over." To which I said, "Amen."

The same holds true in ministering the cup. The eucharistic minister would pause a moment as the person takes the cup and while both are holding it together says, "The blood of Christ."

The effect can be even greater because of the symbolic significance of blood.

Some Corollaries

One advantage of doing this is its immediate good effect upon those (often youngsters) who are hurried or casual, or who take the host with their fingers while already starting to walk away, who don't look up at all, or who mumble an "Amen" either before you have said anything or while they are leaving. Just do it the way I described and usually they stop, and look at you (a little surprised) and say—perhaps for the second time, but in a much more thoughtful way—"Amen." If all who ministered the Eucharist in the parish did it this way every weekend, the cumulative effect would be astounding.

This also points to the wisdom of using the ritual words ("The body of Christ. Amen.") and not changing them to "This is the body of Christ," or the communicant substituting "I believe," or "Yes it is," for the "Amen." All of those changes direct the "Amen" to the real presence. When the focus is directed to receiving the Lord, and all the implications, then "Amen" is just about the only word we can say.

When you think about it, that is quite an "Amen" we are called upon to say at communion. It is a personal and communal crescendo to all that has preceded this moment, which means that eucharistic ministers, with each communicant, are doing something as ritually important as just about anything else that happens at Eucharist.

Preaching Better

Paulist Press, 1999 (excerpts)

Chapter Two
What Is a Homily?

"...In receiving the word of God from hearing us, you received not a human word but...the word of God." (1 Thessalonians 2:13)

Just what is a homily anyway? We've wrestled with this in group after group, and gradually I have come to see homilies differently. This has been far and away the biggest effect upon me.[1]

In years gone by, I pictured the homilist as a cook who looks to see what's in the pantry and the refrigerator (the readings), comes up with a menu (the "main thought"), puts the meal together (the homily), and then serves it.

What I've become more conscious of is that the homilist comes into a kitchen that is filled with the smell of something already cooking, and it is the Lord who is doing it. The liturgy is the Lord's meal all the way around: the menu, the cooking, the serving. We are helpers.

The task of all liturgical ministers, including the homilist, is to help the flow of what *Christ* is doing, for Christ is the leader of all liturgical prayer. The first thing we must do when preparing a homily (or planning a liturgy) is to stand humble before the Lord.[2]

The Threefold Task of a Homilist

If this is true, then the role of the homilist comes down to three tasks: (1) to discern what the Lord is doing/speaking through this event, (2) to help illuminate this for the assembly, and (3) to do all this on behalf of the church.

1. *To Discern What the Lord Is Doing/Speaking through This Event.*

God's word doesn't live in a book. It comes alive within the entire event...which is the convergence of:

these scripture texts (on Sundays there are four texts: three readings plus the psalm)

this liturgical setting (season, feast, occasion)

this historical time and place (all that is going on in our world and church right now)

these people (the real-life circumstances of the people to whom we preach)

This involves exegesis, but it is more than that. We are trying to discern how this text *functions* here and now. Someone once commented to me that homilists so often seem to preach a "historical Jesus"; that is, they explain Jesus "back then." But Jesus isn't back then; Jesus is alive...and not simply living in retirement. Jesus is here-and-now acting upon us, particularly in liturgy. Something is "combusting" in the combination of these scriptures and this event, and we who preach must discover it and help open it up for the people of God.

The word of God at liturgy is always live, never a rerun. When the scriptures are proclaimed, we are not listening to something God *once* said. We are listening to God speaking *live* to us now. This is Catholic doctrine,[3] but I fear that we don't take it seriously enough.

The living character of the Word means not only that God *is* speaking to us live, but also that God's word is *enlivening.*[4] It is a graced word that has a quickening power. It is more than a word that is true and points us in the right direction. It is, to use traditional terminology, an "efficacious sign" that brings about the redemption to which it points. It shapes individuals. It shapes the church.

When Jesus says, "It is the spirit that gives life," he immediately speaks about his *words:* "The *words* I have spoken to you are spirit and life" (John 6:63). Several verses later, Peter says, "Master, to whom shall we go? You have the *words* of eternal *life.*"

Saint Paul says, "For I am not ashamed of the gospel. It is the *power of God* for the salvation of everyone who believes" (Rom 1:16; emphasis added).

The flow of this graced, living, quickening word is what we homilists try to discern.

2. *To Help Illuminate This for the Assembly*

Having attempted to discern what the Lord is speaking to us through this event, the second task of the homilist is to help illuminate this for the assembly.[5]

We homilists need to remember that a great deal has already been happening before the homily. Songs, symbols, prayers, and the word of God have been flowing upon all of us. Our task is to help the flow of what is already taking place. We are not making it happen; we are helping it happen.

> For just as from the heavens
>> the rain and snow come down
> And do not return there
>> till they have watered the earth,
>> making it fertile and fruitful,...
> So shall my word be
>> that goes forth from my mouth;
> It shall not return to me void,
>> but shall do my will,
>> achieving the end for which I sent it. (Isa 55:10–11)

We minister gifts that are not our own, gifts that have more formative power than our eloquence.[6]

3. *To Do All This on Behalf of the Church*

When we preach a homily, we do so *on behalf of the church*. It is not as though we who preach are the recipients of personal revelations or function as freelance spokespersons for God.

We participate in the gift of the Spirit given to the church. We are sharing not simply our faith, but the faith of the whole church. That is why a homily is different from giving personal witness. There can be a time and a place for that, but a homily is wider than personal witness.

Homilists have to be attentive to the faith of the whole church as they discern what the Lord is speaking in this event. We have to express this in a way that is personal (i.e., from the heart), but not in a way that limits the breadth of the message to the width of our own personal experience.[7]

Some Corollaries

If one truly ministers the word of God in the way we've been describing, there are a number of corollaries.

• **The preparation process can be more enjoyable.**

There is a sense of freedom. No longer is it a weekly task to come up with an original talk; instead, we participate in and help with something that is already taking place and is very good. The proclaimed scriptures are flowing, and we are trying to help them along. Discerning the flow will require study, prayer, interpretation; presenting it will require some creativity. But there is not so much depending on ME.

• **We never have to worry about running dry.**

Our own stories and files of material are like the oil reserves with only a fixed quantity, but the scriptures are living waters that never run dry, and the life of the community is not static. Endless riches continually open up when the living word engages with life.

• **We don't have to come up with a new topic every Sunday.**

We can feel more at home preaching several Sundays in a row on the same thought; for example, during the Easter season, the emphasis is on the Spirit, a neglected part of our preaching. (We tend to emphasize the earthly ministry of Jesus.) If we preach about the Spirit one Sunday, the next week we might say, "I've already done that. I have to come up with a new topic." Not true. I can speak about the same topic and even spin out the same basic truth over and over with a freshness each time. Homilies on successive Sundays are not individual talks; they are illuminations of the live scriptures happening each Sunday.

• **Great homilies are within reach of homilists who are not great speakers.**

Attention is less focused on the homilist, more on the word of God. Our respect and love for the word will show through and have an effect. The focus will be more on the God-given insight rather than on the homily or the homilist. Rather than the people being taken with the homily or the homilist, it's more important that they be taken with what the Lord is speaking to us. A good homily still requires basic speaking skills, but these are within reach. We don't have to be gifted raconteurs, entertainers, or even extroverts.

- **Our homilies will have much more diversity.**

When we use the text as a touchstone for something we want to say or for something that strikes us in prayer, each individual homilist—depending on temperament, special interests, where he or she is on the Enneagram, Myers-Briggs, and so forth—tends to gravitate toward topics to which he or she is naturally inclined: interpersonal relationships, social justice, doctrinal teachings.

On the other hand, if we stand humbly before the text and listen to what God is saying to us through this event, we are less apt to give homilies whose sameness of theme is due to our own inherent inclinations. At times, the Lord will lead us where we do not want to go (cf. John 21:19).

- **We will preach more directly about God, Jesus Christ, the Spirit**

I have discovered that people often think that in our preaching we are more focused on the church than on Jesus Christ and his teachings. Think for example of how often people ask us a question by saying something like: "By the way, what does the church teach about such and such?" Seldom do they say, "What does the Lord teach about such and such?"[8]

- **We will preach the basic truths of our faith**

Scripture will be our guide (not a touchstone for our own thoughts). It will take us to the depths of revealed truths and to the depths of human life. Left to our own choice of topics, some of our most fundamental truths will be neglected either because they seem too obvious or too difficult.

This, I believe, has been a great neglect for some time. We don't preach the fundamental truths—God, the Holy Spirit, redemption, grace. Not long ago, I asked a group of grade-school youngsters (K through 8) to tell me about Jesus. They talked about his birth, his miracles, and how he helped people.

When I pressed them as to whether Jesus was God, I was surprised to see most of them shake their heads no. Our first reaction might be to blame this on religious-education programs. But what about our preaching?

One of the problems in today's church is that we've been busy arguing about altar girls, inclusive language, who can be called a pastoral minister—and the good news of the core truths on which we all agree is neglected. (That's one mistake the fundamentalist preachers have not made.)

- **The effect of such homilies will tend to be long term.**

Generally speaking, these kinds of homilies won't individually seem as sensational. They won't sound as innovative or clever. The effect will be cumulative, formative, and the result of continued exposure to the living word of God, much like steadily praying the scriptures in *lectio divina*. And the effect will be powerful, for the word of God is powerful. People will begin to listen to the readings more receptively. The people will be less taken with the homily, and more taken with the deep-down insight that broods in their souls. Their appreciation will tend to be quietly long term rather than instantly ecstatic.

The effects of eating healthily are not strikingly manifest after the first day or week of doing so, nor would we react to every fine meal by calling it sensational. Only over the long haul do we sense the effects of eating well. The same is true of fine homilies.

A Closing Thought

It is not the power of the homilist but the power of the word of God that shapes the church and shapes the individual believer. The *skill* of the homilist comes into play, but it is a skill used to minister the word of God, not our own thoughts.

Pastoral leaders who wish to affect, change, and form their people will do so most of all not by their own persuasiveness or cleverness, not by programs, policies, or organizational ability, but by truly ministering the living word of God—letting this "sacrament" pour its light upon the community and illumine life.

Imagine what would happen if, in churches around the world, the formative power of the word of God were turned loose.

In the Capernaum synagogue, Jesus took on a shouting unclean spirit and commanded it to leave the man. It did. The people "were all amazed and said to one another, 'What is there about his word?'"

What is there about his word? There is everything about his word. It is a graced word that accomplishes more than truckloads of our own.

Notes

1. Defining a homily can become abstract, complicated. I find it more concrete to get at this by asking, "What is the role of the homilist?"

2. Those who select and minister liturgical music are among those who need to take careful note of this. Lay people who participate in the musical selection process (e.g., for weddings or funerals) usually need some brief catechesis on this before getting down to specifics.

3. The "live" character of the scriptures proclaimed at liturgy is taught clearly in the Vatican II Constitution on the Liturgy and in the General Instruction of the Roman Missal.

"He (Christ) is present in his Word, since it is *he himself who speaks* when the holy Scriptures are read in the Church" (Const. On Liturgy no. 7; emphasis added).

"When the Scriptures are read in the Church, *God Himself is speaking to his people*, and Christ, present in his own word, *is proclaiming the Gospel*" (General Instruction of the Roman Missal no. 9; emphasis added).

"In the readings…*God is speaking to his people*, opening up to them the mystery of redemption and salvation, and nourishing their spirit; *Christ is present to the faithful* through his own word." (Ibid. no. 33, emphasis added).

4. In John's Bread-of-Life Section (chapter 6), a great deal of the focus is on the word, and it is a living word. Jesus speaks of himself as the "living" bread that comes down from heaven. See

Raymond Brown, *The Gospel According to John*, Anchor Bible, vol. 29 (New York: Doubleday, 1966), 255–304.

5. One might ask, "Why even have a homily? Why not just proclaim the word and sit down?" Because we believe that the reception of the word can be helped, assisted. We believe that God acts through others, in this case those who preach. The ministry of the homilist is an important part of our liturgical tradition.

6. The homily is more than the external application of an old text to the contemporary scene: It is a faithful ministry of the living word that emerges with new meaning "for us and for our salvation." The Pontifical Biblical Commission in its 1993 document entitled *The Interpretation of the Bible in the Church* speaks of *actualization* (i.e., discovering what the text has to say at the present time) and *inculturation* (i.e., situating the text in a specific community with its culture).

On Actualization: "The Church, indeed, does not regard the Bible simply as a collection of historical documents dealing with its own origins: it receives the Bible as word of God, addressed both to itself and to the entire world *at the present time*" (PBC, IV, emphasis added). "Actualization is necessary because, although their message is of lasting value, the biblical texts have been composed with respect to circumstances of the past and in language conditioned by a variety of times and seasons. To reveal their significance for men and women of today, it is necessary to apply their message to contemporary circumstances and to express it in language adapted to the present time" (PBC IV A1).

On Inculturation: "Inculturation is not a one-way process; it involves 'mutual enrichment'. On the one hand, the treasures contained in diverse cultures allow the word of God to produce new fruits and, on the other hand, the light of the word allows for a certain selectivity with respect to what cultures have to offer: Harmful elements can be left aside and the development of valuable ones encouraged" (PBC IV B).

7. Cf. chapter 18 [of *Preaching Better*] on the need for homilies to be personal.

8. Commenting on the institutions of Christendom just before the Reformation, Pelikan makes an observation that all homilists might keep in mind: "Intended as windows through which

we might catch a glimpse of the Eternal, they (the institutions of Christendom) had become opaque, so that the faithful looked *at* them rather than *through* them. The structures of the Church were supposed to act as vehicles for the spirit—both for the Spirit of God and for the human spirit....Captive in ecclesiastical structures that no longer served as channels of divine life and means of divine grace, the spiritual power of the Christian gospel pressed to be released" (J. Pelikan, *Spirit Versus Structures: Luther and the Institutions of the Church* [New York: Harper and Row, 1968, p. 30; emphasis added]).

The Fundamental Mistakes of Preaching

New Theology Review (February 2001)

In his reflection Bishop Untener recounts his experience of a diocesan-wide program in which he and a group of priests come together to prepare and evaluate their preaching. He provides eight practical admonitions or cautions for preachers to keep in mind....Kenneth Untener is the bishop of the Diocese of Saginaw, Michigan. He is the author of Preaching Better *(Paulist Press, 1999).*

One of the best tips I ever heard about writing or speaking is, "Don't act as if you were superior to your material."

Another, specifically directed to homilists is, "Don't give the impression that your own conversion is complete."

Just those two would help many a homily. But I cite them here in reference to this article. I'm happy to pass along what I've learned so far about homilizing, but I'm still learning.

You need to know how I have learned whatever it is I have learned.

In 1993, with the unanimous support of the presbyteral council, I began a program in the Saginaw diocese that works like this. I go through the list of priests and choose four, plus a deacon or lay preacher,* and send each a letter. They are to tape (live) a Sunday

---

*Bishop Untener wrote this article in 2001, prior to the 2003 edition of the G.I.R.M., and the instruction Redemptionis Sacramentum, issued in 2005.

homily within the next three weeks and send it to me. It is not optional. I also tape one of my homilies and add it to the batch.

Upon receiving these homilies my secretary prepares and mails to each of us a "kit" containing a tape and typed transcript of each homily, and notification of a date and time when we will all meet at my office. Our task in the meantime is to listen to the homilies (including our own) and make notes. We then gather at the appointed time for two hours and talk about the homilies. There is no "teacher"—we are like professional musicians trying to help one another. Besides specific critiques of each homily, our discussions are wide-ranging, for example, what works and what does not, what a homily is supposed to be in the first place, and the joys and sorrows of preaching.

At the end of the two hours, we set another date and do the whole thing again—tape a homily, send it in, and so forth. We do this a total of four times. Then I send a letter to four other priests (plus a deacon or lay homilist) and start the same process with them. And so on.**

We have just finished going through the whole presbyterate, and we are starting over. Homilists, like musicians, authors, and golfers, are never finished perfecting their skills.

Having been part of each session, listened to over a thousand homilies, had hundreds of my own critiques, I have learned a lot. Two years ago I wrote a book in an attempt to summarize and pass on what I have learned. But the learning continues, and there's much more I wish I had said.

In this article I will use the *via negativa*, citing what I perceive to be the most fundamental mistakes we homilists tend to make. I will number them for convenience, but this is not an attempt to rank them.

1. Neglecting the Great Mysteries

There is a fascinating incident in the Acts of the Apostles. When St. Paul first came to Ephesus, he found people who knew

---

**See note on previous page.

about Jesus, but not the whole story. They had been taught by Apollos, who "spoke and taught accurately about Jesus, although he knew only the baptism of John" (cf. Acts 18:24ff). When Paul asked them about the Holy Spirit, they said, "We have never even heard that there is a Holy Spirit."

We do not know how this happened, but let us imagine this scenario: Apollos was one of the first disciples called by Jesus and was with Jesus throughout his entire ministry—except the last two months. He had a job opportunity in Ephesus (about six-hundred miles away) and took it.

In Ephesus, Apollos preached about Jesus—the kind of person he was, the kind of life he led, his teachings on forgiveness, the Sermon on the Mount, the coming of the reign of God, his miracles, the parables. Apollos had been there for all of it. But he never knew the rest of the story.

Think for a moment. What would be missing from what Apollos taught?

Missing would be the part that gives full meaning to all the rest. Apollos would know nothing about the crucifixion, death, resurrection, and sending of the Spirit. These are not simply a few items in a long list of truths. These are the events through which the disciples were later able to interpret everything about who Jesus was and what he did—and what he was still doing.

Now here is the question. Could Apollos have given many of the homilies we preach? I think so.

We tend to neglect the great mysteries—death, resurrection, the Spirit, the Trinity, grace, sin (versus sins), redemption, the mystery of God. We preach on the passion only on Palm Sunday and Good Friday and on those two days, since the whole passion is read, we usually preach briefly. We preach on the resurrection at the *beginning* of the fifty-day Easter season, but we have the resurrection narratives only for two Sundays after Easter. Then we shift to the "good shepherd" section of John's Gospel (Apollos could preach on that one), and for the rest of the Easter season until Pentecost we have John's Last Supper discourse, parts of which are so difficult we resort to the first or second reading.

During much of Ordinary Time we have miracles and parables that seem much more down-to-earth and enable us to draw behavioral lessons for our listeners. The great mysteries lie within all these texts, but we're more inclined to use them to preach/teach behavior.

Homilies are meant to go to the root of what it means to be a Christian. Instead, we tend to preach about how we're supposed to live the faith, without illuminating what underlies it all. Apollos could have given a lot of the homilies we preach.

2. Preaching as Though We Get to Choose What to Say

This gets to the core of what a homily is. On the one hand, we are well aware that we are not preaching *our* message. We preach what Jesus preached and taught, as handed on by the church.

On the other hand, we can treat it as *our* message insofar as we think we can arbitrarily determine what we are going to say as long as it is connected with the scriptures and is within the bounds of orthodoxy. We can easily find ourselves doing something like this: We look at the gospel first, think about it, and say, "Nothing really jumps out at me. I think I will use a line from the second reading and preach about factions in the community."

I describe a homily as trying to discern what the Lord is doing/speaking through this event (*these* scripture texts, *these* liturgical texts, *this* liturgical feast or season, *this* historical time and place, the gathering of *these* people)—and helping to illuminate this for the assembly.

We homilists don't simply choose what we want to say. Our first task is to discern what the Lord is saying. The question is not what Jesus once preached, but what Jesus *is preaching* to us here and now. It is much like ministering a sacrament. Those who minister a sacrament do not decide what effect they want it to have. They are instruments *the Lord* uses to do what *he* is doing. When we preach we exercise a similar role. We are instruments of what the Lord is speaking to us through this liturgical event.

To put it another way, we exercise a function similar to that of the biblical authors through whom God spoke to the people. It is the same Spirit who guides us as we select what is to be said, compose it, and deliver it. When we preach, we are an instrument of what the Lord is doing in this liturgical event. It will take us down new paths. One could use the analogy of Jesus saying to Peter, "You used to dress yourself and go where you wanted" but now "someone else will dress you and lead you where you do not want to go."

3. Using the Scriptures as a Platform to Teach and Moralize

We have been making progress in the relationship of homilies to the scriptures. Within my own life as a priest I can identify three stages.

(1) When I was ordained in 1963, the Archdiocese of Detroit (like most dioceses) issued "sermon outlines" that we were to follow. In effect, they were lesson plans based on the Creed, the sacraments, and the Ten Commandments. They connected with the scriptures after the fact, that is, the author of the outline found a way to connect the lesson *post factum* with something from the scripture readings of the day.

(2) After Vatican II, such outlines disappeared and we were taught to base our homilies on the scriptures of the day. No longer was a predetermined lesson connected after the fact to the scriptures. We began with the scriptures. But we did not go too deeply into them. Most of us were taught to make sure we "applied" them to people's lives. So, after establishing the "platform" provided by the scriptures, we went on to spend the second half of the homily moralizing about human conduct.

Connecting with real life is a laudable goal. But instead of connecting with the "real-life" deep aspirations and questions within the human spirit, most of us tried to connect with the day-to-day stuff of proper behavior. Once finished with the scriptures, we were into our own agenda. If it was social justice, most of our homilies were about social justice. If it was building community, most of our homilies were about building community. And so forth and so on.

In Matthew's Gospel, the first words quoted in the ministry of John the Baptist and Jesus are exactly the same:

In those days John the Baptist appeared, preaching in the desert of Judea and saying, "Repent, for the kingdom of heaven is at hand" (3:1).

From that time on (after the temptation in the desert) Jesus began to preach and say: "Repent, for the kingdom of heaven is at hand" (4:17).

We think of the word *repent* as striking our breast and promising to do better. But the Greek word means to *think again*. The English word actually has the same literal meaning. The word *pensive* has to do with thinking. Thus *repent* means to *rethink* the way we see God, creation, other people, ourselves, and change our lives accordingly.

We do not change people's conduct by telling them what to do. We do this by enabling them to see things differently, which is what the great mysteries of our faith do.

(3) We are gradually moving on to a third stage—opening up the scriptures for and with the assembly. We are gradually moving there, but I think we are still very much caught in the stage of using the scriptures to teach and moralize.

Let us consider the gospel passage in which Jesus says, "You are the salt of the earth…you are the light of the world." The pattern in statement number 2 would be first of all to explain the text and point out why salt and light were so important to ancient peoples. That takes care of our obligation to deal with the scripture text. Then we talk about how we are supposed to make a difference in our world (salt) and give good example (light), and we use down-to-earth examples to apply this to today's world.

For one thing, they have heard it all before. It is predictable stuff. For another, we all go home with "bad marks." For still another, as mentioned above, we do not change people's behavior by telling them what to do. We change behavior by helping them see things differently. That is what a homily is supposed to do— open our eyes to the great mystery of God proclaimed in the scriptures, and thus see life differently.

The mistake is to use the scriptures as the occasion to say something about real life, but without any serious engagement of the text. We use the text as a peg, a thought-starter, and then go on with our own development. We never get into deeper theological reflection on the scriptures, but move quickly toward offering applications. We give pat answers, instead of trying to let the light of the scriptures and God's grace open us up to a deeper, wider perspective, a richer understanding of life. People never get to enjoy basking in great mysteries of our faith—which may be why we have such a difficult time with *mystagogia*.

4. Neglecting the Old Testament

The Old Testament is not an antique in our religious museum. Nor is it the wreckage of something we Christians have left behind. It is the foundation on which stands all that we hold sacred.

Jesus was a Jew. He prayed the Jewish scriptures (the Our Father could be prayed word for word by a Jewish person today). He celebrated the Jewish feasts. He fulfilled the law and the prophets.

The earliest Christian community was Jewish and drew upon the Jewish traditions. They remembered how Jesus fulfilled them, went beyond them, and the memory helped.

We need to regard the Old Testament more highly than we do. We need to pray it more. And we need to preach it more.

Raymond Brown pointed out that the New Testament covers a relatively short period of time—about seventy years—which today is less than one lifetime. The gospels (apart from the infancy narratives of Matthew and Luke) cover only two or three years. The New Testament (especially the gospels) is a success story. Jesus dies and rises. Peter is thrown into prison and is miraculously set free. Paul persecutes and then becomes a Christian. Gentiles are converted.

The Old Testament covers a much longer span of time—nearly two thousand years. There are success stories (e.g., the Exodus) but they take a long time. And there are long stretches of great suffering, lasting not a lifetime, but generations—the exile, a long string of poor leaders, a long drought with no prophets. But through the years the people managed to believe in God's promise, "I will be your God, and you will be my people."

We need to hear this message so that we can trust in God and learn to bear hardships and setbacks over which we have no control. We also learn that sin has consequences, that there is a sameness, a pattern to the way we humans act, the way we fall into sin—from Adam and Eve to Peter. We learn that it is okay to think of God nonphilosophically...to picture God as getting angry, jealous, pleased...to picture God as being able to be talked into and out of things.

We need to take more time with the Old Testament, learn from it, meditate on it, identify with it...and preach it.

5. Giving a Talk Rather than Talking to the People

A homily is always "live" as opposed to a taped message. The truth is, some homilies could just as well be on tape. We prepare it, box it, and give the contents to the people. It may be nicely wrapped (i.e., not a monotone), but we're still "delivering" it rather than speaking "live" from the heart. We do it "live" when our interaction with the people affects what we are saying and how we are saying it. And they can tell the difference.

Sometimes, after discussing a homily in our groups, I ask the person to extemporize briefly what they wanted to say most of all. They begin to speak thoughtfully, from the heart, "live"—and it is ten times better than the homily they gave.

Weekday homilies are usually "live" because we feel free to speak this way. (A very frequent comment from parishioners is, "I wish they'd preach on Sundays the way they do on weekdays.") But on Sundays we go into a different "zone," perhaps because we lose our nerve. It is not easy to speak from the heart to a large group.

In order to speak "live" we have to get hold of our material. What we have to say has to be so much a part of us that we could not forget it, any more than we could forget a great incident we cannot wait to tell a friend about. We could tell it six different ways.

Getting hold of our material is the step in homily preparation that is most often left out. We finish writing the homily, go over it so we can get through it, but never really get hold of it.

This may be a symptom of the number-one problem with most homilies—too many thoughts. To get hold of our material we have to have a "sense of the whole." Sometimes we cannot get a "sense of the whole" because there is no "whole." There is a theme, but not a whole. Instead of one thought with depth (that we could never forget) we have a number of related thoughts strung together.

Generally speaking, the larger, more important the event, the less likely the homily will be "live."

A well-prepared boxed message is not necessarily a bad homily. People appreciate the preparation and the organization. But they thirst for a "live" message from the heart.

6. "Burying Our Lead"

Journalists will tell you that their editor sometimes reviews an article and says, "You buried your 'lead.' Rewrite it and start with what you have here in the middle. Let the rest flow from that."

This is true of many homilies. Time after time in our groups we tell one another, "You have a great thought here on the second page. You should have started with that and stayed with it."

When writing a homily, instead of thinking of a "beginning" as though it were a unit all its own, we should think, "How am I going to get into it?" The "it" is the core thought of the homily into which the homily should flow from the very beginning.

It frequently happens in homilies that we "do a beginning" (which may be quite interesting), then shift into our real message. The listeners catch the shift right away and figure that now we are getting into the "religious stuff," so they more or less tune out the rest. Such shifts reinforce the idea that the real world is one thing, and religion is one step removed from it.

Another problem with beginnings occurs when our first words are not really part of the homily at all. We begin with things that could have been part of the Introductory Rites, for example:

thanking the bishop for coming, or acknowledging the presence of a twenty-fifth anniversary couple who will be renewing their vows after the homily. The homily is part of the flow of the word of God, and inserting such comments between the gospel and the homily is just as inappropriate as inserting them between the first and second scripture reading.

7. Failure to Edit

Editing is more than touch-up work. It can involve drastic changes. When we start writing or outlining our homily, we tend to work in linear fashion—we stay with the development we had in mind when we started, and each unit is an add-on to the previous one. Most good writing, however, involves major changes of direction along the way...and after we have completed the whole text/outline.

Editing along the way. We figure we are about halfway there...and suddenly we see the whole landscape from a different vantage point. What we had intended as a small part of the homily could become the heart of it. But doing this would require a new direction and new material. We are faced with a major overhaul, which usually means that some of the parts will have to be thrown out (always painful). Do we dare it...or just go on?

Editing when we've finished the text/outline. As far as we are concerned the homily is finished, except for some minor tinkering. We do not allow ourselves to wonder, "Is there a better way to do this?" This is the point at which we need to have the nerve to let the creative juices flow, and be open to a major rewrite.

One of the things we do in our homily groups is have a journalist review two of the transcripts at each session, and go over them as if she were an editor. It is amazing to see how many sections get cut or reordered and how many unnecessary or weak words get circled. We have come to the conclusion that most of us were never taught to do this and, in fact, seldom do.

Editing may be the step that could turn a mediocre homily into a great one.

8. Picturing the Homily as the Main Event

The homily is important. But so is the whole Liturgy of the Word, the preparation of the gifts (giving the assembly a sense of their "flow" toward the altar), the eucharistic prayer, the communion rite. I recently received a letter from a layperson that said:

> One realization I've had recently is that...there's a clear danger of the homily eclipsing the rest of the liturgy—in length and "weight." I get tired, just wishing for more really good eucharistic action in addition to a worthwhile homily.

How important is a homily? I have asked different folks. Here are some of the comments:

"It's not what I go to Mass for."

"A poor homily (like poor music) can get in the way, but there's much more than that."

"I'm so happy when it's good."

"I look forward to the homily. There will always be something good even in a bad homily."

"I expect God to reveal himself in the whole event. If it were not so, I wouldn't go."

We would do well to realize that the homily is only one part of the ritual, a relatively small part, and therefore, craft a jewel rather than trying to seize the whole event with our preaching. If we approach it this way, we are more apt to preach well, and preach from the heart.

Postscript

My experience in working with homilists is that they take this ministry seriously and are trying to do their best. They are people of faith, people who have an adequate theological and scriptural background, life experience. They are people of goodwill, open to anything that will help them improve. They simply do not get much help. They get some reactions, encouragements, and kindness.

Church musicians get the same. That helps them survive, but does not help them improve.

I chose the *via negativa* not because I wished to be negative, but because it seemed a way to be concrete and helpful. Homilies, I believe, are much better than they used to be. We are moving in the right direction. We need hands-on help to keep us moving in that direction.

3

Ministry of Mercy

Introduction

I hereby decree that from this day forward...in the Church of Saginaw, every meeting—no matter what its purpose—have as its first agenda item this question: How shall what we are doing here affect or involve the poor?[1]

I dream of the day when...we will stand out in the world because of our mercy as clearly as the Amish stand out because of their horse and buggy.[2]

Bishop Ken Untener was a master at stating a simple thought that easily captured a large idea and gave it practical consequences. He might have written a pastoral letter on the need to be more aware of the poor in our midst, but he did one better. With the "Decree on the Poor" he mandated that for the following three months every meeting in the diocese must open with the same question, "How shall what we are doing here affect or involve the poor?" A lot of practical consequences for the diocese and the poor resulted from this one decree.

This decree was front and center of every diocesan meeting for three months, whether the meeting was large or between two people such as himself and his secretary. The effects lasted much longer than the ninety-seven days of the decree. In "How Should We Think about the Poor?" he makes very practical observations and suggestions about that experience and what he learned for himself.

Without feeling personally deprived by it, Bishop Ken lived what he taught. Many people remember him for his habit of moving from rectory to rectory, nearly sixty rectory moves during the twenty-four years he was bishop, staying several months and then moving on. It was, he said, an almost accidental decision; he didn't want to live in a big mansion by himself. He added, "I don't feel at home in a big house. I don't feel at home in a big car, and I know a lot of people don't. I guess I don't take it away from people who do, but I know where I feel at home." He decided early on, why not live in parish rectories close to the priests and people? He liked ordinary people, liked living in various parishes of the diocese among the pastors and people.

Bishop Ken took care to visit the sick regularly, even taking a turn at living in a hospital for several months. He went out of his way to support BeFrienders, and lay people trained to visit the sick. All knew his concern for the poor and those who were hurting. On one occasion he said that it was seeing goodness in people who deal with the cross patiently that most "undid" him.

While he was bishop, Ken had a personal conversion. Early on, he thought of stewardship in the church as, so to speak, "It's the money, stupid." Later, he said he came to a wholly different conclusion, "It's gift; all of it's gift. None of it's mine or ours; everything is only on loan to be used as good stewards." It makes a difference when it's all gift anyway.

Reflections on the stewardship of a bishop and "stewardship" programs in the diocese also helped bring about that conversion, and in 2003 to 2004 he added to the "Little Books" he was writing for the liturgical seasons, a "Little Burgundy Book" (two of them) on stewardship. His homilies began to reflect that conversion. During the night before he died his niece was sitting up with him for a while. He had been told that he had perhaps twelve to fourteen hours to live. In the night she asked him, "Are you okay with this Uncle Ken?" He answered with peace, "I've already given it all to God."

Notes

1. Chrism Mass, March 6, 1991.
2. "A Church Remarkable for Tenderness and Mercy," *Origins* 16 (May 7, 1987): 826.

A Church Remarkable for Tenderness and Mercy

Bishop Untener to Religious Educators
Origins 16 (November 20, 1988)

Religious educators "must pass on the tradition of a church remarkable for its tenderness and mercy," Bishop Kenneth Untener of Saginaw, Michigan, said in a homily on April 6 during a Mass for the Michigan Religious Education Leadership conference held in Grand Rapids. Untener said it is his dream that one day, "because of our religious formation we will stand out in the world because of our mercy as clearly as the Amish stand out because of their horse and buggy." But, Untener cautioned, "there is something in the church sort of like a prevailing wind that makes us drift toward severity, away from softness." In this he said he was not speaking of individuals in the church. "I believe that church ministers, when dealing one to one with people, generally tend to be very compassionate. I am speaking of what might be called 'corporate severity.'" There is a tendency—not unique to the church—"that keeps moving us away from softness and toward severity," he said. The text of his homily follows.

A strange thing happened to this story—Jesus and the adulteress—on its way to becoming part of John's Gospel. It was hushed up, suppressed. It is missing from the early Greek manuscripts in the East. In the West, it was missing from some early manuscripts, but was included in others.

Because of all this, there have been questions about where it belongs in the gospel. Some feel that it belongs at a different place in John's Gospel. Others say that it doesn't even belong in John's Gospel, but was originally part of Luke and should be placed just before his account of the treachery of Judas. Some of the early manuscripts actually have it there.

Wherever it belongs, two things are clear: The story is part of the early tradition about Jesus. Early attempts were made to hush it up.

Why would people in the church want to suppress it? The answer is quite clear: This story just didn't seem right. Jesus, it would appear, was too soft on sin. The more severe the church became in its discipline—and this happened very early—the more difficult it became to tell a story like this about Jesus. And so it was hushed up.

The Trend toward Severity

We can learn something from this: There is something in the church, sort of like a prevailing wind that makes us drift toward severity, away from softness. I am not speaking of individuals in the church. I believe that church ministers, when dealing one to one with people, generally tend to be very compassionate. I am speaking of what might be called "corporate severity." The posture we take as a church toward the world, toward our own people, the image we present—all these seem to tend toward corporate severity rather than softness. It is like a prevailing wind always moving us in that direction, and I worry about it. Gospel passages such as this one—plus the story of its attempted suppression—give us good cause for worry.

I should point out that this is not unique to the church. It seems true of any organization. For example, think about our country and its immigration laws. Which way has the drift been? Obviously, it has been away from softness ("Give me your tired, your poor, your huddled masses yearning to breathe free") and toward severity. On a smaller scale, think of neighborhood organizations. They start out with the intention of joining together in a common effort to build a pleasant and happy community, and then they become stricter and stricter. The trend toward severity seems to be part of every organization, including the church.

That might be understandable if the church were simply an organization founded by Jesus. But the fact is, Jesus is more than our founder. He is our foundation and we must act as he did—not simply as individuals, but as a corporate body. That is why I worry about our drift toward corporate severity.

Other Examples of This Trend

The attempt to hush up the story of Jesus and the adulteress is just one example of this trend away from softness and toward severity. In Holy Week we are presented with another example: the washing of feet. This wasn't taken out of the manuscripts like the story of the adulteress, but we have other ways of suppressing it. How many of you, for example, have a picture of the foot washing on your wall at home? I'd bet there's not a person here who does. You rarely, if ever, see a picture of this. Also, did you ever notice that this mandate from Jesus (the washing of the feet is called the *mandatum*, and it is why Thursday of Holy Week has traditionally been called Maundy Thursday) is optional at Mass on Holy Thursday? We've made it an optional mandate.

Why isn't the washing of the feet more prominently displayed in the pictures on our walls and in our ceremonies? Probably for the same reason that the apostle Peter had trouble with it at the Last Supper. It just didn't seem right for Jesus to be doing a thing like that.

There is something in the church like a prevailing wind that keeps moving us away from softness and toward severity. There are examples of it all around you in this cathedral.

- Those oils on display over there. They represent softness and compassion and healing. Until very recently we kept them hidden. Very few Catholics could name the three oils the church uses. They have not been part of our emphasis.

- The reconciliation room over there. It represents the tenderness of Jesus toward sinners, as in the story of the adulteress or the prodigal son. We took that softness and changed it into a severe closet, dark and anonymous, with the priest sitting as judge.
- The hosts on the table back there. They are meant to express the sign of real food. They are meant to taste and smell and feel like bread....
- The red wine back there. It is also part of the Lord's Supper and it brings warmth and fragrance to the meal. We took it away from the people for centuries.

There has been in this church a drift away from softness and toward severity. I realize that one should not oversimplify all of this, and one must be careful about unfair caricatures. But the emphasis—at least in the perception of the people—seems to have been on severity rather than softness. How would the people characterize our marriage legislation and our marriage tribunals? Would they identify them with Jesus in this gospel passage or with the people who were demanding that the Mosaic law be carried out to the letter? It is a question of emphasis and the way we are perceived.

We are perceived as severe. Not so long ago, if a marriage was mixed, you had to "celebrate" it at a side altar or a sacristy. We are a church that, not so long ago, would not bury one of our own who committed suicide. Even today, in some of our new approaches and programs, we can be inflexible and rigid.

You as Educators

What has all of this got to do with educators? A great deal. You are people entrusted with passing on our traditions to others. Given the trend away from softness and toward severity, which do you emphasize in your teaching mission? Let me put it another way: Would the people you teach be more likely to be able to recite the Ten Commandments or the Beatitudes?

To borrow a famous phrase, I have a dream. I dream of the day when our religious education will so remarkably stress the gentleness, forgiveness, and love that Christians are called upon to live that this will be our trademark in the world. I dream of the day when our youngsters will find it as natural to help in a soup kitchen as we once found it natural to have a sock hop. I dream of the day when a peace march might be as normal as a paper drive was for us. I dream of the day when youngsters will be able to tell the story of the prodigal son with all the graphic details and drama that we use to describe Dante's hell. I dream of the day when youngsters will be able to recite the gospel passage "I was hungry...I was thirsty...I was a stranger" as perfectly as we could recite catechism answers. I dream of the day when because of our religious formation we will stand out in the world because of our mercy as clearly as the Amish stand out because of their horse and buggy.

There has been a prevailing wind in the church moving us away from softness and toward severity. But John XXIII brought a fresh wind, and it moved us in the other direction. Ask anyone out there what they think of "good Pope John" and the image clearly comes through. It was a fresh emphasis on mercy and love. But we're not sure how to handle this new breeze, just as the early church wasn't sure how to handle the story of Jesus and the adulteress. Our tendency will surely be to stifle it. You educators have an enormous role to play in determining which breeze will prevail. You must pass on the tradition of a church remarkable for its tenderness and mercy.

I close these reflections by reminding you of the closing scene in the gospel passage. Everyone had gone, and Jesus and the woman were left standing alone. It is a magnificent scene, described beautifully by St. Augustine with the words: *"Relicti sunt duo, misera et misericordia."* "And two were left...one filled with misery, and one filled with mercy." There is a lot of misery in our world, and it desperately needs a merciful church. I pray that the church you proclaim will be a church manifestly filled with mercy.

Bishop Untener's Chrism Mass Homily

March 26, 1991

This morning, before the assembled representatives of the church of Saginaw, I hereby issue two decrees.

First Decree

The first decree has to do with these oils about to be blessed. I hereby decree that wherever and whenever these oils are used, they be used generously.

Jesus, in his hometown inaugural address, announced that a new era had begun, a time of God's favor, God's graciousness, a special time of God's merciful love that would mark his whole ministry. These oils are a sign of that. They are a sign of God's kind, gentle, soothing touch, and God's largesse. This largesse must characterize everything the church does, and perhaps, if we use these oils generously, they will remind us to act as Jesus did.

I looked up adverbs and phrases in Roget's *Thesaurus* that express this "largesse," and found:

liberally, freely, generously, munificently, handsomely, unselfishly, ungrudgingly, unsparingly, unstintingly, bountiful, bounteously, lavishly, profusely, openhandedly, freehandedly, openheartedly, bigheartedly, large heartedly, great heartedly, with open hands, with unsparing hand, without stint, with a full heart.

I think you get the idea. And so my first decree: I hereby decree that wherever and whenever these oils are used, they be used generously.

Second Decree

My second decree has to do not with the oils, but with another centerpiece of the church's ministry: meetings.

I hereby decree that in the church of Saginaw, from this day forward until July 1, 1991, every meeting—no matter what its purpose—have as its first agenda item this question: How will what we are doing here affect or involve the poor?

We tend to define the word *poor* in a way that makes it elusive. But I mean *the poor*. If we start with the poor, then the rest will be included too. The words in Roget's *Thesaurus* under *the poor* sum up what I mean when I use that phrase: the needy, the have-nots, the down-and-out, the forgotten ones.

That last phrase—the forgotten ones—is the reason why we need to do this. Despite the best of our intentions, we have so many things to do just to keep doing what we're doing, that the poor tend to be forgotten, or at best, receive our leftover attention and leftover resources.

Jesus and the Poor

For Jesus it was not so. The poor were front and center. They were at the center of his inaugural address in Luke's Gospel, and they were a constant theme of his preaching afterward. They will come up again and again in Luke's Gospel:

"And raising his eyes toward his disciples he said:
'Blessed are you who are poor,
for the kingdom of God is yours.'" (6:20)

"And he said to them in reply, 'Go and tell John what you have seen and heard: the blind regain their sight, the lame walk, lepers are cleansed, the deaf hear, the dead are raised, the poor have the good news proclaimed to them.'" (7:22)

"Rather, when you hold a banquet, invite the poor, the crippled, the lame, the blind." (14:13)

"Then the master of the house in a rage commanded his servant, 'Go out quickly into the streets and alleys of the town and bring in here the poor and the crippled, the blind and the lame.'" (14:21)

"And lying at his door was a poor man named Lazarus, covered with sores....When the poor man died, he was carried away by angels to the bosom of Abraham." (16:20–22)

"When Jesus heard this he said to him, 'There is still one thing left for you: sell all that you have and distribute it to the poor, and you will have a treasure in heaven. Then come, follow me.'" (18:22)

"But Zacchaeus stood there and said to the Lord, 'Behold, half of my possessions, Lord, I shall give to the poor, and if I have extorted anything from anyone I shall repay it four times over.'" (19:8)

"He said, 'I tell you truly, this poor widow put in more than all the rest.'" (21:3)

If the poor were central to the ministry of Jesus, they must be central to the ministry of the church of Saginaw. And so I decree that the poor be first on the agenda of all our meetings for the next three months—all our meetings, whether a clergy personnel board meeting, an education meeting, a liturgy meeting, a youth-ministry meeting, a staff meeting, or even a meeting to plan another meeting. The first agenda item must be: How will what we are doing affect or involve the poor?

There will be times when the question won't quite fit, and when it may seem contrived even to ask it. But ask it anyway. Just having asked the question will have an effect. Maybe we should do it forever, but my decree for now is that we do it for the next three months.

The Anointing at Bethany

It's interesting how these two themes—the oil and the poor—come together in the passage in John's Gospel read on the Monday of Holy Week. At Bethany, Mary anoints the feet of Jesus with considerable largesse, and Judas complains that the money spent on the oil could have been given to the poor.

Judas missed the point. Sometimes we do too. Concern for the poor doesn't mean being meager and miserly, nor does it mean simply giving the poor some money now and then. What it does mean is seeing the world through their eyes, holding them in our hearts as we plan, set our priorities, design our programs, shape our church and our world. An occasional nod in their direction doesn't do it. The poor must be front and center. If they are not front and center, despite our best intentions, they will end up outside the gate looking in, and we will barely notice them.

As we leave here today with these newly blessed oils I ask that you display them in your churches, and that you use them generously. Let them be a sign of God's gracious extravagance toward all people, especially toward the poor. And to make sure of that, I ask that you put the poor first on every agenda, which is exactly where they belong in a community that bears the name of Christ.

The Decree to Discuss the Poor: What Was Learned

Origins 21/10 (August 1991)

"I have learned eight things in particular these past ninety-seven days" about the poor, as well as about others, Bishop Kenneth Untener of Saginaw, Michigan, said in a set of reflections he issued at the beginning of July. He was reflecting on the impact of his March 26, 1991, decree that all meetings held under diocesan auspices from then until July 1 begin with this agenda item: "How shall what we are doing here affect or involve the poor?" Untener said that during this period he learned that "we tend to forget the 'poor' poor" and the "the poor are often invisible." He said, "The real-life poor do not come as easily to mind as, say, the sick." Because of their invisibility—because, for example, the poor don't get the parish bulletin—they tend not to know of services available to them in the church. They might not know, for example, of tuition assistance available at schools. Untener said, "If you want the poor to take advantage of help to the poor, you must reach out to find them." And, "to find the poor you must go out of your way." Untener said he learned that "helping the poor is not always a pleasant experience," that "sometimes the poor are overwhelmed into inaction," but that "the poor also help the poor." Again, he said, "food baskets at Thanksgiving and toys at Christmas are good as far as they go, but they don't go very far." The text of Untener's reflections follows.

And now, after ninety-seven days, the decree on the poor has ended.

Never have I talked about and listened to so much about the poor. On some days I had four or five meetings, and each began with the poor.

I learned a lot, not only about the poor but about us and how we think about (or don't think about) the poor. Believe me, I am no expert on the poor. But I have learned eight things in particular these past ninety-seven days.

1. We Tend to Forget the "Poor" Poor

A typical scenario: The chairperson begins the meeting by saying something like, "Well, the bishop has asked that we begin each meeting with a discussion about how this affects or involves the poor. So we're going to spend a few minutes doing that. I'll throw it open for anyone who would like to say something."

Silence.

Then someone says, "Well, people can be poor in a lot of different ways. There are some people, for example, who don't have friends, and they are poor."

I interrupt. "I agree with you. But this decree has to do with the *poor* poor. They are the ones who are left out because they're no part of what I did yesterday or today. The other kind of poor people are part of our lives, and we need to be concerned about them. But I want us to connect with the *poor* poor. If we deal with them, all the rest will follow. The *poor* poor are the ones who rarely if ever are first on an agenda. So let's talk about them."

Mental note: Always start with the *poor* poor.

2. The Poor Are Often Invisible

We rarely sat through those awkward group pauses that drive everybody nuts. Thankfully, someone was always present who could speak firsthand about an experience with a poor person. Once they did, others began to think of things to say about the poor.

The real-life poor do not come as easily to mind as, say, the sick. After the ice was broken, a person might say, "Well, now that you mention it, I did hear about such and such family and how they haven't been around much lately, and that they've been having a hard time of it." Then somebody else would tell of someone they knew or heard about, and we would all be somewhat surprised. We didn't expect poor people to be in our neck of the woods.

Poor people are everywhere, and once we tune in to them a whole new world opens up. Tuning in to the poor, however, is no small trick.

The poor around us (as opposed to the ghetto or some distant country) are often invisible. They aren't in our same "networks":

- They aren't at the same gatherings.
- They don't belong to councils or committees.
- They aren't on invitation lists.
- They don't always go to church (and if they do they try hard not to look poor).
- They don't bump into us at the mall or the supermarket.
- Take tuition assistance at schools. We offer help for those who cannot pay full tuition or cannot pay any tuition. But the poor often do not come forward. Why? It is announced in the parish bulletin. There are even fliers about it.

But the poor don't get the parish bulletin. They don't see or respond to the fliers. If you want the poor to take advantage of help to the poor, you must reach out to find them.

To find the poor you must go out of your way. You must look with different eyes, for the poor feel that we do not want them in those parts of our lives. So they disguise themselves or absent themselves.

Mental note: It takes initiative, creativity to reach the poor.

3. The Biggest Problem Is the "Undeserving Poor"

Place a child before us with a hungry face and ragged clothes, and we jump at the chance to help.

Children, you see, haven't done anything to make themselves undeserving. They haven't made the bad choices that landed them in this mess. They haven't failed to lift a finger to help themselves, because children can't help themselves anyway. They really can't help it if they are poor.

Poor children don't make it hard to help the poor. Poor adults who have had bad luck don't make it hard to help the poor.

The problem is the undeserving poor. They are the ones who have made the bad choices or failed to make any choice at all. They are the ones who have been helped before, and it didn't help. They are the ones who seem to expect us to bail them out and who hardly say thank you when we do. They are the ones who seem to take advantage of the system, of other people.

Help them anyway. If you start to distinguish between the deserving and the undeserving poor, you are finished—at least as far as the gospel is concerned. Who is really to decide if they are undeserving?

I do not mean that we shouldn't try to help them help themselves. As the saying goes, "Give me a fish and you feed me for a day. Teach me to fish and you feed me for life."

We should always try to help the poor help themselves out of their poverty. But be careful about metering out your help too carefully. Jesus was never overly careful about metering out his mercy too carefully. He was criticized for his largesse, his "reckless" mercy toward undeserving sinners. The memory of Jesus helps us deal with the "undeserving poor."

The "undeserving poor" remind us that something deeper needs to change—whatever it is that makes them feel so hopeless and helpless. We need to address that something deeper. In the meantime, help them. Do not be judgmental or overly careful.

Mental note: If you're going to err, err on the side of largesse.

4. If You Try to Help the Poor, You Will Sometimes Get Taken

Every parish minister can tell stories of people who have come with a sad tale. You check it out very carefully, give them money, and later find out that they did the same thing at three or four neighboring parishes.

Helping the poor has its risks. You will sometimes get taken. (The same is true of forgiveness. If you try to forgive seventy times seven, you will sometimes get stepped on.) It's a darn shame. Be generous anyway. Don't be foolish, but don't overdo the safety rules.

It's like playing racquetball. You're going to get hit with the ball now and then, and it hurts. You can wear safety goggles and learn how to step out of the way of certain shots, but you are still going to get hit now and then. The only way to avoid it is to stand in the corner.

If you are going to be generous to the poor, you are sometimes going to get taken. The only way to avoid it is to stand in the corner.

Mental note: Learn to write off your losses.

5. Helping the Poor Is Not Always a Pleasant Experience

It's no picnic helping the poor. There is often no feeling of fulfillment. It's work, like a lot of virtue is work, like taking care of an elderly parent is work.

The poor, as fate would have it, are just like us. They are mixtures of virtues and vices. Like us, they are not always grateful. Like us, they don't always trust. Like us, they don't always respond. Like us, they are both generous and greedy. Like us, they are sometimes wonderful and sometimes awful. Whatever happened to the noble poor? Some are out there, but mostly they are in Charles Dickens.

The *poor* poor are not always so noble, and they are the hardest to deal with, which is probably why we don't.

Mental note: When you help the poor, you always receive more than you give, but it may not seem that way at the time.

6. Food Baskets at Thanksgiving and Toys at Christmas Are Good as Far as They Go, but They Don't Go Very Far

People easily talk about direct help to the poor on special occasions—clothes, food, money. Those fine things shouldn't be taken lightly. But that is the easy part. The hard part is trying to do something about the poor's state in life.

The discussion always slowed when we tried to focus on this. Where do you begin? What do you do?

It's hard when you deal with the causes. How can we give them basic skills to manage their lives? Can we make loans available to them through our own credit unions—at considerable risk? Shouldn't the state make better provision for dependent children? What about health insurance? How do we help them find work? How do we help them find work that pays a living wage? Why are single parents, usually women, abandoned so easily by a spouse?

Mental note: Direct assistance is good. Tackling the causes is better.

7. Sometimes the Poor Are Overwhelmed into Inaction

People who deal with the poor can tell a hundred stories about how they waste money and opportunities. You bring food to their home and notice a large-screen television. You give them money, and they buy groceries at the nearby convenience store where prices are much higher and send their youngster to the mall to have a good time. You arrange to have their car fixed and find out it is a Buick Skylark. Whenever you visit, they are watching television.

Why? Let's try to put ourselves in their shoes.

You are thinking about cleaning the garage (or the basement or your desk). Actually, you have been thinking about it for weeks.

Well, to tell the truth you have been thinking about it since last winter when you were trying to find room in the garage for the snow blower.

It is a hopeless mess, but today is the day you are going to tackle it. Getting started is the problem, because with a mess like that there is no logical place to begin.

So you decide to have a beer first and watch a couple of innings of the ball game.

Hold that thought. Right there, in that moment, you are in their shoes. You may spend only half an hour watching the game, and you will eventually get to your task, but in those thirty minutes of doing nothing you know exactly how they feel all day, every day. At least with cleaning the garage there is an end in sight. But for the poor the task seems to have no beginning and no ending. They can't get enough together even to get started—a down payment, transportation, protection from an abusive husband, and education.

Their life is like that all the time. It is too big a mess even to know where to begin. So they try to forget it by enjoying some "luxuries," having a beer and watching television.

Mental note: Don't judge their "laziness" too quickly.

8. The Poor Also Help the Poor

People who work with the poor can tell a hundred stories about the "generous poor." The family who took in a neighbor's child without a second thought because the child needed to be taken in somewhere. The person who has next to nothing gives money to someone who has nothing at all, simply saying, "Well, they need it more than I do." A poor family in a small house takes in another family because they had their heat turned off in the dead of winter. Food is shared even though there isn't enough to begin with.

There are a hundred true stories about the "generous poor." The widow's mite wasn't a parable that Jesus made up. It was a true story that unfolded before his eyes. And it still happens every day in poor communities.

Mental note: God loves a cheerful giver, which is one of the reasons why God loves the poor.

Now, after ninety-seven days, the decree on the poor has ended. Is it all over? Can we now get back to normal?

Yes. We can get back to normal by realizing that *normal* means talking about the poor at normal meetings and finding ways to translate our words into actions. *Normal* means focusing on the poor as much as Jesus did.

I hope that the decree simply primed the pump. I hope we have only just begun. For there is more to learn, more to do.

The decree has been successful, but it is like the success of people who joined Weight Watchers and reached their goal by losing thirty-seven pounds. They are congratulated, cheered by all at the meeting, and given a pin. But the true measure of success is whether they will change their eating habits in the weeks and months and years ahead. Some do, and some don't.

Congratulations, church of Saginaw. We have achieved our goal of talking about the poor at our meetings for ninety-seven days. Now we must see if we have changed our meeting habits, and if we will think and act differently. The true measure of success lies in the weeks and months and years ahead.

May God, who has begun this good work in us, sustain us along the way as we strive mightily to live what we have learned.

Pastoral Letter on Sex Abuse

May 18, 2002

My Brothers and Sisters in the Lord,

I intend this to be a very frank and personal letter about the sexual abuse of minors by priests.

Let me start off by setting aside my "bishop's hat" and speaking to you as a person who comes from a large family. I'm the seventh of nine children, and I have nineteen nieces and nephews whom I dearly love. If I found out that someone—anyone—had sexually abused one of my nieces or nephews during their childhood, I would want to find that person and forget everything I believe about nonviolence.

Now, I know it's a mistake just to go out and act on my feelings. But I also know that it's healthy to *acknowledge* my feelings. I readily acknowledge them. Children come first. There may be other factors to take into account, but they are all a distant second. Children—and their safety—come first.

When we have strong feelings, we have to decide what we're going to do with them. They're a powerful force that can be used for good or evil. What I need to do and what we all need to do is to use the energy of our feelings as a force for good.

I intend to do that. I intend to do whatever I can to eliminate the problem of child abuse. Not reduce it. Eliminate it.

The Situation in Boston

Let's step back and take a look at what's been happening these past few months. In order to do that, we have to put this in perspective so that as a society we don't lull ourselves into the complacency of thinking that child abuse is simply a "church problem." It *is* a church problem. And it is also a *societal* problem.

The situation in Boston is dominated by two terrible cases—terrible not only in the crimes committed, but also in the way they apparently were handled. This has produced an extraordinary climate of mistrust not only in Boston, but across the country. The fumes of those two cases have infected every diocese in the United States and have influenced people's perceptions of how cases of child abuse have been dealt with everywhere in the church. I want to face this issue head on.

The U.S. Catholic Church

In years past, each bishop simply tried to deal with cases of abuse as best he could. To understand why there hasn't been a national policy, we need to step back and look at the structure of the Catholic Church. Our church is not as "centralized" as most people think. Individual dioceses, while in communion with all the dioceses of the Catholic Church, operate independently. For example, each diocese is independent financially. No other bishop, no group of bishops, no one in Rome has access to the money held by each individual diocese.

The same is true administratively. Individual bishops from other dioceses can't tell a bishop what to do in his own diocese. That's one of the reasons why each diocese has its own policies on the sexual abuse of minors. We bishops will take up this issue as a group at our national meeting in June.

Almost all the cases of which I have personal knowledge or have read about are from many years ago. This doesn't lessen by one iota the evil or harm done. The abuse of a minor is a terrible thing *whenever* it happens. The procedures used in the past simply are not adequate by today's standards.

Was airport security adequate before the Twin Towers' disaster? We thought so, but by the new standards, no. Was security in high schools adequate before the Columbine tragedy? By today's standards, no. Something happened that made us reexamine everything.

Were procedures adequate in dealing with priest offenders in past years? By today's standards, no. Something has happened that is making us relook at everything. And we are. Saginaw was among the first dioceses to have procedures for dealing with the abuse of minors. These were promulgated in 1989 and were developed with the help of representatives of Child Protective Services and the Department of Social Services. We are currently doing a thorough review of these procedures in the light of what society now knows about child abuse. And we continue to be committed to working with law enforcement personnel in our efforts.

Dealing with the Wider Problem

Sexual abuse of young people is a huge problem. By the time they are eighteen years old, one out of seven youngsters in the United States has been sexually abused by someone.

Most victims don't tell anyone. They keep it to themselves because it seems shameful, or because they don't want to get the abuser or themselves in trouble (most abusers are family members, other relatives, or people whom the youngster considers a friend). Or because they think no one will believe them. Some victims learn to manage the hurt themselves and are able to move on with their lives. Some don't. But it stays a secret.

Now, in the light of all that has taken place, they no longer feel they have to carry this secret alone. Victims, some after many decades, are coming forward. Stories long kept secret have begun coming out in the open. This is unprecedented, and we have to recognize it as something good, because victims deserve first consideration.

With this new openness, many are finding the freedom to tell their story to someone who can help. It is painful for them, and for all of us, but it is something good and we need to recognize it as such.

Some Closing Thoughts

These past few months have been painful and embarrassing for all of us. Day after day we read reports of past abuse by priests. This is the most agonizing experience I have ever had. It's not a thorn in my side. It's a sword in my soul. The pain comes from knowing that some youngsters have been hurt. The pain also comes from knowing that you have suffered as a member of the Catholic Church. It's on my mind every waking hour.

It is the role of a bishop to stand before his people as a representative of the whole church. In that capacity, I want to apologize to you for the failings of our church. I truly am sorry that all this has happened.

Most of St. Paul's letters were written in response to problems that existed in the communities to whom he wrote—factions, the rich ignoring the poor, sexual immorality, drunkenness. But Paul's letters were always filled with hope. He never forgot how he himself fell flat on his face when he encountered the Risen Lord on the road to Damascus. He discovered that his strength was in the Lord, not in himself.

On this feast of Pentecost we celebrate the Lord's gift of the Holy Spirit upon us. Our hope does not ultimately rest on the abilities of bishops or popes, or good public relations departments, or even on the goodness of the grass roots. Our hope rests on the unbreakable bond of the Spirit who is with us for better or for worse, until the end of time.

The Spirit does not guarantee us a perfect church. It works through all of us, saints and sinners, always leading us to reform. But the Spirit does guarantee us a well-grounded hope even in difficult times, including difficulties of our own making.

It is my prayer that all of us will open ourselves more fully to the Holy Spirit who is the Lord's own gift to each of us and all of us—the Holy Spirit given to the whole church, not just to a select few. May we together find the light and strength to walk more faithfully in the footsteps of the Lord.

Sincerely in the Lord,
Ken Untener,
bishop of Saginaw

"The Lord Hears the Cry of the Poor"

Millennium Monthly (September 1999)

The Jubilee Year in ancient Israel wasn't practiced to perfection. But *some* debts were canceled, *some* servants set free, and *some* land returned to those who had lost it through foreclosure. One of the reasons for this was their economic system. Unregulated interest rates, for example, resulted in huge, unpayable debts, and many lost their property and/or ended up in servitude. This was not good for their economy, and the periodic Jubilee Year was a good "course correction" because it set a lot of people back on their feet.

The millennium is a time for course corrections. Maybe a better image is the corrective lens put on the Hubble Space Telescope because it was out of focus. We need to correct our focus when it comes to the poor, not just in the year 2000 but into the future.

In his apostolic letter, *The Coming Third Millennium*, Pope John Paul II is very clear:

> It will be necessary, especially during this year, to emphasize the theological virtue of charity…love of God and neighbor…the summing up of the moral life of the believer. From this point of view…how can we fail to lay greater emphasis on the Church's preferential option for the poor and the outcast?…Christians will have to raise their voice on behalf of all the poor of the world (no. 50, 51).

Why does the pope talk so much about the poor? Why do preachers talk so much about the poor? Come to think of it, why did Jesus talk so much about the poor (eighteen times in the gospels)? There's a lot more to living a Christian life—like raising our kids right, doing an honest day's work, taking care of aging parents. Why single out helping the poor? There's a reason. Perhaps an analogy will be helpful.

The "Key" in Sports

Most sports involve complicated moves, and athletes try to find the "key"—one thing that makes the rest happen. For example, the racquetball swing: In a split second you coordinate the movement of your arm, wrist, knees, feet. You can't think about all those at once, so you try to focus on the key. For me, it's the elbow. If the elbow is ahead of the rest of my arm as I'm coming at the ball, the rest happens.

In hockey, meanwhile, the key is to skate with the puck while looking up, not down. That forces you to skate well, handle the puck well, and pass well. (It also helps prevent you from getting clobbered.)

The Key to Goodness

I know what the key is in real life. I learned it from the gospels. I learned it by watching good people lead good lives. The key is the poor. There's a lot more to leading a good life than simply being kind to the poor. But if we do that, the rest will happen.

That's why Jesus talked so much about the poor. Caring for them is not simply one item in a long list of good works. It's the key.

The Jesuit poet Gerard Manley Hopkins recognized this. Robert Bridges, a fellow poet, was struggling with his faith and wrote to Hopkins for advice on how he could learn to believe. Hopkins sent back a two-word letter: "Give alms."

In trying to rear a child well, parents have hundreds of things they want to pass on. If I were a dad I would teach my children how to tie their shoes, how to play "Chopsticks" on the piano, how to swing a bat, to say *please* and *thank you*. I would try to pass on to them the love of good music, the value of good friends. And for sure I would teach them to see God's face in the face of the poor, to hear God's voice in the cry of the poor, and regularly to give to the poor. I'd want to plant this in their hearts from their earliest days because it would affect everything else: their attitudes toward money, people in general, life, and God.

This past Lent, the parents of a three- and a four-year-old let them earn money for the U.S. bishops' rice bowl collection by doing small tasks around the house. One day, shortly after Lent ended, they came to their mother and said, "We want to do some more work for the poor." As a result, these youngsters now have a bank with a slot for "savings" and another for "spending" and another for "the poor." The effects will be long-range, and nothing but good.

Getting It Right

The word *righteous*, used so frequently in scripture, can have for us a negative ring, probably because we may connect it with self-righteous. The meaning of righteous, however, is wholly positive. Simply put, it means getting it right, seeing things as they are: Two plus two equals four. The earth is round. We are all brothers and sisters. The earth is the Lord's and all that is in it. If we see things any other way or act as though these things were not true, we don't have it right.

In the parable of the rich man feasting at his table and the poor man lying at his gate, each was looking from a different angle and their views were different. The rich man was looking over the top of his table and across the lawn down to the gate. The beggar, however, was looking up from the ground and through the gate. Imagine how the food looked to the rich man and how it looked to Lazarus. Imagine how the house looked to each man. Imagine how they saw one another. Imagine how life itself looked to them. Which one saw things accurately?

Jesus does not leave us without an answer, as is clear when both men die. The rich man wants to send Lazarus back to explain things to his brothers because they think as he did, and he had it all wrong.

Jesus had a way of turning things upside down and explaining that this way of seeing things was actually more accurate: The last are first; the least are the greatest; death is the way to life. It is the narrow door, not the wide one, that leads to life. The way to deal with violence is kindness. We should love all people, including our enemies, and give to those who ask of us.

I'd have sworn a lot of those were the other way around. I must have had a bad angle and missed something, which is why some sports use the instant replay. The angle can make a big difference, as the rich man learned after he died.

God's Money Managers

If indeed the earth is the Lord's and all that is in it, then we are God's money managers. It would be a strange money manager who thought that the funds entrusted to him were "gifts" for his own use. Talk about not getting it right.

After we die we're going to be asked about how well we managed the goods entrusted to us by God. How do I know that? Because in his last sermon in Matthew's Gospel, Jesus gave us a sneak preview of the judgment, and in this advance look we see the Risen Lord take the judgment seat and talk about the distribution of food, drink and clothing—about the people on the margin ("strangers"), the sick, the imprisoned.

We might imagine a conversation that goes something like this:

"Well, Lord, along the way I contributed to some good causes now and then."

The Lord: "We're here to look at the whole sweep of your life, not isolated sins or isolated good works. All the things that were given to you were given so that you could put them to good use, accomplish something with them."

"Now, Lord, you keep saying that these things were 'given' to me. They weren't just given. I worked for them. It wasn't easy to get a good education, to earn a good living, to build up a savings account. I worked for all these things."

The Lord: "Some acquire money and possessions by chance, and some by hard work. But both groups keep them by choice. Regardless of how you got them, you knew that 'The earth is the Lord's and all that is in it.' So I want to get back to the question of how you managed my goods and what you were able to do with them."

Those certainly aren't the exact words of the dialogue, but we can be pretty sure about the gist of it. The Lord has told us that in advance.

Room 436

Every three or four months I move into a different parish in the diocese and make that my temporary home. One time, when I was about due to move on to a new parish, I was visiting someone at St. Mary's Hospital in Saginaw, and it occurred to me that it might be a good idea to live there—in one of the regular patient's rooms. So, after making sure that I wouldn't be depriving anyone of necessary space, I moved into Room 436.

Room 436 soon became home to me, the way any dwelling becomes home. Everything around you triggers the familiar feeling of being home: the sights, the smells, the sounds—especially the sounds. I got used to the announcements on the intercom, the helicopter coming in, a patient down the hall moaning in pain, carts and equipment being wheeled down the hall. They were all signs that I was home, like the sound of a train to someone who grows up near railroad tracks. I got to know the people on my floor, both the nursing staff and the patients. It was a surgical floor, so the medical problems varied from minor to major. These people became my neighbors. Some died while I was there. Others were there for a long time.

I became familiar with the whole place. There was no resident chaplain so I told the staff that I would take the night calls. When I came in late I always walked through the emergency room and saw action there. I'd often notice the windows in the operating room, its lights frequently burning all night long.

The strangest thing happened to me. I had visited hospitals hundreds of times in my thirty-two years as a priest. I had dealt with emergency-room crises, death, grieving families in shock—plus deaths in my own family. But these were all extraordinary situations outside the inner circle of my normal life. I could rise to the occasion, and then it was over and life was regular again. But now this was my home. Sickness and death became the regular stuff of life.

It wasn't simply a matter of getting used to it. It was a matter of letting all this become absorbed into the core of my life. I had to find a way to make sense out of life with these things in the center of it. No longer could I just rise to the occasion as though this was the exception. My whole life had to widen to include it. My faith had to deepen to include it.

What strikes me is that we hardly ever do that with the poor. They are exceptions to the normal run of our life. We "visit" them sometimes in our thoughts and sometimes literally. We rise to the occasion to help them. But they're not part of our inner thoughts, our regular, real life.

We need to put them there. Then, everything changes. They are family, our brothers and sisters. We don't have to be poor, any more than I had to be sick or dying. We simply take them into our heart. When that happens we can make the Lord's words our own: "What you did to the least of these you did to me." When that happens, we've found the "key."

Bishop Ken Untener Pleads for the Poor

The following is a statement made by Bishop Ken Untener on behalf of some religious leaders of Michigan at a press conference in the Capitol. Reprinted by The Catholic Weekly, *December 20, 1991.*

We are here today to address the leaders of our state government and the citizens of our state, and to speak on behalf of our sisters and brothers in need. There are many things to say about conditions in our state. I will speak about some very basic convictions.

We recognize the complexities involved—decreasing revenues, the prevailing winds of antitax sentiment, the wish to downsize government.

But I picture a mother as family Christmas plans are being made, and some family members are being left out. I picture her saying, "We can't do that. I don't care how hard it is—we have to find a way to include everyone." And others might argue with her and say that it isn't practical or even possible—the car is too small or the house is too small or the dinner table is too small—and she would say, "Well, we're just going to have to find a way, because we're not going to leave anyone out."

As we stand here this morning, we see family members being left out—left out in the cold, left out of food, left out of health care—and we are saying, "We can't do that. We know there are problems, but leaving out family members who are in need, no matter how they got that way, no, this we simply cannot do. We have to include everyone, even if it means that those with more will have less, so that those who have nothing will have something."

Darwin's law does not apply to human beings. The survival of the fittest may work with other species, but it doesn't apply to human beings. We feed the weak first, not last. We house everyone, not just the strong. We carry our wounded; we bring along those who travel more slowly, even if it means that we cannot travel as fast. We have the power to intervene to help the weak.

So gentlemen and gentlewomen—sisters and brothers—we must not do what we are doing. This cannot be. It is not in the tradition of Christianity or Judaism, Islam, Buddhism, or any other of our religious traditions. It is not in the tradition of the United States—or of the State of Michigan.

It is not like us to act this way. For the sake of those in need—for the sake of ourselves—we must find another way.

Thoughts on Stewardship

Little Burgundy Book, 2002

The Word *Stewardship*

The word *stewardship* is the English translation of a secular Greek term formed from two words: *manage* and *house*. A steward is someone who *manages* someone else's *house* (that is, all the owner's possessions).

The word *steward* (or *stewardship*) is found eighty-seven times in the New Testament. For example, Paul speaks of himself as a "steward" of the gospel. He has received the "good news" from the Lord, and it has been given to him so that he can share it with others.

In two passages of Luke's Gospel, it is even on the lips of Jesus.

New Testament writers use the words *steward* and *stewardship* to make the point that in reference to God, all people are stewards, because everything that exists belongs to God.

Laws about ownership can help to keep good order in society. But legal "ownership" can be deceptive. A person only "owns" something in the sense that other human beings can't claim it of themselves. For example, to take another person's car is auto theft.

But in relation to God, no one ultimately *owns* anything. God is the owner of everything that exists. God created it, and it is God who continually keeps it in existence.

That is the fundamental meaning of stewardship: Everything belongs to God.

Time/Talent/Treasure?

Literature on stewardship traditionally uses three categories: time, talent, and treasure. These sum up the gifts we have been given by God, and which we—as stewards—are to "manage" for God's purposes.

These categories can seem somewhat artificial. For example, it's not always easy to distinguish between giving our *time* and giving our *talent*. Maybe more contemporary terms would help. For some, it might be easier simply to speak of "skills" and "money."

Skills: We may or may not have *highly specialized* skills, but we all have skills. If we listed them, we might surprise ourselves. Many of the things on the list would seem simple and normal. But the truth is, we all have many skills that we use just to get through a day.

Money: Whereas "treasure" may evoke thoughts of riches, "money" is something that is just plain part of life. We speak of our wages as "earning a *living*."

Stewardship poses the question: How do I make use of my skills and my money? In other words, do I handle these as gifts belonging to God, which I am meant to manage on God's behalf and for God's purposes? Or do I consider my skills and my money as belonging to me—possessions that I occasionally bestow on others?

That is *the* question, and how we answer the question makes all the difference in the world. And the difference, by the way, deals not so much with the effects upon *others*, but with the effects upon *me*.

That is a key to stewardship. Not the needs of others to receive. But my need to give.

A Flash of Insight

Some basic truths are right there before everyone's eyes, but not perceived. When such a truth is discovered, it's not because of a long process of reasoning. It simply comes in a sudden flash of insight. It just plain dawns on a person.

For example, children, even teenagers, sometimes think that everything their parents do for them is simply what mothers and fathers do—wash the clothes, make and serve the meals, earn the money, care for them when they're sick, stay at home with them in the evenings. Children take all this for granted, like the air they breathe.

When do sons and daughters suddenly realize that all this was hard work, sacrifice? Many adults say that they themselves didn't get this flash of insight until they had children. Suddenly, they saw everything differently.

When do God's sons and daughters realize that everything they have really comes from God, belongs to God, and that they are stewards and managers of goods that don't belong to them...that God intended that they use these gifts for the benefit of others?

It dawns on some people early in life, some on their deathbed, and others miss it entirely.

If and when it does come, it usually doesn't come from a long reasoning process. It's one of those deep-down truths that simply dawns on a person in a flash of insight. It is, in the end, a grace from God.

To catch that insight, and live by it, is called stewardship.

4

Consistent Ethic of Life

Introduction

"That they may have life"
—Bishop Ken Untener's motto

"Every human being has a fundamental dignity that they cannot lose. For this reason we are opposed to abortion, euthanasia, assisted suicide, capital punishment and nuclear war."

"A person says, 'I am pro-life.' That deserves some examination. Are they 'pro-life' for the children in Iraq who lack medicine? Are they 'pro-life' for criminals on death row? Or are they 'pro-life' only when it applies to life in a mother's womb?"[1]

"It cancels out the message when we call for reverence to all human beings and then fail to reverence some human beings."[2]

Bishop Ken's controversial positions, whether on birth control, women's ordination, morality of war, or right-to-life issues, frequently attracted negative press or inaccurate reporting. One of these involved his questioning of the morality of the Persian Gulf War. The media inaccurately portrayed him as counseling conscientious objection and teaching Catholic students how to dodge the draft. Inaccurate media coverage and negative responses in personal mail did not prevent Ken from speaking out and acting upon his principled theological convictions.

In 1991, Bishop Ken wrote a pastoral letter on abortion after a year's study with a diocesan task force. Words alone are cheap, so in his pastoral letter he invited all of the people of the diocese to sign the letter along with him and take some practical action. He asked parishes to provide services to alleviate the practical problems that result in abortions and to seek volunteers who would actively work on legislation and education. The Office of Christian Services and

Catholic Family Services coordinated efforts for the program named "A Friend for Life," which included: (1) a pregnancy, birth, and child support program that would provide practical assistance, including counseling, transportation, referrals, and finances where needed, (2) a diocesan legislative advocacy network called the Catholic Voice, which is still operative, and (3) an 800 care-line number and volunteers to provide listening, confidential help, and referrals. Ken promised that the diocese would "walk with them" and foot the bill wherever this was needed. And the people responded.

All of Bishop Ken's activity for life-and-death issues, social reforms, health care, as well as liturgy and the word, were grounded in a contemplative prayer life to be envied. This included mystical experiences that he occasionally spoke about with friends. He remarked more than once that he frequently ended prayer with, "Lord, I have a loaf and two fishes, but what are these among so many? I trust that you will multiply them."

In his articles and talks on assisted suicide, Bishop Ken tackled the delicate and controversial moral issues surrounding the termination of life. He believed that God is author of both life and death. We do not hold the power of either in our hands. In our prayers for the dying, there is no attempt to ward off death as evil or a reality to be avoided at all cost. It is the doorway of life. There are times when the terminally ill should be allowed to die. That is vastly different from helping them to die.

In a "Statement on the Anniversay of *Roe v. Wade*," Bishop Ken noted his belief that in general Americans do long for a moral framework that will help them deal with abortion and other complex life-and-death issues, including the death penalty for crime. He believed we already have that moral framework in "a clear and consistent ethic of life." This consistent ethic of life includes health care services especially for the poor, as well as abortion and end-of-life issues. The Christian Service Office worked with the diocesan parishes to advocate legislation for health care issues as well as a ban on abortion and assisted suicide.

Lest one think that Ken's concern for life focused only on monumental moral issues, the picture on the cover of this book appears to be a head photo of Bishop Ken thoughtfully at work, but actually it catches him coloring Easter eggs with Franciscan Poor Clare nuns for the diocesan staff. The diocesan staff and others spent one morning of every Holy Week coloring Easter eggs for a Saginaw soup kitchen, where Ken later mingled with patrons and played the piano for them. There were many such seasonal and holiday activities that enhanced community life in the diocese and simultaneously reached out to the less fortunate in the community. Ken loved life—all of it, not just its beginning and its ending. He wanted each and all to prosper and be well.

Notes

1. Statement on the Anniversary of *Roe v. Wade*, 2001.
2. Pastoral Letter on the War in the Persian Gulf, 1991.

Pastoral Letter on the War in the Persian Gulf

January 23, 1991

I offer this pastoral letter not as an answer to all questions about the war, but as an attempt to set forth moral reflections that can help provide a framework for answers. It is sometimes very difficult to apply our faith to concrete and complex human situations. I hope that these reflections, based on the gospel teachings that live on in our church tradition, will help you face the inevitable questions that every disciple of the Lord must face in these difficult days.

Our Immediate Concern

Our first and immediate reaction to the war should be the same as in a car accident: concern for the people involved. Instinctively, without thinking about anything else, we look to see if anyone has been hurt, and we tend to the victims.

And so, our thoughts turn first to the people on both sides of the line in the sand who are in immediate danger. We want them all to be safe, and we are concerned about those already injured or killed. Our hearts go out to their families who worry about them hour by hour. May God give strength and protection to all the members of the human family.

Natural Reactions

There is something else that happens quite naturally, at least to me. It happens at the level of feelings, and there are many, many feelings within me. I am competitive by nature. I want to win. I am also proud of my country, and I want the United States to win the Ryder Cup or the Davis Cup or the Olympics or whatever. I am fascinated by high technology, and in the earlier days of the space program I was glued to the television every time a rocket was launched. I also admire skill and bravery and teamwork whenever I see it.

Finally, I resent cruelty and unfairness, and whenever I see them I get angry inside.

All those feelings are there as I watch the war. At the level of feelings I want to win, I am in awe of the technology, I admire the bravery and skill and teamwork of our military, and I have hateful feelings toward Saddam Hussein—especially when I see prisoners humiliated on Iraqi television.

Deeper Reflection

But feelings are an uncertain guide. The mature, healthy person is one who can acknowledge feelings and reflect on them, and also reflect on deeper values and wider truths. We try to teach youngsters to do that.

I remember a youngster watching the television newscast of the San Francisco earthquake. Someone with a video camera had taken pictures of the Oakland Bay Bridge as part of it collapsed, and you could see a van driving along and suddenly plummet downward through a gaping hole in the pavement. The youngster said, "Neat!"

It was a youngster's natural reaction to something like that on television. He had not yet learned to reflect, to be attentive to the deeper truth of what was taking place.

I can find myself watching this television war the same way.

As an aside on this, I would like to observe that on the first day of the war I saw on television an adult version of what that youngster did. At the end of trading, the stock market was up over a hundred points. The people on the exchange floor cheered. Understandable, perhaps, but the deeper reflection was missing.

Moral Considerations

I appreciate the difficulties our president and our government leaders face. I do not for a moment believe that they have evil intentions. I believe our military when they say that they are not targeting civilians. However, I also believe that we all need to take fuller consideration of values that are often left out of the conduct of human affairs.

Saddam Hussein's invasion of Kuwait cannot be justified. By all accounts, he has been and is a serious threat to the peace and good order of our world, and he must be stopped.

Our country has decided to stop him by going to war. It is a well-planned, well-coordinated military effort. But one must ask the question: Is this the only way to do it, and is it morally justifiable?

Our traditional morality teaches that war is not simply one of many options. We believe that killing is forbidden by the fifth commandment. In the New Testament, Jesus went even beyond the fifth commandment when he said, "You have heard that it was said to your ancestors, 'You shall not kill'…but I say to you.…" He then went on to forbid even a murderous heart. He said, "You have heard that it was said, 'You shall love your neighbor and hate your enemy.' But I say to you, love your enemies, and pray for those who persecute you."

Now, we have taught and continue to teach that there can be exceptions to this teaching. One must be very careful whenever making exceptions to the very clear teachings of Jesus, and this is no small matter. Some Christians would question whether we can ever do this, but in the Catholic tradition we have done this under carefully defined moral criteria.

Those criteria are commonly referred to as the "just war principles." I would like to outline them for you and comment as I go along.

Just War Principles

Morally speaking, the presumption is always against war. These principles are meant to make war not easier, but harder. All of them—not most of them—must be fulfilled to justify crossing the terrible line of war.

(1) Just cause: Is there a real and extraordinarily grave danger that can only be resolved by war? Iraq's flagrant violation of international law has given the United States and the world community good reason to mobilize political opposition and economic sanctions. Does it justify war? It needs to be pointed out that you can have a just cause, but it may not necessarily justify war.

Again, war is not simply one of many options you may use when dealing with evil. It can only be used in the most extreme circumstances. In the case of the Persian Gulf, we need to look at the other criteria to see if this just cause justifies war.

(2) Competent authority: Individuals or groups of individuals cannot simply decide to go to war. Only appropriate and lawful authorities can authorize the use of the deadly force of war. Given our political system, the issue of competent authority does not seem to present a major problem in this case.

(3) Right intention: You cannot go to war primarily out of vengeance, anger, impatience, because it is quicker or more efficient, to prevent economic problems, to prove your military might, or any number of other reasons. Your intention must be to prevent a terrible evil, and the reasons set forth for going to war must be the actual reasons for doing it. I will accept the reasons our country has set forth for this war.

(4) Last resort: A nation must pursue fully all political, diplomatic, and economic means to secure justice. This criterion places an enormous burden of proof on those who say that the time has come to go to war.

For me, this presents a major problem in the war against Iraq. I do not believe that this criterion has been met. I can understand the anger, but I have already dealt with the question of feelings. I can understand the impatience of many people to get on with this, but this criterion requires enormous patience—not passive patience, but active patience: the patience of the farmer who works very hard plowing, planting, and cultivating, but knowing that the results will not come quickly.

We are a result-oriented, quick-fix culture. It is one of the reasons why drugs are such a problem. I am uneasy about the number of times I have heard people say, "Let's get it over with." We need to be reminded that patience and tenacity are not signs of weakness. They are signs of strength.

(5) Probability of success: Is the prospect of success sufficiently clear to justify the human cost? I am not an expert in the military and political analysis of this situation, and I cannot say that this criterion has or has not been met. I would observe, however, that success has to be measured in long-range terms. Some look back and wonder if the invasion of Panama, with the drug trade reportedly flourishing there again, the problems with the economy and the government, and the tremendous cost to the United States, could be called a success.

(6) A sense of proportion: Are the objectives sought proportionate to the damage to be done—the damage to human life, to human resources, to relationships in the human family, to our earth? Does the good outweigh the evil?

Our response to this crisis sets an important precedent for our attempts to shape a new world order. The use of political and non-violent means would contribute greatly to the future of our world. War sets it back. The time has come, and seemed so near, when we could break precedent and no longer see war as the logical or necessary response to serious problems. With the crumbling of the Berlin Wall, the remarkable global coalition opposed to Iraq's aggression, the time had come, or so it seemed, to demonstrate that justice can be achieved by a determined solidarity among nations, rather than resorting to the primitive solution of war. The time had come, or so it seemed, when we could fulfill the words of Pope Paul VI when he said to the United Nations, "War…war…never again!"

The long-range effects of this war are frightening. We are creating a well of bitterness from which we will have to drink for generations to come. I have no idea whether the value of oil will go up or down, but the value of human life will definitely go down. Youngsters are learning a lesson as they watch this war on television, and it is not the lesson we usually try to teach them.

Given these wider, long-range considerations, I believe that the good to be achieved in this case does not outweigh the damage done.

Words of Other Religious Leaders

In setting forth these reflections, I am making a judgment. While there can be legitimate disagreement with my judgment, I would not want you to think that I stand alone, or almost alone among religious leaders in arriving at this judgment. Many religious leaders have spoken very forcefully on this. Just before Christmas, twenty-three leaders of Catholic, Orthodox, and Protestant churches throughout Michigan signed a joint statement saying "we believe that war is not according to God's will."

Archbishop Roach, on behalf of the U.S. Catholic Bishops Conference a week before the January 15 deadline, expressed to the U.S. Senate our "profound concern that offensive action in this situation could well violate traditional moral criteria, especially principles of proportionality and last resort."

Two days before the war, Pope John Paul II said, "A war would not resolve the problems, only aggravate them....More than ever this is the time for dialogue, negotiations and the pre-eminence of international law."

Then on January 17, the day after the war began, in a much longer statement the Holy Father said this:

> The news which has reached us during the night concerning the drama taking place in the Gulf region has evoked in me and, I am sure, in all of you feelings of deep sadness and great unease. Up to the last moment I prayed and hoped that this would not happen, and I have done everything humanly possible to avert a tragedy.
>
> My sorrow derives from the thought of the victims, the destruction and the suffering which war can cause. I feel particularly close to all those who because of it are suffering, on both sides. This sorrow is made even more acute by the fact that the beginning of this war also marks a grave defeat for international law and the international community.
>
> In these hours of great dangers, I would like to repeat forcefully that war cannot be an adequate means

for completely solving problems existing between nations. It has never been and it never will be!

I continue to hope that what has begun will end as quickly as possible. I pray that the experience of this first day of conflict will be enough to make people understand the need for the aspirations and rights of all the people of the region to be made the subject of a particular commitment on the part of the international community. It is a question of problems the solution of which can only be sought in an international meeting at which all the interested parties are present and cooperate frankly and calmly.

I still place my hope in courageous gestures which can shorten the time of trial, reestablish international order and enable the star of Peace which one day shone over Bethlehem to cast its light once more over that region which is so dear to us.

Predictions in Scripture?

I must say a word about some who find predictions in scripture about what is taking place in the Gulf.

Such a use of scripture is, according to our beliefs, a misuse of scripture. The Bible is not a coded message for those who can break the code, nor does it have predictions about the future hidden in the text.

Scripture is a collection of writings that give us very basic and timeless truths—truths about God, about the meaning of life, and how people relate to God. The human struggles and conflicts of past ages can sound very much like evils in our own age. When we see a similarity, it is not as though the author had any special knowledge about us. The author was simply describing the problems human beings have faced from the beginning of time.

This is a time when we should turn to scripture—but not for secret messages that provide answers to those who can decode them. Rather, we turn to scripture to hear the word of God spoken for all peoples of all times and places.

Family Members and Friends in the Gulf

Many of you have family members and friends in the Gulf. What does all this mean for them, and for you?

These are people who are committed to serve their country, and that is something to be greatly admired. They deserve our respect, our concern, and our prayers. We must be concerned about their safety, as well as the safety of all people who are in danger.

Your family members and friends were not in a position to decide whether our country should go to war, nor are they in a position to decide that our country should continue this war. If we disagree with that decision, our disagreement should not be directed at them.

In calling for a stop to this war, I am expressing genuine concern for their safety. If there were a cease-fire tomorrow, they would be the first beneficiaries. They are among the important reasons why I believe we should all be praying and working to stop the war.

I like the symbol used at the peace vigil on the east side of Saginaw last Monday night. Small yellow ribbons were passed out for people to pin on their lapels, a reminder of our concern for people in the Gulf. But attached to it was another ribbon—a purple one. This is our traditional color for penance, and it was a reminder of the need to pray for reconciliation and to reflect on the underlying sinfulness that causes war. The symbol was a good one. Neither color canceled out the other. Concern for our loved ones and concern about the war itself go hand in hand.

Conscientious Objection

We do not have a military draft at this time, but the possibility needs to be addressed. This raises the very sensitive question of conscientious objection.

The first thing to say about conscientious objection is that it is conscientious. There are many ways to object, many kinds of objectors, but here we are talking about something that comes from love, not fear; something that comes from courage, not cowardice; from concern for our country and our world, not apathy;

from a willingness to take on a difficult issue, not dodge it; from a desire to get involved, not cop out; from dedication to duty, not desertion; from prayer and conscientious belief and not from anything else. That, as you can see, is a very special kind of objection.

The Catholic teaching on conscientious objection is expressed concisely and clearly in the Pastoral Letter on War and Peace promulgated by the U.S. bishops in 1983. I quote that section in full:

> A dominant characteristic of the Second Vatican Council's evaluation of modern warfare was the stress it placed on the requirement for proper formation of conscience. Moral principles are effective restraints on power only when policies reflect them and individuals practice them. The relationship of the authority of the state and the conscience of the individual on matters of war and peace takes a new urgency in the face of the destructive nature of modern war.
>
> Catholic teaching does not question the right in principle of a government to require military service of its citizens provided the government shows it is necessary. A citizen may not casually disregard their country's conscientious decision to call its citizens to acts of "legitimate defense." Moreover, the role of Christian citizens in the armed forces is a service to the common good and an exercise of the virtue of patriotism, so long as they fulfill this role within defined moral norms.
>
> At the same time, no state may demand blind obedience. Our 1980 statement urged the government to present convincing reasons for draft registration, and opposed reinstitution of conscription itself except in the case of a national defense emergency. Moreover, it reiterated our support for conscientious objection in general and for selective conscientious objection to participation in a particular war, either because of the ends being pursued or the means being used. We called selective conscientious objection a moral conclusion which can be validly derived from the classical teaching of just war principles. We continue to insist upon respect for and

legislative protection of the rights of both classes of conscientious objectors. We also approve requiring alterna-
tive service to the community—not related to military
needs—by such persons.

This is a decision I cannot make for another person. But when
it is made in good faith, it must be respected.

Prayers, Vigils for Peace

There are many people who believe, as I do, that the ultimate
effects of this war will work against peace, not for peace. They
share the belief that there is a need to remind ourselves and others
that we hold truths often left out of the public debate. There is a
need to speak them openly, and thus there are gatherings, vigils,
marches for peace.

But there are marches and there are marches. I do not support
marches, rallies, or meetings conducted in a spirit that contradicts
the message of peace they are meant to preach. I find no passage in
the gospel that condones being disrespectful to our president, or to
our government leaders, or to anyone, for that matter.

It cancels out the message when we call for reverence to all
human beings and then fail to reverence some human beings. It
serves no good purpose to use violent words to protest violent
actions. The medium is at least part of the message, and we simply
cannot preach peace in an unpeaceful manner. There is no place for
insulting slogans, no matter how catchy or rhythmic; no place for
burning the flag of our nation, or any nation; no place for taunts,
put-downs, harsh rhetoric, personal attacks, or gestures that are
just plain uncharitable.

But, some might say, all of this is permitted by free speech. It
is perfectly legal. That may be true, but we believe that what is legal
is not necessarily right, and abortion is not the only example.

I respect those who gather, speak, and march peacefully for
peace, and I have gladly joined them. It is unfair, I believe, to characterize these as "antiwar protests." The word *anti* can be very
misleading. One who thoughtfully dissents from something is

really assenting to something he or she believes to be a greater truth.

Do prayers and vigils for peace undermine our troops in the Persian Gulf? Not if they are truly peaceful. To call for peace is not to care less about the men and women on the front. It is an attempt to care more. A cease-fire would ensure their safety.

The Ultimate Solution

The only ultimate solution to the problem of war is the recognition of a world order that can deal with such conflicts. There will be other Saddam Husseins; there will be others who threaten to use chemical weapons; there will be other countries acquiring nuclear weapons. If each country claims total and complete sovereignty, war after war is inevitable.

The only way we can bequeath a peaceful world to our children and our children's children is to recognize that we are one human family. We say this, but we haven't found ways to translate our words into actions.

Let me quote again from the U.S. bishops' pastoral letter on peace:

> An important element missing from world order today is a properly constituted political authority with the capacity to shape our material interdependence in the direction of moral interdependence.

Pope John XXIII stated the case in the following way:

> Today the universal common good poses problems of world-wide dimensions, which cannot be adequately tackled or solved except by the efforts of public authority endowed with a wideness of powers, structure and means of the same proportions: that is, of public authority which is in a position to operate in an effective manner on a world-wide basis. The moral order itself, therefore,

demands that such a form of public authority be established.

Just as the nation-state was a step in the evolution of government at a time when expanding trade and new weapons technologies made the feudal system inadequate to manage conflicts and provide security, so we are now entering an era of new, global interdependencies that require global systems of governance to manage the resulting conflicts and ensure our common security.

Closing Thoughts

There are many religious truths that we believe insofar as we don't deny them. But there are some that we reflect upon and take to heart, and they become part of our way of life. Those waters are not easy to cross.

This is a time when we are forced to ask ourselves how deeply we believe those truths we have never denied but have not yet taken fully to heart. This is a time when we realize that baptism is a vocation, a call to a different way of life. This is a time when we begin to realize that we are indeed a strange people who have chosen as our logo the cross.

At a parish Mass last weekend I read a gospel passage we have all heard many times before. You could have heard a pin drop. The words sounded so different with war in the air.

> You have heard that it was said, "You shall love your neighbor and hate your enemy." But I say to you, love your enemies and pray for those who persecute you, that you may be children of your heavenly Father, for he makes his sun rise on the bad and the good, and causes rain to fall on the just and the unjust. For if you love those who love you, what recompense will you have?
>
> Do not the tax collectors do the same? And if you greet your brothers and sisters only, what is unusual about that? Do not the pagans do the same? So be perfect, just as your heavenly Father is perfect. (Matt 5:43–48; NAB)

We are called to an unusual way of life. I close with words Pope John Paul II spoke several years ago:

> Violence destroys what it claims to defend: the dignity, the life, the freedom of human beings.
>
> Violence is a crime against humanity, for it destroys the very fabric of society....To all of you who are listening I say: Do not believe in violence: do not support violence. It is not the Christian way. It is not the way of the Catholic Church. Believe in peace and forgiveness and love, for they are of Christ.*

---

*Speech in Northern Ireland, 1979.

Statement on the Anniversary of *Roe v. Wade*

January 22, 2001

This week we mark the twenty-eighth anniversary of the 1973 *Roe v. Wade* Supreme Court ruling that legalized abortion in the United States.

The presidential election and last weekend's inauguration have put the phrases "pro-life" and "pro-choice" very much in the air these days. Yet, as they are commonly used, neither is an adequate slogan.

People say, "I am pro-life." That deserves some examination. Are they "pro-life" for the children in Iraq who lack medicine? Are they "pro-life" for criminals on death row? Or are they "pro-life" only when it applies to life in a mother's womb? If so, it is "partial pro-life" and very inadequate, for it favors the premeditated and intentional killing of some human beings. Better that such people didn't simply call themselves "pro-life" but rather spoke honestly about their restricted beliefs in such matters.

People say, "I am pro-choice." That deserves some examination. Are they "pro-choice" in believing that people ought to be able to make their own choice on things like wearing seatbelts? Are they "pro-choice" in believing that parents should be able to choose whether or not their infant receive immunization against deadly disease, or undergo a life-saving operation? Or are they "pro-choice" only when it applies to having any kind of abortion at any stage for any reason whatsoever, including gender preference or the wishes of their male partner? Better that such people didn't use the catch-phrase "pro-choice," but rather spoke honestly about their restricted beliefs in such matters.

Rhetoric and slogans get in the way. They are high-sounding and misleading, and fortunately people are gradually seeing through them. People know that some who fiercely speak of "pro-life" have a very narrow scope of people whose lives they're really for. People know that pro-choice rhetoric is thin and that very few abortions have anything to do with health, rape, or incest. Why do they know this? Because they know the people who have abortions, and they know why they have the abortions.

A short while back, the *New York Times*, comparing a survey it did in 1989 and another in 1998, found that there has been a notable shift in our country away from a general acceptance of legalized abortion. The *Times* found much public dissatisfaction with our current permissive laws. Other scientific polls corroborate this trend.

Sometimes the issue can seem impossibly complicated. Not surprisingly, millions of Americans are hungering for a moral framework to help them deal with the increasing human life issues that face us. Such a moral framework is available. The Catholic Church has a clear and consistent ethic of life.

We believe that God is the source of all life. We believe that Christ offers to all people a risen human life that lasts forever. We believe that human beings are living temples of the Holy Spirit. As such, all human beings have a fundamental dignity that they cannot lose.

For this reason we are opposed to abortion, euthanasia, assisted suicide, capital punishment, and nuclear war. The U.S. Catholic bishops have been clear on this, and Pope John Paul II has spoken loudly and clearly on all of these questions. We have also spoken clearly on the need for all of us to be concerned about the quality of human life at every stage, and the need to establish a more just and humane society.

The late Cardinal Bernardin was right when he said that respect for life is a seamless garment. Maybe public opinion is finally moving in that direction. May we all do our part on behalf of this human life that we share, and in a special way on behalf of those who are most vulnerable.

Those Struggling with Abortion Decision

Origins 21/32 (January 16, 1992)

Teen-age girls and young women afraid to tell their parents they are pregnant should ask for moral and material support from concerned Catholics, Bishop Kenneth Untener of Saginaw, Michigan, said in a December pastoral letter. "If you don't believe us, try us....We have hundreds, thousands of people willing to come forward and volunteer their services," Untener said in addressing "all people who struggle with problems that might lead to abortion." Untener urged Catholics of his diocese to sign his letter, which promised direct support and companionship to any woman contemplating abortion. "Words alone will not carry the day" when it comes to communicating the pro-life position, Untener wrote. "The time has come to put our beliefs into practice." The pastoral follows.

This pastoral letter was due several weeks ago, but I just couldn't seem to find the words. Actually, that is not true. I had too many words, and three or four drafts to show for it.

It seems that everything that ought to be said about abortion has already been said. Hundreds and hundreds of very good articles have explained the pro-life position. I myself have written articles about it, preached about it, made a video, and issued a pastoral letter to all Catholics in the diocese four years ago.

I have finally come to the conclusion that words alone will never carry the day. Perhaps people aren't sure that we really believe our own words. If that is true, then the time has come to put our beliefs into practice. So I have written a pastoral letter, but I want you to sign it with me. It is addressed to the general public and it goes like this:

Dear Friends,

We address this to all people who struggle with problems that might lead to an abortion. We want you to choose life instead of abortion, and we stand ready to help you with whatever problems you face.

- If you are young and afraid to tell your parents that you are pregnant, we'll go with you and help you tell them.
- If you are under pressure from someone else to get an abortion, we'll stand with you to take the pressure.
- If you don't have transportation to get to a doctor for prenatal care, we'll drive you there and stay with you.
- If you can't pay for the medical services you need, we'll find a way to assist you.
- If the problem is money, and you simply can't afford another child, we'll find a way to help.
- If you don't know how you will care for your child afterward, we'll help you.
- If you feel isolated and alone as you face these decisions, we'll walk with you.
- If you have family problems, we'll work with your family to deal with them.

Let us know what you are struggling with and we'll help you.

You may not know about services that are available, and we'll help you find them. We have many services of our own through Catholic Family Service (including adoption and foster care), our Christian Service Office, and through our parishes. We offer them to you. If the services you need aren't available, we'll find a way to provide them.

We'll do more than that. We'll work together to get the legislation and programs and services that mothers and fathers and children and families need. We'll work on the underlying causes, particularly attitudes toward women.

If you don't believe us, try us. We have the heart for it. We'll do anything to help, everything to help. We have hundreds, thousands of people willing to come forward and volunteer their services. We have 115 parishes in these eleven counties that stand ready to help.

We believe that every human life is worth more than the flowers of the field, the birds of the sky. And that includes your life. If you have had an abortion and are struggling with guilt, we'll help you too, because we care about you. Or if you have experienced domestic abuse and are still troubled by that experience, we'll help you.

Whatever your problem, just call us and we'll be there.

Sincerely,
The Catholic Community
of the Diocese of Saginaw

Pastoral letters are usually issued by the bishop, but we need to do this one together. I want you to put your signature to it, as I gladly put mine.

All of this will cost money. Do we have enough? I don't know. We'll manage. We'll find a way. We'll simply start doing whatever we can, and we'll keep doing whatever we have to do. We'll put our trust in the Lord.

When the disciples looked at the great crowd of men, women, and children who were hungry and tired, they wanted to send them away to get what they needed. But Jesus said, "You help them." The disciples responded, "We don't have enough—just a couple of loaves and fishes." Jesus said, "Bring me what you have." They did and it was enough.

We aren't doing this all on our own. We are a eucharistic people, and in the procession of gifts at Mass we bring everything to the Lord. We will bring this to the Lord. In his hands, it will be enough.

There is a time for words and a time for action. When someone experiences a death in the family, words aren't all that helpful. The best thing you can do is put your arms around them and be with them. Abortion is about death, and we need to respond, not with words but with actions. Abortion is also about life, and we need to be a friend for life.

A Pastoral Letter for Respect Life Sunday

Respect Life Sunday, 1989

My Sisters and Brothers in the Lord,

I have been intrigued by something St. Catherine of Siena wrote in her book of "Dialogue" with God. She heard God say:

"The service you cannot render me
you must do for your neighbors."

Now that deserves some thought. It gives a different slant to a truth we've been taught since we were little children.

First of all, what service can we render to God? None. We can love God, talk to him, make offerings to him. But there is no service we can render to him. Does loving God nurture his growth? Does conversation with God enhance his sociability? Do offerings to God improve his economic position? Of course not. When it comes to God, then, do we love someone for whom we can really do nothing? It would seem so...until we hear God tell it.

Jesus described the last judgment scene in graphic terms. Remember the question people kept asking him?

Lord, when did we see you hungry and feed you,
or see you thirsty and give you a drink?
When did we welcome you away from home or
clothe you in your nakedness?
When did we see you ill or in prison and visited you? (Matt 25:37–39)

You know what the answer will be. But I want you to think about those words from Catherine of Siena and see if they don't help us see this familiar gospel text in a new light. Look at the two texts side by side.

The service you cannot render me you must do for your neighbors.	As often as you did it for one of my least ones, you did it for me.

Service rendered to our neighbor is not simply something that "counts" in our favor. It is service rendered *to God*.

Another Way of Looking at It

At the risk of becoming a bit abstract, I would like to suggest another way of approaching this same truth with fresh insight.

God does not usually relate to us directly. God speaks to us, acts upon us, and relates to us most often through people and created things. We Catholics particularly emphasize this, and it is a characteristic of our sacramental life. We use the term *mediation*.

Now consider this from the other end—the way we relate to God. We often do not relate to God directly. We relate to him through people and created things. Once again we are dealing with "mediation."

I'm not sure we think about it that way when it comes to our relationship to God. But it is just as true, just as real.

Our conduct toward people and created things is not simply behavior that God will judge as good or bad. It is part of our relationship with God—part of the way we "treat" God. I have been particularly struck by this. Whenever I think about it this way, it affects my behavior.

This could be the basis for a pastoral letter on the way we treat our "God's good earth." I will leave that for another time.

For now I would like to make it the basis for some reflections on the way we treat human beings. Two particular issues deserve our special attention on this Respect Life Sunday—abortion and health care.

Abortion

The mother and father of a child developing in the womb must realize that everything we have been saying applies to them. Their relationship to God is mediated through this child.

What will their response to God be? Love, care, nurturing? Or, rejection, neglect, abandonment?

Society may tell them to think in terms of economics, social acceptance, their own personal rights under civil law, convenience. But the crux of the matter is this: Their relationship to God is mediated through this child.

This is a different perspective on abortion. It is both simple and profound. It makes us realize that our beliefs make all the difference in the world. It forces us to ask if we really mean it when we sing, "We walk by faith and not by sight." It challenges us to see if we can translate words into deeds, allow belief to affect behavior.

As often as you did it for one of my least ones, you did it for me.

The service you cannot render me you must do for your neighbors.

The words will not go away…and they apply very much to the issue of abortion.

Health Care

There are many human-life issues before us today. We must address all of them. From time to time we give particular emphasis to one of them and this year, on Respect Life Sunday, we are giving special attention to health care concerns.

We are facing today a health-care crisis. Increasing health-care costs and health-insurance pressures are leaving "no room in the inn" for more and more people. We would all be surprised to discover how many people in our own parish no longer have adequate health insurance…and as a result are not getting proper health care.

When we think of the "poor," many stereotypes come to mind. The "health-care poor" often do not fit these stereotypes.

They are the elderly, the children, the unemployed within our own parish. They are our "neighborhood neighbors."

Materials on this have been prepared by our Christian Service Office, in cooperation with St. Mary's Medical Center and St. Francis's Home. I ask that you give them careful attention. We must find ways to reach out to those around us who are in need of help. We must advocate legislation that will enable us to live up to the words that John Paul II spoke to the people of this country when he visited Detroit:

> Your greatest beauty and your richest blessing is found
> in the human person: in each man, woman, and child,
> in every immigrant, in every native-born son and daughter.

The abortion debate will gradually escalate in the United States. Some have suggested that it will surpass the intensity of the Vietnam debate in the 1960s. We must prepare ourselves to enter into this. The Diocese of Saginaw will, in the months ahead, provide assistance to you as our society moves into this great debate.

It is very important that our position on abortion be grounded in our basic beliefs about all of human life. Consistent concern about the wide range of issues involved strengthens rather than dilutes our stance on abortion. Together we must reflect on and strengthen our belief in human life and have the courage to speak out whenever and wherever it is threatened. We must see this not simply as a duty, but as part of our relationship to God.

> The service you cannot render me
> you must do for your neighbors.

I close with some very forceful words from the Epistle of James: "What good is it to profess faith without practicing it? If a brother or sister has nothing to wear and no food for the day, and you say, 'Good-bye and good luck! Keep warm and well fed,' but do not meet their bodily needs, what good is that? So it is with the faith that does nothing in practice. It is thoroughly lifeless" (Jas 2:13–17).

God bless you,
Ken Untener

Bishop Untener Writes on Assisted Suicide

I'll make four statements that I hope will shed light on the Catholic position on assisted suicide.

1. *We believe there is a night-and-day difference between allowing a person to die, and helping people kill themselves.*

Allowing a person to die is to accept that God is God and we are not—that God is the Lord of life. Helping people kill themselves is to claim that we are a law unto ourselves, and that every possible choice is good as long as we choose it. It is to consecrate "choice" and make it a god.

There are some life decisions that are not ours to make. There are times when we say with the Lord: "Father, if you are willing, take this cup away from me; still, not my will but yours be done" (Luke 22:42).

2. *We believe that those who are terminally ill should be allowed to die without being forced to undergo every possible procedure to extend their life by days, months, or even years.*

In our Catholic ritual, we have prayers for the sick—we ask God for healing. But we also have prayers for the *dying*—we ask God for a holy and peaceful death. Our approach to death is governed by the belief that death is the doorway to life. We pray for the dying with no pretense that we are trying to ward off death at all costs.

There comes a time when, with trust in God, we turn the page and pray to help someone die. I said some of these prayers for my own mother when it became clear that medicine could do no more:

"I commend you...and entrust you to your Creator. May you return to God...may you see your Redeemer face to face...."

In his last months of life, Cardinal Joseph Bernardin of Chicago said it well: I want to accept death as a friend.

3. *We believe everything should be done to eliminate the pain of those who are terminally ill.*

We do *not* believe that suffering is good in itself. The terminally ill should be spared pain as far as possible. This includes the use of powerful drugs. Much more can be done, and *should* be done to eliminate the pain of those who are dying.

4. *We believe that dependence is not always something bad.*

The truth is, we are totally dependent on God, although there are times throughout life when we need to be reminded of this. There is something in us that says, "I don't want to be a burden on anyone." That's understandable, even praiseworthy at times. But it's not an absolute. Love involves not only giving, but also receiving. In our first years of life, and sometimes in our last years of life, there is more receiving than giving.

There are times when we grow in love by accepting the love of others. We come to terms with the truth that we are worth loving, and we learn to trust in the love of God, and in the love of those who care for us.

I close with this thought. To think that we should be able to write the script of our *whole life* is to deny the first commandment: "I am the Lord your God."

We can't write the script of birth, although some might want to do that through abortion. We can't write the script of death, although some might want to do that through assisted suicide.

In birth, and in death, we follow the Lord—who wrote neither script for himself. To follow the crucified Lord means to give ourselves trustfully into God's hands—to say as Jesus did in Gethsemane: "Not my will, but yours be done."

We do *not* claim the power to die as we choose. We claim only the freedom to accept the death it is given us to die. Jesus showed us the way. He freely accepted a death he did not choose—and he showed us the path to life.

5

Ministry of Prophet

Introduction

I am going to zero in on one aspect of that prophetic role… by adding just one word to the description. I am going to focus on "speaking God's hard truth.[1]

Beware of the prophet who has everything all figured out. John XXIII didn't. Archbishop Lefebvre did.[2]

The role of prophet is not an easy one, but Bishop Ken was prophetic on both local and wider church levels.

Beginning in 1990, the Diocese of Saginaw gradually moved toward cluster parishes that share ministries of education, Christian service, and worship. Cluster parishes replace the current pattern of closing parishes common to many other dioceses across the United States. As clusters, communities are able to maintain their own distinctive heritage and parish configuration and at the same time deal with the fact that there are not enough priests to go around. Pastoral administrators, both religious and laywomen, have supplied the gaps in parishes without a resident priest, together with ministries of service among the laity. They attend presbyteral planning meetings and truly "pastor" the parish of which they are the administrators.

Early in the 1980s, Bishop Ken spoke out against sexism and sexist language in the liturgy, with reference to the people of God and God language. Accordingly, the Saginaw diocese changed patterns and customs to avoid it.

Bishop Ken thought the horizons should widen in the whole church on the question of who can be ordained. He spoke about this at the USCCB and wrote about it. He did not specifically ask that married men or women be ordained, but that the question be openly discussed by the bishops, since the rest of the faithful have been discussing it for some time. He also brought up the question of birth control, and wrote about it, asking "what has it done to us" when the laity have ceased to listen to us or even care what bishops think about the question of birth control? They have made up their minds on their own, and we still will not discuss it openly. Among other things, it erodes authority when bishops will not deal with issues that concern the lives of the faithful.

He wrote that bishops and cardinals need more open conversation among themselves and how they understand many issues. They need to take the same care about facts when criticizing one another that they take when writing pastorals, and not reiterate a party line using even the same words [the particular case he cited: criticisms by four cardinals of the United States of the writings of Archbishop Quinn and Archbishop Bernardin without sufficient care for the facts].

It took courage, he admitted, to speak out on these issues without support from others. Although afterward some bishops might come up to congratulate him for speaking out on birth control and the ordination issue, they were silent in the sessions.

Ordination of seminarians was an ongoing question from the days when Ken was rector/president of St. John's Seminary. Convinced that seminarians are formed and educated to serve the laity (more than 98 percent of the total body of the faithful are laity), he thought they should also be educated *among* the laity, in an ecclesial (not a monastic) style of spirituality for their work with the laity. After becoming bishop, he sent seminarians on to Catholic universities rather than to a seminary in the archdiocese or elsewhere in the country. They were under a diocesan formation director and council, but educated among men and women of the faithful at universities. Did it pay off? Time will tell.

During the homily for Bishop Untener's funeral, Archbishop John Quinn, quoting from an earlier letter to Ken, said: "You have given all of us bishops a striking, powerful but gentle challenge to live the Gospel in a clear way. I have seen how you have been criticized and misrepresented, and how, following the Gospel injunction, you have not reacted with rancor or bitterness....Your simplicity of life is a true fulfillment of the

Council's call for bishops to recognize the signs of the times and respond to the apostolic ideal of the Gospel."

Notes

1. *Origins* 21/2 (May 23, 1991): 36–40. Quote from p. 36.
2. Ibid., 39.

What a Prophet Does and Does Not Do

Origins 21/2 (May 23, 1991)

(An address on April 30 to the National Federation Priests' Councils convention in Orlando, Fla.)

You have probably heard a number of definitions of the prophetic role in this past day and a half. I am going to use as my working description this one: The prophetic role is simply that of speaking God's truth. Every disciple of the Lord is called upon to exercise that role.

I am going to zero in on one aspect of that prophetic role. It is specified by adding just one word to the description. I am going to focus on "speaking God's hard truth."

I am also going to focus on the diocesan priest, or at least the person ministering in a parish setting. There are others who have more specialized roles, and there are more specialized prophets. I hope that what I have to say will include and pertain to all, but I am looking at this through the window of parish ministry.

Finally, I am going to look at this through the window of my own experience, as I was asked to do. That is not, by temperament, my first inclination. In a way, I would be more inclined to analyze the prophetic role as described in Vatican II, compare that to the way it was seen before the council, look at the trajectory of development since then, and apply all that to parish ministry. However, there are times when it is helpful to speak out of personal experience. Some of us have to be nudged to do that. Others need to be restrained. There is something good about speaking from personal experience as long as it doesn't become self-centered, and as long as we don't make ourselves the norm.

Some Personal Examples

I will begin by citing and commenting on six examples when I have, successfully or unsuccessfully, properly or improperly, tried to speak the hard truth.

1. After the 1983 National Conference of Catholic Bishops' peace pastoral, I found myself speaking out on the issue of war and peace, nuclear weapons, the arms race, and the policies of our country relative to all of this. These were hard truths, and I did not enjoy speaking them. There were the expected reactions—what is the church doing getting involved in politics, why are you being so unpatriotic, soft on communism, and so forth. I gave a talk at a local university in which I attempted to address the basic issue of the relationship of the church to the world. Along the way I pointed out that the issues can be very complex, and slogans and bumper stickers don't help. For example, "Better dead than red," can be used to justify anything, even a nuclear holocaust. Would all the people of communist countries be better off if we wiped them out with nuclear weapons? Are there times when you could say "better red than dead"? The media was there, and the headline of the article in the local newspaper the next day was "Untener: Better Red than Dead."

Among other things, this made my mail quite interesting. However, I really should have anticipated this sort of slant on the story. That's the way newspapers get the attention of their readers, and I should have remembered that. You put a line out like that and of course it is going to get picked up. I shouldn't be surprised or complain if that happens. It was my own fault. I spoke something true, but it was not good communication. It is never enough just to be right.

2. The second example has to do with sexism and particularly sexist language. I have been brought along by others in my aware-ness of this, and I have spoken out on it. It is a hard message, espe-cially when it touches upon the way we refer to God. Still, I have spoken out on it and continue to do so, and I get some flak for it.

3. The third example occurred at the November 1990 meet-ing of the NCCB. We were discussing a document that referred to our teaching on birth control and said that our arguments on this

were compelling, and we called upon those who disagree to rethink carefully their position. I raised four questions about this, including whether we really believed that the arguments were compelling, whether we really listened to the *sensus fidelium* on this, whether the time had come for us to take a careful look at our position, and whether we weren't acting like a dysfunctional family that is unwilling to talk about something that everyone knows is there. This was reported widely, and I have received a lot of mail. Interestingly, most of it—about ten to one—has been positive. I think it was a good approach, insofar as I asked questions. That can be an appropriate way to exercise the prophetic role.

4. The fourth example relates to the Persian Gulf War. Immediately after it began, I issued an eight-page pastoral on the war. I spoke of how I had to work through my feelings—feelings of pride you have when your country is winning the Olympics, feelings of hatred toward Saddam Hussein, and so forth. We teach youngsters, I explained, not to act simply on feelings but to learn to reflect upon wider truths. Then I set forth the principles of a just war and said that, in my judgment, these had not been met and that our action was unjust. I explained that my purpose was to provide a moral framework for reflection and that some might disagree. All I asked was that they reflect upon it in a moral context.

The pastoral was received reasonably well. At about the same time, however, I did something else. I participated in a presentation to Catholic high school students about conscientious objection. My role was to talk about the just war principles, and then a draft counselor explained the procedures for conscientious objection. The media were there and it was on the six o'clock news, and the next day it was in the local paper with a headline that read, "Catholic Students Taught to Dodge Draft."

The response was swift and fierce. If you can remember the feelings in those first days of the war, you can just imagine what it was like. Here again, I think I made a strategic mistake. The message was right; the timing was bad. It got in the way of the main message of my pastoral, and thus it was bad communication. It is never enough to be right.

5. My fifth example has to do with the ordination of women. In January of this year I published an article in *Worship* about the

use of the phrase *in persona Christi*. I pointed out that it is a mistranslation of 2 Corinthians 2:10, which really means "in the presence of Christ" (which is how most contemporary translations read). The phrase was used infrequently in history to describe the ordained priesthood, but more recently it has been used very much. Furthermore, it is now used to describe the priest as "impersonating" Christ, which presents further problems. I suggested that a proper understanding of this phrase could eliminate one of the major objections to the ordination of women.

This, too, was picked up in the media, and I have been receiving mail from around the country. Those who read the article are almost all positive. Those who read about it are mixed. Again, I raised questions rather than claiming to have all the final answers, and it is my hope that it will contribute to the ongoing discussion.

6. Finally, at the Chrism Mass in our Saginaw cathedral a few weeks ago, I issued a decree that from that day forward until July 1, 1991, every meeting held under the auspices of the church at the diocesan or parish level, no matter what its purpose, no matter how few or many people are there, must have as its first agenda item: How shall what we do here affect or involve the poor?

This has been very well received. We are all doing it, and it is affecting the way we think and act. Our consciousness is being raised in geometric proportions. It is working. I'll have to think about that and look more carefully at it to figure out how that same success can be translated into other areas.

Some Characteristics

We are, of course, speaking of true prophets. The fact is, however, that every prophet thinks that he or she is a true prophet. Imagine asking youngsters what they want to be when they grow up and getting the answer, "I want to be a false prophet."

False prophets usually think they are true prophets. They look like true prophets, they act like true prophets, and they often have a piece of the truth. How can you tell the difference? How do you check to make sure that you are a true prophet?

I am going to offer three characteristics of the true prophet. These are not *the* three characteristics. They are simply three that come out of my experience and reflection. They may be helpful for you.

Called Here and Now

A prophet is someone *God* chooses to announce something. God chooses the person for God's own purposes, which the prophet may not even know. In many cases, the prophet is God's instrument because he or she just happens to be in the right place at the right time for God's purpose.

Of course, the call usually has to come through something. Beware of the prophet who has heard a voice or feels called directly by God. There are some few called that way, but very few. Most who think they are, aren't.

I'll tell you how the call will surely come to the diocesan priest in parish ministry. It will come through the Lectionary. The Lectionary will call you if you will only let it. This is one of the best ways to be called.

In order to allow yourself to be called in this way you have to take the Lectionary seriously and prayerfully. You have to let the readings speak to you and let them say what they say. That is one of the reasons why I do not like to change the readings assigned by the season or the feast, no matter what the event. There are exceptions, of course, but they should be rare. Rather than finding a reading that says what you want it to say, take the readings that are there and let them shine their light upon this gathering. Some of them will call you to speak the hard message.

It is very helpful, in this regard, to step back and see if you generally preach only one kind of homily. There are many kinds of homilies, and we should preach them all at one time or another. I used to teach homiletics, and I came across a list of different kinds of homilies—you could use different categories, but this list will give you an idea.

- Catechetical (instructive)
- Scriptural (simply opening up the readings)
- Liturgical (a feast or season)
- Pastoral (a particular need)
- Prophetic (the hard message)
- Exhortative (urging them on)
- Inspirational (consoling, reflective)
- Thematic (following a theme for several weeks)
- Special (for example, stewardship)

Beware of the preacher who only preaches one kind of homily. I remember a priest years ago who always managed to preach about Mary, no matter what the readings. One time the gospel was the parable of the prodigal son, and I wondered how he was going to work Mary into that one. After reading the gospel, he began by saying, "The problem here is that this boy didn't have a good mother to guide him," and you can guess the rest.

I sometimes use the piano to demonstrate this. I can play a tune and make it sound like chimes by playing a certain combination of notes two octaves above middle C. It sounds very beautiful, with the crystal ring of chimes. But when I play exactly the same notes down in the normal range, it does not sound pleasant at all. The dissonance that creates the chime effect two octaves above simply sounds dissonant in the normal range.

Some of the *hard* teachings of the gospel really fit well only in the kingdom. They will ring nicely only "up" there. Here below, when the kingdom is only begun, not achieved, they do not quite fit. They are dissonant. For example, forgiveness will only "work" perfectly when the entire community is forgiving, which is the kingdom. Down here, if you are forgiving you will sometimes get hurt and be stepped on. The same is true of the message of peace. Peace will work only when all creation is brought together in the kingdom. Until then, the message of peace is dissonant, and it will not always sound good to people. If you are generous to the poor, you will sometimes be taken. And on and on. The Beatitudes, the Sermon on the Mount, will fully make sense only in the kingdom.

Now here is the problem. I can make that music sound good when playing it down in the normal range. Do you know how?

Simply by changing some of the notes. Not many, just a few notes, and it will no longer be dissonant. That is the temptation. That is what happens when we do not let the Lectionary speak its message. We change some of the notes. We touch it up just a bit and never have to speak the hard, dissonant message.

One other thought on the "call" of the prophet. The true prophet usually has some reluctance, and that is usually a good sign. Down deep, the reluctance isn't because of the flak. It is because of the focus on me. If you preach the hard message, you are standing out there, a little ahead of or apart from the others, and you are claiming to know better than the rest. You are doing something that you usually try not to do. You seem to be less collaborative, less communal, less tuned in to the *sensus fidelium*. Sometimes we have to do that, but a feeling of reluctance is a healthy sign. Beware of the prophet who wears the mantle of the prophet too easily.

I think of John XXIII. He did not set out to be a prophet. He was an earnest old man of conservative bent who was simply in the right place at the right time for God's own purposes. He sensed God calling the church to new pastures in these modern times. So he threw open the windows without intending or foreseeing or fully understanding all the consequences. John XXIII did not look or act like a prophet. He looked like someone who should be selling pizza. Beware of the prophet who sets out to look and act like a prophet.

Freedom

The second characteristic of the true prophet is freedom. The true prophet has to be free in both directions—free to speak the hard message for the right reasons and free not to speak it for the wrong reasons or at the wrong time because of some compulsion that is ultimately selfish.

My favorite images in the gospels are those that revolve around the shepherd and the sheepfold. It's interesting. If one were to give a caricature of religion, it might be that of bringing people into the sheepfold. The process of conversion might be described as bringing people from the wide-open spaces to the safety and the parameters of a sheepfold. Religion brings restrictions, a framework, a limited horizon within which people must think and act.

But Jesus used exactly the opposite image. He described the shepherd as one who comes to the sheepfold and leads the sheep *out* of it. The shepherd brings them to the wide-open spaces, green pastures, wider horizons, where they can have a freedom they never knew before. The truth shall set you free. To forgive is to be free. To be able to give things away is to be free. To dream great dreams is to be free. This is precisely the freedom the prophet must have, and the freedom the prophet must give to others.

I believe that there is a lack of this freedom among bishops today—not on all issues, by any means, but on some. The bishops of the United States are very courageous on social issues. I am proud to stand with them. They have carried me forward to places I would never have gone. They have taken great risks.

But on issues within the church, I am embarrassed. We have seemed fearful to speak on church issues that are right before our eyes, but that are unmentionable. We are like a dysfunctional family, unwilling to talk openly about things that are on everyone's mind even when we are together at an NCCB meeting.

Why is this so? I don't think it is necessarily a desire for larger or more prestigious dioceses. It is much more subtle. It is the wish to look good, to maintain "credibility" with influential church leaders who would confuse disagreement with disloyalty. So you join what someone called a "conspiracy of silence" on certain matters. You tell yourself that it isn't for yourself that you are doing this. You will be able to do so much more good this way—be more credible and be able to accomplish more. It isn't for yourself; it is for a good cause. Once you buy into that, you start to be very careful about what you say, especially in matters that pertain to the church. The priests can talk about them, but you can't.

One of the paradoxes of this is that we ask everyone else to take risks. We ask you priests on the front lines to take risks. We ask lay people to take risks. Our pastoral letters on peace, on racism, on economics have exhorted people to put themselves on the line, even to put their jobs on the line. Yet, when it comes to matters within the church, we ourselves back away from the same kinds of risks. I don't know what to say about that, except that I feel very sad.

John XXIII was not afraid to take risks even on church matters. Perhaps it was his old age that gave him the freedom to do it. I don't know. But he was free.

Another aspect of this freedom has to do with realizing that it is the Lord who builds the house. There was a time when I wanted to be the master builder, the architect. But more and more I have come to realize that my task is to craft something small, something good, that the master builder will use. I think this is a perspective the prophet must have. It is the freedom to let the Lord build the house. Beware of the prophet who has everything all figured out. John XXIII didn't. Archbishop Lefebvre did.

When faced with the decision to preach a hard message, I always want to ask myself, or ask the person doing it, "Why are you doing this?" And I want to listen carefully to the answer, the tone in their voice, the look in their eyes. If you were to use the Enneagram, I wouldn't say, "Beware of the prophet who is an eight or a one." I would simply say to the eight or the one, "Beware of the driving force behind your prophetic message."

Wisdom

Wisdom can be defined in many ways. For our purposes here I am going to described it as "truth—plus love."

The truth has to come from somewhere. So I want to ask prophets questions such as, What do you read? To whom do you talk? How are you connected with things happening in our world? Tell me about your relationship with God.

The prophet must be a person of wide horizons, much wider than the specific "hard truth" they proclaim. That is a very important characteristic. The truth proclaimed by the prophet must not be a one-dimensional obsession. Their mind must not have a narrow focus, must not be locked in on one thing, for the world never revolves around one thing. It revolves around faith, hope, and love. The prophet must be a person whose horizons are wide enough even to include the other side. Beware of the prophet with narrow horizons.

And then there is love. Wisdom means not only knowing the truth, but also knowing how to use it to achieve good. John XXIII again comes to mind. It is interesting that he is called "Good Pope John." He had a goodness about him, and he exemplified "truth plus love." In contrast, Archbishop Lefebvre seemed to wave the truth like a battle flag, demanding the unconditional surrender of all who disagreed with him.

It is never enough to be right. You have to know how to use the truth. Beware of the unloving prophet.

One of the temptations of prophets is to court martyrdom. They speak a distasteful message (which often must be done), and they do it in a distasteful way (which is never the objective). A prophet must be a communicator, and a communicator always asks: How can I get this message across to these people? Sometimes, when we get into the "prophetic mode," we suddenly put aside everything we know about good communication. We seem to say, "It's a hard message and they're not going to like me," and we make sure they don't. And if they don't like our message, we always have that excuse. We seldom ask if it is our own fault for communicating it badly.

Jesus seemed honestly bothered when people rejected him. You can almost hear the pain in his voice when he asked, "Do you want to leave me too?" Then, of course, there is the very sad scene when he wept over Jerusalem.

A final thought on this: Each of us could look back and chart the development of our prophetic awareness. It is probably a long road, with many turns in it and many bridges crossed. You could visualize a map showing where you began, the twists and turns along the way, the bridges crossed, and then put an X where we finally have arrived. Too often, it seems to me, we then get up and preach the hard message—which is the conclusion of a long trip—and wonder why the people aren't right there with us. The truth of our message, the connection with the gospel, the relationship to our tradition—all these things are perfectly obvious to us. But it took a long time for us to get there. And we had a lot of help—our training, people who helped move us along, reading, reflection. It should not surprise us that many people who have not had these advantages are at a different place on the road, with many bridges yet to cross.

Closing Comments

We are celebrating the one-hundredth anniversary of Leo XIII's landmark social justice encyclical *Rerum Novarum*. This doesn't mean that we have been preaching social justice for a hundred years. As a matter of fact, Pope Pius XII, in his long pontificate during which he wrote forty-one encyclicals, did not write any on social justice. Many of the people to whom you preach were raised on Pope Pius XII. Social justice was not part of their formation. It is not the only dimension of the prophetic role, but it is a significant part of it, and many people resist the involvement of the church in these political, secular issues. It is not a popular message, and we take a lot of flak when we preach social justice.

On top of all this, we take a lot of flak just for being who we are. I sometimes feel very weary and sore from being identified with the "wrong" group on just about every issue these days.

- In this age of the laity—I am a priest.
- In this age of feminism—I am a man.
- Blacks call for justice—and I am white.
- Hispanics assert their rights—and I am Anglo.
- The Third World is emerging—and I am a citizen of the First World.
- We talk now about the southern hemisphere emerging— and here I am in the northern hemisphere.
- The vocation of marriage is receiving its proper emphasis— and I am unmarried.
- We are told to have a preferential option for the poor—and I am middle class.

Whenever a minority or an oppressed group steps forward, I am identified with the oppressor. It doesn't matter how I feel about the issues. I am who I am, always identified with the clerical, male, white, Anglo, First World, middle-class oppressor, and I can feel the looks, hear the criticism. I feel like someone wearing a Notre Dame sweater in the Orange Bowl when Notre Dame is playing Miami and Notre Dame is going to lose. I can decide not to wear that sweater, but I can't change the color of my skin, and I don't want to stop being a priest. So I take it, and you take it, and we accept it because after all we are white, male, Anglo, and so forth. But it's hard never, ever to be identified with the right side.

On top of all that, we're supposed to preach the hard message. We shall. We must. But the whole thing takes its toll on us.

My closing thought: There is a gospel passage seldom read in the Lectionary, because it is assigned to a Saturday morning. It reads as follows:

> After Jesus had cured the man with the withered hand on the Sabbath, the Pharisees went out and took counsel against him to put him to death. When Jesus realized this, he withdrew from that place. Many people followed him, and he cured them all, but he warned them not to make him known. This was to fulfill what had been spoken through Isaiah the prophet:
> "…Behold, my servant whom I have chosen,
>   my beloved in whom I take delight;
> I shall place my spirit upon him,
>   and he will proclaim justice to the Gentiles.
> He will not contend or cry out,
>   nor will anyone hear his voice in the streets.
> A bruised reed he will not break,
>   a smoldering wick he will not quench,
>   until he brings justice to victory.
> And in his name the Gentiles will hope."
>   (Matt 12:14–21)

Instead of fighting, Jesus withdrew, and Matthew uses the quote from Isaiah to show that this did not come from fear or weakness. It came from faithfulness to his call to be servant—the courageous, gentle leader described by Isaiah.

There is something that rings true here about the role of pastor. You have to preach the hard message, but you also have to be the pastor of the whole parish community. You are not a specialist. You are the servant-leader of everyone.

We are less the storm troopers...more the shepherds.

We deal less with the sensational things...more with the joys and sorrows of ordinary life.

We deal less with global issues...more with issues like whether there can be a pastoral solution to a broken marriage.

We do not often fill the air with prophetic shouts...but more with weekday and weekend homilies.

We are not so much in the streets as in the homes.

We deal less with great structures...more with bruised reeds.

We cannot pick our issues and focus on one or two. We take the ones that come, and they seem to come in the thousands (all you have to do is look at your desk).

The servant model in this gospel passage speaks very much to those of us who have the pastoral care of a community. There is a difference between a Dan Berrigan and a pastor. God bless them both. We need both. But there is a difference.

The servant model is no mean model. There is greatness there—not the kind of greatness people usually measure, but the kind measured in the kingdom.

Know that what you do in trying to be good shepherds is greatness. How to do that and also preach the hard message is something that no one can come here and tell you exactly how to do. There is no formula for it. But if we are prayerfully attentive to God's call, if we accept the risks of freedom, if we open ourselves to the gift of wisdom, we will surely find the way to do it.

Forum: The Ordination of Women: Can the Horizons Widen?*

Worship (January 1991), 50–59

We live in a galaxy called the Milky Way. It contains millions of stars, one of which is very close to us: the sun, a medium-sized star. There are millions of "suns" in our galaxy. The Milky Way is about a hundred-thousand light-years from one end to the other, which means that something traveling the speed of light would take a hundred-thousand years to cross our galaxy. The earth is about thirty-thousand light-years from the center.

Until the 1920s it was thought that the vast expanse of our galaxy was the whole universe and included all created reality. Some suggested that there might be more out there, perhaps even another galaxy, but most argued against it. In arguing against it and attempting to prove the cogency of their data, they probed the edges of this galaxy and looked at it from different angles. In the course of doing so they found something they were not looking for: another galaxy. Actually, they found more than another galaxy. They found many galaxies, and we have since come to know that

---

*Bishop Untener wrote this article in 1991, *prior to* the publication of the Apostolic Letter *Ordinatio sacerdotalis* (OS), issued by Pope John Paul II in 1994. *Ordinatio sacerdotalis* is a non-infallible document that gives a definitive teaching on ordination to be held by all of the faithful. The pope stated: "I declare that the Church has no authority whatsoever to confer priestly ordination on women and that this judgment is to be definitively held by all the Church's faithful" (OS, 4). The text of this Letter can be found on the Vatican website at http://www. vatican.va/holy_father/john_paul_ii/apost_letters/documents/hf_jp-ii_apl_ 22051994_ordinatio-sacerdotalis_en.html.

there are billions of galaxies. This opened up an entirely new horizon, a totally different perspective.

One might have thought that this happened because of more powerful telescopes that enabled scientists to see distant galaxies never before seen. But such was not the case. They had "seen" these galaxies all along, but thought they were stars or clusters within our own galaxy. By studying them more carefully and looking at them from different angles they discovered that they were outside our galaxy and were actually other galaxies. Thus it came to be that a whole new horizon was opened up, and the debate was resolved. It wasn't quite as simple as one side being right and the other side wrong.

I think that there is some parallel here to the discussion on the ordination of women. Perhaps there are wider horizons that can give us a new perspective. Let me illustrate with an example from another area of church doctrine. In the year 1441, the Council of Florence, the seventeenth ecumenical council of the church, decreed the following:

> The Holy Roman Church believes, professes, and preaches that no one remaining outside the Catholic Church, not just pagans, but also Jews or heretics or schismatics, can become partakers of eternal life; but they will go to the "everlasting fire which was prepared for the devil and his angels" (Matt 25:41), unless before the end of life they are joined to the Church. For union with the body of the Church is of such importance that the sacraments of the Church are helpful to salvation only for those remaining in it; and fasts, almsgiving, other works of piety, and the exercise of Christian warfare bear eternal rewards for them alone. And no one can be saved, no matter how much alms he has given, even if he sheds his blood for the name of Christ, unless he remains in the bosom and the unity of the Catholic Church (DB 714).

Five hundred and twenty-three years later, the Second Vatican Council referred to those whom the council of Florence had called "heretics" and "schismatics" as brothers and sisters. Vatican II then said of the Jewish people: "...this people remains most dear to God, for God does not repent of the gifts He makes" (LG 16). The council then went on to speak about non-Christians: "But the plan of salvation also includes those who acknowledge the Creator. In the first place among these are the Moslems....Those also can attain to everlasting salvation who through no fault of their own do not know the gospel of Christ or His Church, yet sincerely seek God....Nor does Divine Providence deny the help necessary for salvation to those who, without blame on their part, have not yet arrived at an explicit knowledge of God..." (LG 16).

These conclusions that seem totally opposite were reached by two councils, both of which affirmed the traditional principle: Outside the church no salvation. How was it possible for Vatican II to affirm this same principle and take a position that apparently contradicted the Council of Florence? The horizons widened. Our understanding of "church" and the ways of relating to the church broadened and provided a new perspective that could now include those who formerly were thought to be excluded from salvation.

We can apply this, at least as a possibility, to the issue of the ordination of women. The magisterium teaches that the ordination of women to the priesthood would be contrary to our doctrine, particularly the teaching that the priest acts "in the person of Christ." From the point of view of the magisterium the issue seems to be settled definitively. But there is a question that must be asked: Can the theological horizons widen?

The key to solving the question of "outside the church no salvation" was finding an aspect that admitted of enough expansion to include both positions. In reference to the ordination of women, the question is whether there is something in this issue that admits of expansion the way our understanding of "church" did. We may find several "expandables," but I will focus on just one.

Having attempted to set a perspective, I would now like to focus on a theological question—a question I believe to be a key one for this issue. It centers around the Latin phrase, *in persona Christi*. It is now commonplace to speak of the ordained priest as acting "in the person of Christ." Where does the phrase come from, and how has it come to be understood?

The Congregation for the Doctrine of the Faith in its "Declaration on the Admission of Women to the Ministerial Priesthood" doesn't answer the first question but does answer the second. It says that in the Mass the priest "acts not only through the effective power conferred on him by Christ, but *in persona Christi*, taking the role of Christ, to the point of being His very image, when he pronounces the words of consecration." The declaration goes on to say that those who would take the role of Christ must have a natural resemblance to him and therefore be of the male sex. As the Declaration puts it, "...His role must be taken by a man."

Is this the traditional meaning of *in persona Christi?* Does it mean that the priest "impersonates" Christ at the Eucharist? Let us go back and look at the origin and meaning of this key phrase.[1]

Scripture. First of all, is this phrase found in the New Testament? It appears to be used once, but closer examination shows this to be a faulty rendering of the original Greek. In 2 Corinthians 2:10, Paul writes: "For indeed what I have forgiven, if I have forgiven anything, has been for you *in the presence of Christ*...." The Greek reads, *en pro 'opo Chris tou.* St. Jerome translated this into Latin *"in persona Christi."* This carried over into English as "in the person of Christ," and in the approved English translations up until the revisions in our own time, it was translated "in the person of Christ."

Biblical scholars from early on recognized that in this passage the phrase really meant "in the *presence* of Christ." The sense would be something like saying "before the face of Christ." Current English translations done under Catholic auspices read as follows:

Jerusalem Bible: "in the presence of Christ"

New American Bible: "before Christ"

Revised New American Bible: "in the presence of Christ."

We can say, then, that the use of this phrase in scripture allows for a much broader horizon than is often understood.

Thomas Aquinas. In the early centuries we do not see this phrase used to describe the role of the ordained priest. For one thing, the word *person* would not be understood then in the same sense as today. Actually, the first significant theological use of this phrase in the context of ordained priesthood was in the thirteenth century by Thomas Aquinas. He says that the priest acts *"in persona Christi"* because Christ acts through the priest in the sacraments, especially the Eucharist. It is very important to note that Aquinas explains this in terms of instrumental causality. Referring to the eucharistic words of consecration he says, "...for since these words are uttered in the person of Christ, it is from His command that they receive their instrumental power from Him" (*Summa Theologica*, III, 78, 4).

Aquinas says that an instrument acts not by the power of its own form, but by the power of the one who moves it. Thus, Christ makes use of the instrumentality of a priest in the sacraments in the same way that a physician makes use of a scalpel— as an instrument, although in this case, an animate instrument. The interpretation that Aquinas gives to his use of this phrase is significant. As we shall see, in recent years the phrase has been used in a way that goes far beyond the notion of instrumental causality.

Council of Florence and Council of Trent. In the middle of the fifteenth century we have the first use of the phrase *in persona Christi* by a council. Referring to the Eucharist, the Council of Florence says, "The priest effects this sacrament by speaking in the person of Christ." The council does not give a reference for this phrase and does not explain it.

Strangely enough, the Council of Trent did not use the phrase, although it might have served well in its efforts to counter some of the teachings of Martin Luther on the priesthood. Perhaps the council was reluctant because it was known at the time that the phrase itself came from Jerome's questionable translation.

Mediator Dei. Some five hundred years after the Council of Florence the magisterium picked up this phrase and began to use it with increasing frequency. In 1947, Pius XII used it in *Mediator Dei:* "Christ is present at the august sacrifice of the altar both in the person of His minister and above all under the Eucharistic species" (no. 20).

There are two other closely related uses of the phrase in the encyclical: "Only to the apostles, and thenceforth to those on whom their successors have imposed hands, is granted the power of the priesthood, in virtue of which they represent the person of Jesus Christ before their people" (no. 40). "The priest (in the sacrifice of the altar) is the same, Jesus Christ, whose sacred Person His minister represents. Now the minister, by reason of the sacerdotal consecration which he has received, is made like to the High Priest and possesses the power of performing actions in virtue of Christ's very person. Wherefore in his priestly activity he in a certain manner 'lends his tongue, and gives his hand' to Christ" (no. 69). It is interesting that Pius XII does not cite 2 Corinthians. His only reference is to Aquinas. This means that despite what the language itself might seem to say, the meaning does not go beyond Aquinas who, as we saw, says that the minister is an external, instrumental cause.

It is also interesting that we have the beginning of something that has continued right up to the present, namely, the use of the phrase "in the person of Christ" as accepted theological terminology, without necessarily giving any reference. Whereas Thomas Aquinas had cited 2 Corinthians, and Pius XII cited Thomas Aquinas, subsequent use of the phrase will be increasingly without reference. It will also be used much more frequently. But that is getting slightly ahead of ourselves.

Vatican II. Vatican II explicitly uses the phrase in reference to the ordained priesthood five times. Other constructions are used that are quite close, but I will cite only those texts that actually speak of the priest acting in the person of Christ:

"Moreover, the prayers addressed to God by the priest who, in the person of Christ, presides over the assembly..." (SC 33).

"The ministerial priest...in the person of Christ...effects the Eucharistic sacrifice..." (LG 10).

"...bishops, in a resplendent and visible manner, take the place of Christ himself, teacher, shepherd and priest, and act as his representatives" (LG 21).

"However, it is in the eucharistic cult or in the eucharistic assembly of the faithful that they [priests] exercise in a supreme degree their sacred functions; there, acting in the person of Christ..." (LG 28).

"...priests...are signed with a special character and so are configured to Christ the priest in such a way that they are able to act in the person of Christ the head" (PO 2).

Note that Vatican II does not cite 2 Corinthians or Aquinas. The council reflects the increasing practice of using the phrase without any reference, or with a reference to Fathers who do not explicitly use the phrase, or with a reference to contemporary usage—as in the case of *Presbyterium Ordinis*, which cites *Lumen Gentium*.

Post–Vatican II. After Vatican II the phrase begins to be used very frequently. We find it in the writings of Pope Paul VI, in the 1970 *General Instruction on the Roman Missal*, and in the 1971 Synod of Bishops. The Congregation for the Doctrine of the Faith began using it in 1973 and has used it repeatedly after that. John Paul II uses it frequently.

Thus a phrase used very infrequently for nineteen centuries has become standard terminology in our own times. This raises a theological question that deserves careful examination. Theologically speaking, the usage of this phrase is relatively recent and relatively unexamined. A great deal of work is needed on this crucial point.

In a 1975 article, Edward Kilmartin probed the question and asked whether the priest directly represents the church and thus represents Christ, or whether the priest represents the church *and also* directly represents Christ. It is his position that the former is the case. "As an activity of the Church, pastoral office can only represent and act in the name of the Lord when it represents the life of faith of the Church."[2]

He then goes on to apply this to the question of the ordination of women:

> Since the priest directly represents the church united in faith and love, the old argument against the ordination of women to the priesthood, based on the presupposition that the priest directly represents Christ and so should be male, becomes untenable. Logically the representative role of priest seems to demand both male and female office bearers in the proper cultural context; for the

priest represents the one church, in which distinctions of race, class, and sex have been transcended, where all are measured by the one norm: faith in Christ.[3]

This is an interpretation that needs theological examination. It suggests the possibility of a broader horizon for understanding the way in which the ordained priest represents the person of Christ.

It should be noted that even if one understands the priest as directly representing Christ there are problems with "in persona" as solely a male representation of Christ. St. Irenaeus taught that what was not assumed has not been redeemed.[4] Christ has assumed the whole of human nature, and to say that a male has to represent the whole of human nature raises many questions. Gregory of Nyssa, in his *Great Catechism*, says, "He united himself with our nature so that by its union with the divine it might become divine." Again, if Christ has united himself to the whole of human nature, one has to ask why a man has to undertake this representative role.

Independent of the historical usage of the term "in persona Christi," one can also understand the phrase in a wider horizon when it is viewed from a liturgical perspective. In the old rubrics, when the priest bent down and directed the words *"Hoc est enim Corpus meum"* to the host, it seemed as though he were speaking to the bread in the first person and thus "impersonating" Christ. But the priest is not speaking to the bread or to the wine. He is speaking *to* the Father *about* Christ.

From beginning to end, the eucharistic prayer is primarily addressed to God the Father. The priest proclaims a great prayer of thanksgiving to God the Father. In so doing the priest recalls the great events of our salvation, and recalls in a particular way what Christ did at the Last Supper. Rather than impersonating Christ, he is recalling to the Father and to the assembly what Christ did: "The day before *he* suffered *he* took bread in his sacred hands and looking up to heaven to *you* Father, he gave you thanks and praise. *He* broke the bread, gave it to his disciples, and said: Take this all of you and eat it: this is my body..." (Eucharistic Prayer 1). The priest proclaims all of this, to use St. Paul's phrase, "in the presence of Christ" (2 Cor 2:10). If one understands "in persona Christi" in this sense, and if one looks carefully at what is actually taking place, it is difficult to see why the person proclaiming these words to the Father must be understood as impersonating Christ.

Another helpful liturgical perspective comes from a careful examination of the epiclesis in the eucharistic prayers. Eastern liturgical theology and practice have given far more emphasis to the importance of the epiclesis. The words in the eucharistic prayer that become absolutely critical are those that call forth the Spirit upon the bread and wine, transforming them into the body and blood of Christ. In speaking these words it is even clearer that the priest is addressing God the Father, and there is less of a tendency to see him as "impersonating" Christ.

"And so, Father, we bring you these gifts. We ask you to make them holy by the power of your Spirit, that they may become the body and blood of your Son, our Lord Jesus Christ, at whose command we celebrate this Eucharist" (Eucharistic Prayer 3).

"We bring you bread and wine and ask you to send your Holy Spirit to make these gifts the body and blood of Jesus your Son. Then we can offer to you what you have given to us" (Eucharistic Prayer 1 for Masses with Children).

"God our Father, we now ask you to send your Holy Spirit to change these gifts of bread and wine into the body and blood of Jesus Christ, our Lord" (Eucharistic Prayer 2 for Masses with Children).

"Father, we ask you to bless these gifts of bread and wine and make them holy. Change them for us into the body and blood of Jesus Christ, your Son" (Eucharistic Prayer 3 for Masses with Children).

When these words are given their proper importance and meaning, the representative role of the priest is seen in a different light.

These are areas that deserve further examination, with the possibility of broadening our horizons in understanding the phrase "in the person of Christ."

As has been noted, the phrase "in persona Christi" has been used much more frequently in recent times. More significantly, there has been a major shift in the way it is interpreted. Thomas

Aquinas interpreted it in terms of instrumental causality. A major shift came about when "in the person of Christ" was used to describe the priest as taking on the role of Christ, that is, not simply representing him as an ambassador represents someone (Corinthians in another place uses the term "ambassador"), but "impersonating" Christ in somewhat the same way that an actor takes on a role "in the person of" someone else. The Congregation for the Doctrine of the Faith interprets it in the latter way when it says, "His [Christ's] role must be taken by a man." Based on the historical and liturgical meaning of that phrase, such an interpretation is open to much discussion.

Finally, I would like to add a very brief thought about the manner in which this discussion is conducted. The truth is, we believe that each of the baptized is configured to Christ. "For all of you who were baptized into Christ have clothed yourselves with Christ. There is neither Jew nor Greek, there is neither slave nor free person, there is not male and female; for you are all one in Christ Jesus" (Gal 3:27–28). In this discussion, as in many others going on in the church today, we must remember, all of us, that we are acting "in persona Christi." I would hope that we could conduct the discussion with an openness and a spirit that expresses the fullest and most authentic meaning of what it means for the church to be the body of Christ, and for all of the baptized to act in the person of Christ.

I do not claim to be able to predict where this discussion will lead us. However, we must at least accept the possibility that there may be new horizons out there. The astronomers in the 1920s diligently pursued their research and discovered broader horizons that they had not anticipated. We, who ponder great mysteries beyond our comprehension, must always be open to the possibility of new horizons. If together we focus on the deeper questions, rather than engage in a tug-of-war confined to our own turf, we may find a new perspective and a truth more comprehensive than we now perceive.

Notes

1. In discussing the history of the use of this phrase, I am indebted in many ways to a master's thesis by Jerome Thompson (Marquette University, 1987), although we come to different conclusions.

2. E. J. Kilmartin, SJ, "Apostolic Office: Sacrament of Christ," *Theological Studies* 36, no. 2 (1975): 260.

3. Ibid., 263. See also his treatment of the representative role of the ordained priest in his more recent book *Christian Liturgy* (New York: Sheed & Ward, 1988), 361–64.

4. Cf. *Ad Haereses*, V, chapters 14 and 21.

Teaching Does Not Mean Ruling

The church needs dialogue on ordination of women.*

Compass (May/June 1992)

As bishop of Saginaw, I am often approached by Catholics who wonder about the integrity of their continued membership in the church. They find themselves in disagreement with an increasing number of decisions of church authority, usually issuing from Rome. Should they still belong to a church with which they feel more and more out of step?

Many experience pain, frustration, and anger. They are embarrassed when friends ask why they still identify with a church that excludes altar girls, does not permit the washing of women's feet on Holy Thursday, bans all forms of artificial contraception, does not ordain women, does not ordain married men (unless they were ministers in another faith), opposes liberation theology, and maintains a host of other policies and practices that many find objectionable. In the eyes of church leaders, these issues have been

---

*Bishop Untener wrote this article in 1992, *prior to* the Apostolic Letter *Ordinatio sacerdotalis* (OS) issued by Pope John Paul II in 1994. *Ordinatio sacerdotalis* is a non-infallible document that gives a definitive teaching on ordination to be held by all of the faithful. The pope stated: "I declare that the Church has no authority whatsoever to confer priestly ordination on women and that this judgment is to be definitively held by all the Church's faithful" (OS, 4). See the Vatican website http://www.vatican.va/holy_father/john_paul_ii/apost_letters/documents/hf_jp-ii_apl_22051994_ordinatio-sacerdotalis_en.html for the complete text.

settled, yet they are far from settled in the minds of so many in the believing community. To make matters worse, discussion of them appears to be either forbidden or ignored by church authority.

What does one say to such people? They are Catholics through and through. They love the church. Many are very actively involved in it (a factor that increases rather than decreases their pain). They readily accept the need for authoritative leadership: the office of teaching, ruling, and sanctifying. But the way these functions are sometimes exercised leaves them feeling less and less at home in the church.

The church has both the power to govern and the power to teach, but each of these has its own methods and spheres. I believe that the root cause of many people's frustration is the increasing tendency of church leadership to use its governing power for the purpose of teaching.

Faith and Theology

Faith is our experience of God. Theology is any attempt to think or talk about this experience. We do so in our own language and out of our own cultural, social, and philosophical background. Of course, words and concepts are inadequate to grasp or express this experience of God. But we must think about it and speak about it, and do our best with whatever words, images, and symbols are available.

Once we become conscious of our faith, it cannot exist without theology. There are, and ought to be, as many "theologies" as there are descriptions of a sunset. Some descriptions of a sunset are better than others. And some might be wrong, like a claim that the sun is square. But we would be deprived if only one description were allowed. Each falls short, and all of them together fall short, but the variety brings out the richness of the experience and brings us closer to the truth.

Does this mean that we are entirely at sea, with no reference points, no compass, surrounded by thousands of theological expressions of the faith, and not knowing which ones are more accurate, less accurate, or wrong?

Not at all. We share the content of our faith with a community, and that community has a history and a Tradition. Tradition is the whole body of beliefs handed down to us as the faith of the church, expressed in a theological form. We distinguish it from *traditions*, which are the ways we have historically acted out our Tradition and are changeable. Distinguishing Tradition from traditions is not always easy. It is a slow process that must involve the lived experience of the whole community, the work of theologians, and the teaching authority of the church leadership. The relationship of the three components of this process appears to be the root of many of the tensions experienced today.

Church Authority

Bishops have the office of teaching, ruling, and sanctifying. The Second Vatican Council's Constitution on the Church states that the primary function of a bishop is that of teaching: "They are authentic teachers, that is, teachers endowed with the authority of Christ, who preach to the people committed to them the faith they must believe and put into practice."

But this teaching office is increasingly exercised through jurisdictional power, a kind of power that is more appropriate to ruling than to teaching. Theologian Yves Congar has observed that formerly jurisdictional power was used only to add "the reality of obligation" to an authentic truth of our Tradition. When a doctrine was still under discussion and not clearly determined to be part of Tradition, it was understood that only truth had authority. Recently, however, authority has been used to "establish" truth rather than to add the reality of obligation to a clearly established truth of our Tradition.

This becomes even more of a problem when ruling power is used to establish a particular theology as though the faith could be understood in terms of this theology alone. "Faith seeking understanding" gives way to "jurisdiction imposing a theology."

In his opening address to the council, Pope John XXIII said that the authentic doctrine of the church "should be studied and expounded through the methods of research and through the literary forms of modern thought." He then spoke of dealing with error:

> The truth of the Lord will remain forever. We see, in fact, as one age succeeds another, that opinions follow one another and exclude each other. And often errors vanish as quickly as they arise, like fog before the sun.
>
> The Church has always opposed these errors. Frequently she has condemned them with the greatest severity. Nowadays, however, the spouse of Christ prefers to make use of the medicine of mercy rather than that of severity. She considers that she meets the needs of the present day by demonstrating the validity of her teaching rather than by condemnations.

John XXIII saw the role of teaching as teaching, not as ruling. This approach takes time. It requires close attention to the work of theologians and the lived faith of the community. When all of this is stifled prematurely by jurisdictional power, it creates the unhealthy situation that I believe we have lived in for nearly two centuries, excepting the years surrounding Vatican II. We are reminded that the foundations are in place for a different way by the event of the council, and by the documents that emerged from it or were inspired by it. The pastoral letters of the U.S. bishops on peace and on the economy, for example, illustrated the difference between teaching and ruling.

The difference between traditions and the Tradition and between ruling and teaching is well-illustrated by the question of the ordination of women. Theologian Herve Legrand writes, "The non-ordination of women to pastoral ministry is an undeniable historical fact, but it is not 'Tradition' in the strong sense of the term." He describes it as a "constant custom" that may have been appropriate to conditions in which the church once found itself. However, the church up to now "has not examined critically this way of acting."

Many other theologians share his conclusion. Where does that leave us? If the issue has not been examined critically, then it is a task we must face with honesty and courage. It will not be resolved by jurisdiction, and attempts to do so damage the health of the church. There are simply too many unresolved questions.

In the meantime, the official church exercises its ruling power by saying that women cannot be ordained. But at this point, it is more an exercise of jurisdiction than the establishment of truth. The sorting out of traditions from the Tradition has not been completed, and there is no short cut to its completion.

After I was quoted in newspapers as saying that I personally saw no scriptural or theological reason that necessarily excluded the ordination of women, some newspaper headlines said, "Bishop Defies Pope." In an article addressed to the people of the Diocese of Saginaw, I commented,

> I trust you will not be surprised to know that I have no intention of defying the Pope on this or any other matter. I could not imagine myself ever doing so. Among the other theological articles I have published, I have pointed out the need for a strong papacy and I have explained the distinctive role of the Vicar of Peter in our Roman Catholic tradition.
>
> It is one thing to have differing opinions. It is quite another to defy someone. For example, husbands and wives sometimes disagree. This should not be construed as "defiance." And what should they do when they disagree? They should talk. That is what I think needs to be done on the ordination of women—as well as other issues—and that is why I gave my opinion.

Collegiality

The College of Bishops is an important part of the teaching function of the official church. What does the College of Bishops hold on the ordination of women and other matters, both doctrinal/theological and disciplinary? We don't know, because without free discussion it is impossible to tell whether a bishop supports a particular position primarily because of a sense of loyalty, because he feels that to say otherwise would cause disunity, or because he truly believes it. If the Holy Father, for example, announced that he thought the time had come to begin the regular practice of ordaining married men, I have a feeling we would discover that many bishops were supportive of the idea.

But the College of Bishops, in communion with its head, shares responsibility for the whole church. The council clearly pointed out the collegiate nature and function of the role of bishops. As Peter and the apostles formed an apostolic college, so do the pope and all the bishops. From "ancient times," the communion of churches have consulted one another, and councils—local, regional, and ecumenical—have met to settle major questions through the advice of many.

The Constitution on the Church states,

> Although the individual bishops do not enjoy the prerogative of infallibility, they can nevertheless proclaim Christ's doctrine infallibly. This is so, even when they are dispersed around the world, provided that while maintaining the bond of unity among themselves and with Peter's successor, and while teaching authentically on a matter of faith or morals they concur in a single viewpoint as the one which must be held conclusively.

Without freedom of conversation, how are the bishops to arrive at this collegial mind so that the Spirit can speak through them, individually and collectively, toward the truth?

Concluding Thoughts

I return to my original question. How does one respond to those who ask why we belong to this imperfect church? My response would be fairly modest, as was Peter's. When Jesus asked the Twelve if they wanted to leave, Simon Peter answered, "Master, to whom shall we go?"

Where else shall I go? Here is where I was born into the community of disciples, and where I continue to be nurtured in the faith. Here is where Christ has been mediated to me. Here is where the Spirit has been poured out upon me. Here is where I am in touch with Tradition and rich traditions. Here is where I find the fullness of the sacramental life.

To be sure, I have also found here failure, imperfection, and sin. I have found here sexism, authoritarianism, and most of the *isms* I find in the world. But if the church is a seed of the kingdom, as I believe it is, then there is within this seed the force to overcome the sins of the world.

"Humanae Vitae": What Has It Done to Us? And What Is to Be Done Now?

Commonweal (June 18, 1993)

I have been asked to describe the effects of *Humanae Vitae* on the church. One should be able to do this regardless of whether one agrees or disagrees with the contents of the encyclical.

In measuring the effects on the whole church, we are dealing primarily with people's perceptions. Most people haven't read *Humanae Vitae*, although they know that in one section it reaffirmed the teaching against artificial birth control. They also know that the findings of the papal study commission on birth control—which recommended a change in the church's teaching—were not accepted, and they have watched how dissent has been handled. Their reactions are generally negative.

The encyclical is certainly not the sole cause, but it appears to have contributed to an attitude among Catholics that authoritative teachings can be brushed aside, and that church discipline (for example, Sunday Mass attendance) is less binding. It has made it more difficult to defend our position on abortion and exacerbated the negative attitude of many women toward the church. Those who teach and preach have felt less confident in attempting to provide guidance in sexual matters. Lay people are increasingly suspicious of the willingness of the hierarchy to listen to them on important matters. The surge of freshness and hope felt by so many during and just after Vatican II seems to have taken a downturn since the encyclical.

It could be argued that 1968 was about the time when most or all of these things would have begun happening anyway, and

Humanae Vitae is being made the scapegoat. It teaches a hard message, but it is the long hard road that must be taken against prevailing attitudes toward sexuality and marriage.

Whatever the merits of that assertion, we are still left with the public perception of the way in which *Humanae Vitae* came to be, and how the church has dealt with the widespread dissent that followed. In the eyes of many people, the teaching church has committed a teacher's cardinal sin: It has become more concerned about itself than about truth.

No analogy is perfect, but the following may help explain how many people see the church on the issue of birth control.

Picture early maps drawn by explorers of North America. You can recognize Florida, the Great Lakes, the outline of both coasts. The contours are real, not figments of their imagination, for they walked the terrain, climbed the hills, and sailed the lakes and rivers. Gradually the maps changed. The terrain didn't. The maps did.

They changed because others also walked the land and sailed the waters, and because new technology gave us additional data. It was the same continent, but now we knew it differently. If in the face of all this, early map makers insisted on the correctness of their original map and refused to listen to the cumulative experience of others who had walked the land, or refused to accept the new information provided by technology, we would begin to suspect their motives. They would appear to be more concerned about defending their map than the truth of the terrain.

In the formulation and subsequent handling of *Humanae Vitae*, many people look upon the church in this way. In their eyes, we opted to cling to the contours of our earlier teachings on birth control without regard for the data we have subsequently received—from married people who have walked the terrain, from science, from theologians, and from pastoral leaders. We simply put aside the findings of the study commission and reissue the same map. Then in the years that follow we have official conferences and invite speakers who a priori are committed to the defense of the map. We pretend before all the world that our best and brightest and holiest believe that the map is true. Indeed, those who speak at such conferences may well be persons of the highest integrity who believe the map is true. But everyone knows that they are a select minority, and the ultimate criterion for their selection is their loyalty to the map.

Observers begin to suspect our motives. The terrain no longer appears to be our issue. Our map is the issue. We fear that if we make even the slightest change, we will lose some of our authority as map makers. Again, whatever your judgment on the contents of *Humanae Vitae*, this is the perception of many people on the formulation and subsequent handling of the encyclical. It has damaged our credibility.

Credibility

It is hardly a subtle insight to suggest that since *Humanae Vitae*, the church's teaching authority has been less credible in the eyes of many people, including many Catholics.

If the reason were simply that people turn us off when we preach hard truths, then this is something we must endure. Our task is to preach the gospel in season and out of season, and we must not become alarmed if people don't like what we say.

I believe, however, that there is a different reason for the loss of credibility. Like it or not, justified or unjustified, the fact is many people think that church leaders say one thing publicly and another privately. When we profess our public support for *Humanae Vitae*, or when we engage in "a conspiracy of silence," they feel we lack integrity.

This presents a very serious problem. It is one thing when people angrily disagree with us, as in many social and economic issues. It is quite another when people cynically dismiss us as dissemblers. In the eyes of many, the issue has shifted. It is no longer an honest evaluation of the moral implications of artificial birth control. The issue is loyalty to church authority.

In an address describing ways in which dissent from *Humanae Vitae* has had adverse effect, Avery Dulles, SJ (*Origins*, April 22, 1993) pointed out what others have frequently observed, namely, that it is used as a loyalty test. Qualified theologians who have expressed reservations about the encyclical are "excluded from sensitive teaching positions and from appointments to episcopal committees." He also noted that priests who dissent appear to be ineligible to be appointed as bishops. If this be true, something has gone awry.

The Approach to Truth

There is another effect of *Humanae Vitae* that is less obvious but deserves attention. It has to do with our approach to truth.

In the decades before Vatican II, there began to reemerge an approach to church teaching that seemed very healthy. I say "reemerge" because it was not new—Thomas Aquinas, among others, had used it. This model emphasized that every effort to conceptualize or put into words the mysteries of our faith falls short. Our teachings need continually to be rethought so that we can understand them more fully, not simply explain more effectively what we already know perfectly well. Human science, culture, philosophy, and experience enable us to shape our understanding of the great truths. The truths themselves endure, but we are able to penetrate them in new ways and thus be more true to these truths.

In his address at the solemn opening of Vatican II, John XXIII affirmed this approach. He pointed out that our duty is not only to guard the precious treasure of our doctrine, "as if we were concerned only with antiquity, but to dedicate ourselves with an earnest will and without fear to that work which our era demands of us." He went on to say:

> ...the Christian, Catholic, and apostolic spirit of the whole world expects a step forward toward a doctrinal penetration and a formation of consciousness in faithful and perfect conformity to the authentic doctrine, which, however, should be studied and expounded through the methods of research and through the literary forms of modern thought. The substance of the ancient doctrine of the deposit of faith is one thing, and the way in which it is presented is another. And it is the latter that must be taken into great consideration with patience if necessary, everything being measured in the forms and proportions of a magisterium which is predominantly pastoral in character.

Compare this to the approach represented by Pius X in his 1907 "Syllabus Condemning the Errors of the Modernists." Among the sixty-five errors condemned was the following: "The dogmas the church holds out as revealed are not truths which have fallen from heaven. They are an interpretation of religious facts which the human mind has acquired by laborious effort."

That statement was condemned as false, and ultimately it is. But if we look upon its reverse, as one looks at a negative in photography, the opposite statement would seem to affirm that revealed truths indeed have fallen from heaven, and there is little need for the laborious efforts and interpretations of the human mind as we try to understand them. It is almost as though the church keeps truths in hermetically sealed containers, and our understanding of them is unaffected by culture, science, human experience. The latter may help us explain these truths more effectively, but our understanding of the truths themselves is not at all shaped by developments in the world around us.

Again, prescinding from whether you think that *Humanae Vitae* is correct or incorrect in its position on birth control, the process by which it was developed and the way in which it has been handled these twenty-five years seem to represent this latter approach. This has had a wide effect that I believe to be negative. It set back the reemergence of an approach that is desperately needed as we move into the postmodern world.

What to Do?

The only solution, it seems to me, is to have honest and open discussion, at least in acknowledging that after twenty-five years *Humanae Vitae* hasn't been accepted by the majority of Catholics.

I expressed some of these concerns to the assembled bishops of the United States at our November 1990 meeting. We were debating a document on guidelines for education in human sexuality, and one section referred to the teaching on birth control in a way that seem to imply that it was one of those "givens" that everyone accepted. It was in that context that I spoke, and I shall close by quoting this hitherto unpublished statement:

I believe that the proposed document on guidelines for education in human sexuality is well written, and that the section on birth control is written with much sensitivity. Yet, as I read that section, I found myself asking questions, and I wonder if the time has come to ask the questions out loud. I have four questions.

1. In the text we briefly restate the teaching on birth control and say, "We hope that the logic expressed here is compelling." I wonder how we can claim credibility when we make a statement like that knowing in fact that the logic is not compelling. It is not compelling to people in general...not compelling to the Catholic laity...not compelling to many priests...and not compelling to many bishops. When we know this, and don't say it, many would compare us to a dysfunctional family that is unable to talk openly about a problem that everyone knows is there.

2. We also say, "It is our earnest belief that God's Spirit is acting through the magisterium...in developing this doctrine." This is true, but it is not the entire truth. It is also the earnest belief of our church that the Spirit acts through the entire people of God in developing doctrine.

The *sensus fidelium* is, of course, more than an opinion poll. But when people disagree with us, we cannot simply assume that it is mere opinion.

The *sensus fidelium* is more than a head count, but the beliefs in the heads and hearts of our people must count for something. Thus, my question: Do we have adequate structures and procedures to listen to the *sensus fidelium*, particularly on this issue?

3. In the same text we call for those who dissent to study and pray over their position. Could they not say to us, "We will, if you will...and let's do it together?" Would such a process weaken the authority of the bishops, or would it in fact strengthen our authority?

4. Yesterday we passed a document of Family Ministry, and we renewed our commitment "to listen perceptively, trustingly, and compassionately to what

people are saying about their Christian understanding of marriage, sexuality, and family life." I tried that last week with our Saginaw pastoral council. You must understand, these are not dissidents. These are a wide mixture of people, totally dedicated to the church. They found great problems with this particular section on birth control. (I note that the bishops' advisory council also had problems with this section.)

After some discussion, I passed out slips of paper and asked them to write down "yes" or "no" on whether they agreed with this section. They were not to sign their names. The count was one yes and twenty-two no. I am wondering what would happen if you did the same with your pastoral council. I am wondering what would happen if you did the same with your priests. I am wondering what would happen if we did it among ourselves right here.

Those are my questions, and I pose them as questions. I ask them up front and out loud, in the conviction that if we do not ask them, we are unintentionally causing great damage to the credibility and the unity of this church that we love.

When asked what he thought about the laity, Cardinal Newman said something like, "Well, the church would look strange without them." We are without them on *Humanae Vitae*, and we look strange. We've go to do something about that.

How Bishops Talk

America (October 19, 1996), 9–15

Two papers of special significance appeared this summer. The first is the address given by Archbishop John Quinn, the recently retired archbishop of San Francisco, at the centennial celebration of Campion Hall, Oxford University. The second is *Called to Be Catholic: Church in a Time of Peril*, a statement with which Cardinal Joseph Bernardin of Chicago has associated his initiative for more understanding within the church. (I will refer to the latter as the Cardinal Bernardin paper.) The first paper was published in *Commonweal* on July 12; the second appeared in *America* on August 31.

An interesting thing happened. Five U.S. cardinals responded quickly and publicly to these two papers—Cardinal John O'Connor to the Quinn lecture and Cardinals Bernard Law, James Hickey, Adam Maida, and Anthony Bevilacqua to the Bernardin paper. (This leaves only two other cardinals who head U.S. archdioceses: Cardinal Roger Mahony, who is already part of the Cardinal Bernardin initiative, and Cardinal William Keeler, who has not commented.)

This public, written exchange provides an unusual opportunity to look in on a discussion among bishops and see not only what we discuss, but *how* we discuss. By comparing the responses with the original texts I will attempt to point out some characteristics that I think are frequently present in discussions among bishops.

By now these papers have drawn more responses. This article, however, will focus on the first and most widely reported responses, those of the five cardinals.

What do we learn from these discussions? One of the obvious things is that there are disagreements at the highest levels about structures and procedures in the church—as there have been since the days of Peter and Paul. Further, such disagreements can be acknowledged and dealt with openly, a sign of a healthy church.

And not only dealt with openly, but respectfully. Perhaps the brightest side of these discussions is their tone. Participants are mutually respectful, do not question motives, and presume the goodwill of one another. Even when expressing sharp disagreement, they are not sharp-tongued or acrimonious. Many a pastor today wishes that all disagreements in the church could be dealt with this way.

It appears to me, however, that while the tone of the discussion was good, its quality left much to be desired.

The High Ground

There is an occupational hazard among religious leaders to seize the high ground in discussions, speaking forth truths that are not in question at all or that the other person has already clearly affirmed. For example, we have the following from three of the responses to the Cardinal Bernardin paper:

Cardinal Law: "The crisis the church is facing can only be adequately addressed by a clarion call to conversion."

Cardinal Maida: "...the way to unity within our church itself is not so much through dialogue, but rather through conversion which is the result of prayer and fasting."

Cardinal Bevilacqua: "Rather, what is needed is that common vision illuminated through prayer to see Jesus as he himself asked to be seen: the way, the truth, and the life."

The Cardinal Bernardin paper seems to have gotten all this quite right in the first place. Some samples:

> Jesus Christ, present in Scripture and sacrament, is central to all that we do; he must always be the measure and not what is measured.
>
> Ultimately, the fresh eyes and changed hearts we need cannot be distilled from guidelines. They emerge in the space created by praise and worship.

Cardinal Law cites the first of these two quotes above and says the thought is introduced too late: "I would have preferred to have the statement begin at that point."

It did. The fourth sentence of the three-thousand-word statement reads: "American Catholics must reconstitute the conditions for addressing our differences constructively—a common ground centered on faith in Jesus, marked by accountability to the living Catholic tradition...."

Two other illustrations of this tendency to make cautionary statements about things never questioned or already affirmed come from Cardinal O'Connor's response to Archbishop Quinn. The first has to do with the motives and dedication of members of the Roman Curia, which Cardinal O'Connor defends in a number of plates. For example:

> Were those [Curia members] who might have preferred that the Second Vatican Council not occur, too aggressive in their objections? Can I automatically assume nefarious motives or "ultra conservatism" on their parts, or did they act out of a sincere love for the Church?

Their motives and/or their love for the church were never called into question by Archbishop Quinn. He is speaking on a different level—that of structure, not of moral reform. He even makes detailed suggestions on how a joint commission might recommend such structural changes to the pope.

The second illustration from Cardinal O'Connor's response deals with possible changes in the manner of appointing bishops. He offers cautions:

> Surely that [the appointment of bishops by emperors, kings and other rulers] would be the last thing we would want to return to.
>
> Would anyone want any President of the United States, of any party, involved in appointing bishops?
>
> Another old-time usage was for "cathedral chapters" to appoint bishops. If one is looking for a way to

broaden input on appointments or to make them more "democratic," this would hardly be the way to go.

As for the election of the bishop by the priests and people...it would seem to me—but I have no empirical data or personal experience—that it would be an extraordinarily difficult approach, subject to great emotional forces, dependent on enclaves of individuals who know a prospective candidate personally and so on.

One would get the impression that Archbishop Quinn was advocating some or all of these approaches or was unaware of the problems involved. But that was not the case at all. As it turns out, Archbishop Quinn himself had noted:

There are, indeed, certain things to recommend the existing procedure. It distances the appointment of bishops from local factions and pressures. It prevents the development of pressure groups favoring one candidate and rejecting another. In some instances it also removes the possibility of the State becoming involved in the appointment of bishops. Yet, honest fraternal dialogue compels me to raise the question whether the time has not come to make some modifications in this procedure.

Accuracy

Another concern about the discussion's quality has to do with accuracy. We should expect of public discussions at this level the same standard of accuracy in representing the original paper as, say, in a book review. I did not find that to be the case here, and I believe it led to unintended misrepresentation. I will give an example related to the Cardinal Bernardin paper and another related to the Archbishop Quinn paper.

In the Cardinal Bernardin paper, the proposal for "dialogue" seemed to evoke the strongest reactions. For example:

Cardinal Law: "The fundamental flaw in this document is its appeal for 'dialogue' as a path to 'common ground.'...Dissent from revealed truth of the authoritative teaching of the church cannot be 'dialogued' away. Truth and dissent from truth are not equal partners in ecclesial dialogue....Dialogue as a way to mediate between the truth and dissent is mutual deception."

Cardinal Hickey: "But we cannot achieve church unity by accommodating those who dissent from church teaching—whether on the left or on the right. To compromise the faith of the church is to forfeit our 'common ground' and to risk deeper polarization....If the Church is to be strong and convincing now and in the next millennium, it must preach the Gospel without compromise."

Cardinal Maida: "This statement may create some confusion for people since it seems to suggest that Catholic teachings are open to dialogue and debate....Dialogue is a helpful tool and step in a larger process, but of itself, it cannot solve religious differences."

Cardinal Bevilacqua: "[Catholic common ground] is an ordinary, everyday term, open to uncontrolled interpretation, including even the meaning that 'Catholic common ground' signifies 'lowest common denominator.'...A polite debate or a respectful exchange of divergent views about what would be the most commonly acceptable Catholic teaching is not sufficient to adequately address and heal the differences which exist among the faithful."

The Cardinal Bernardin paper did not talk at all about accommodation, compromise, or lowest common denominator. Nor is that the meaning of dialogue. Dialogue—as etymology, definition, and usage make clear—means simply to talk together. The respondents seem to have confused dialogue with debate, arbitration, compromise, forging a consensus. The purpose of dialogue is clarity, not compromise. It is the basic first step in trying to understand each other's position.

The church always needs dialogue, not only with those outside the church but among its own members. In his major encyclical on the church, Pope Paul VI uses the word *dialogue* sixty-seven times. Each time, he uses it positively. Consider this section specifically addressing dialogue *within* the church:

> We address Ourself finally...to the one, holy, Catholic, and apostolic church....How greatly we desire that this

dialogue with Our own children may be conducted with the fullness of faith, with charity, and with dynamic holiness. May it be of frequent occurrence and on an intimate level. May it be open and responsive to all truth, every virtue, every spiritual value that goes to make us the heritage of Christian teaching. We want it to be sincere. We want it to be an inspiration to genuine holiness. We want it to show itself ready to listen to the variety of views which are expressed in the world today. We want it to be the sort of dialogue that will make Catholics virtuous, wise, unfettered, fair minded and strong (*Ecclesiam Suam*, no. 113).

The negative interpretation of dialogue read into the Cardinal Bernardin paper by those who criticized it does not reflect a high standard of discussion.

A similar misinterpretation occurs in Cardinal O'Connor's response to the Archbishop Quinn lecture. Cardinal O'Connor says:

First, my surprise at attributing the decline in numbers of priests in any way to the Curia. I simply don't understand that one, much less as an impediment to Christian unity....I do not know of any other bishop who has cited any obstacles to vocations caused by the Curia.

What Archbishop Quinn actually said was that many Christians of other faiths are hesitant about full communion with the Holy See "*because of the way* issues are dealt with by the Curia" (emphasis added.) Archbishop Quinn then gives examples of some of these issues:

The concern has to do with the appointment of bishops, the approval of documents such as the *Catechism of the Catholic Church*, the grave decline in the numbers of priests and the consequent decline in the availability of Mass for the people, the cognate issue of the celibacy of the clergy, the role of episcopal conferences, the role of women and the issue of the ordination of women.

Clearly Archbishop Quinn did not say that the Curia was impeding vocations. He said the Curia *was impeding Christian unity* because of the way it deals with many issues, among them, discussion of the declining numbers of clergy and the cognate issue of celibacy.

Generalizations

The cardinals' responses also tended to make general statements critical of the others' position, without citing specifics. For example, commenting on the Cardinal Bernardin paper, Cardinal Law says:

> Throughout there are gratuitous assumptions, and at significant points it breathes an ideological bias which it elsewhere decries in others.

This broad accusation of "gratuitous assumptions" is itself a gratuitous statement. What are these gratuitous assumptions "throughout" the document, or the ideological bias it "breathes"? Not one reference or example is given. Such a serious and sweeping criticism ought not to be made gratuitously.

One might counter by saying that Cardinal Law's statement was too brief to have space for these citations. But that will not do. If one is going to be severely critical in the public forum of a lengthy document written with careful thought and precision, then short and undocumented indictments are not appropriate. Otherwise we are caught in the "sound bite" approach we decry in others.

Opinion Versus Data

Another occupational hazard of religious leaders is to resolve something with personal conviction and/or opinion rather than available data. Cardinal O'Connor does this several times in his critique of Archbishop Quinn's talk. For example, he disagrees with

Archbishop Quinn's list of issues, saying that many of them are not ecumenical concerns:

> It is my own conviction that the crucial obstacles to Christian unity remain doctrinal, including the very concept of the primacy of the pope, and not simply the mode of exercising the primacy.

Granted Cardinal O'Connor's own convictions, formal ecumenical discussions have given us some data on this. For example, the Anglican-Roman Catholic International Commission, after eleven years of discussion, issued a final report in 1981. It said in part:

> Much Anglican objection has been directed against the manner of the exercise and particular claims of the Roman primacy rather than against the universal primacy as such (*Agreed Statement on Authority in the Church*, I: Elucidation, no. 8).

There are indeed still questions about primacy, but the manner of its exercise is also a high ecumenical concern.

Another example of citing personal opinion rather than data is Cardinal O'Connor's question about whether the pope was really inviting Catholic leaders to respond to his invitation for suggestions on the way in which the primacy is exercised. Placed at the beginning of his critique, it calls into question the appropriateness of Archbishop Quinn's whole lecture:

> I had personally interpreted the Pope's call to dialogue in this encyclical as an invitation to "church leaders and their theologians" of other Christian persuasion, rather than to Roman Catholics.

Let us look at the data. The Pope says at the beginning of his encyclical:

> I myself intend to promote every suitable initiative aimed at making the witness of the entire Catholic community understood in its full purity and consistency, especially

considering the engagement which awaits the church at the threshold of the new millennium....The present Encyclical Letter is meant as a contribution to this most noble goal. Essentially pastoral in character, it seeks to encourage the efforts of all who work for the cause of unity.

If there are any further questions about the appropriateness of Archbishop Quinn's effort to offer suggestions about the exercise of primacy, these questions are put to rest by a document promulgated by the Vatican's Congregation for Bishops. It deals with the proper role of bishops and says in part:

> With due reverence the bishop offers the Pope advice, observations and suggestions, and he points out dangers to the church, occasions for doing good or *other opportune ways whereby the ministry of the Primacy may become more useful* and church offices and institutions more fit to fulfill their duties (*Directory for the Pastoral Ministry of Bishops*, no. 45, emphasis added).

"Reception"

Three of the four cardinals who criticized the Bernardin paper expressed major concern about the matter of "reception." The manner in which this was done raises a number of questions. First of all, in the Cardinal Bernardin paper, the term *reception* is mentioned only once. Note that it occurs as a background reference to the need for consultation regarding church policies:

> ...an essential element of Catholic leadership must be wide and serious consultation, especially of those most affected by church policies under examination. The church's ancient concept of reception reminds us that all the faithful are called to a role in grasping a truth or incorporating a decision or practice into the church's life.

Now let us look at excerpts from the cardinals' criticisms:

Cardinal Hickey: "[The statement] even seems to say that church teaching must be 'received,' that is 'accepted' by a majority of Catholics before it can be regarded as authentic. Every day we Americans learn of yet another new poll telling us what we believe about the issues of the day. That might be how politics works and it might be how news is made—but it is not how church teaching is determined."

Cardinal Maida: "We cannot measure Catholic teaching the way the media might suggest in the sense that some teachings are 'accepted' or not accepted by a majority of Catholics. Perhaps that is how politics works, but it is not how Church teaching is determined."

Cardinal Law: "The statement raises the issue of the faithful's 'reception' of a truth or in the incorporation of a decision or practice into the church's life....Reception by the faithful cannot be measured by polls which are subject to all the pressures of contemporary culture, however, anymore than the schism of all the bishops save one in Henry VIII's England can be ascribed to an exercise of collegiality."

When one considers the length of the Cardinal Bernardin paper, the selection of this issue by three of the four cardinals and the emphasis on it (one fourth of Cardinal Law's statement) is striking, almost as if they were improvising from the same script.

But what is more striking and disturbing is the imputation of such a low notion of reception to the Bernardin paper, which does not even hint that reception has anything to do with polls and politics. I have never heard a bishop or theologian remotely suggest that reception means this at all.

Reflect for a moment on the meaning of this ancient and beautiful concept: Reception has to do with the church, the body of Christ, incorporating a teaching into its own being—bringing something from the outside to the inside. Our teachings are not dead letters or museum pieces. They live in the community. Reception is the process by which they take root and come alive. The local churches or individuals receive the faith of the whole church into their lives, even when it may be difficult to do. It is part of the struggle of faith. In the last century Cardinal John Henry Newman criticized those "who will believe anything because they believe nothing" or who "think that to believe is as easy as to obey."

When one realizes what reception is, rereads the reference to it in the Cardinal Bernardin paper, and then reads the critiques, one cannot help but be concerned about the level of discussion.

Substance

One last illustration has to do with the importance of dealing with the substance of what the other person has said.

A major part of Archbishop Quinn's lecture deals with collegiality. He cites his experience working with the pope during the Seattle consultation and also his appointment by the pope in 1983 as pontifical delegate for religious life. He speaks positively of the "brotherly collaboration" he experienced with the pope in both cases. He then says:

> Yet these are instances *not so much of* collegiality as they are of collaboration by bishops in a task undertaken by the pope at his initiative....And so collaboration by bishops with the pope in a task he specifically entrusts to them is *not the full measure of collegiality.* "Collegiality" is predicated of the bishops precisely because—with the pope—they have from Christ a true responsibility for the whole Church. Hence bishops by this fact have the responsibility from Christ to take initiative in bringing forward problems and possibilities for the mission of the Church. Collegiality does not exist *in its fullest sense* if bishops are merely passive recipients of papal directives and initiatives. (emphasis added)

Cardinal O'Connor makes the following observation:

> From my viewpoint, one of the most interesting issues Archbishop Quinn addresses is that of collegiality vs. collaboration. A key illustration he uses to suggest that the Holy Father tends to act "collaboratively" rather than "collegially" is particularly fascinating to me....[Cardinal O'Connor then speaks about the Seattle consultation and

continues....] What surprises me now is what I considered to be the collegiality of the process. Archbishop Quinn apparently considered it to have been not collegiality, but collaboration.

A careful reading of Archbishop Quinn's text indicates that it is not accurately represented by setting collaboration and collegiality as mutually exclusive by the use of phrases like "collegiality vs. collaboration," or "Archbishop Quinn apparently considered it to have been not collegiality, but collaboration."

An accurate representation would have been, for example, in the latter quote: "Archbishop Quinn apparently considered it to have been *not the full measure* of collegiality, but collaboration...."

Besides the accuracy of the quote, there is also the matter of getting at the substance of the issue. One of the fundamental theses of Archbishop Quinn's entire lecture is this: If the church, on the institutional level, has the office of governing, teaching, and sanctifying precisely as a college of bishops in union with the pope as member and head of the college, then the college with its head should be in truth and practice, not in name only or sporadically or passively, the governing, teaching, and sanctifying organ of the church. Is the full measure of this borne out in the way the church actually functions?

Archbishop Quinn says that it is not. Cardinal O'Connor says that in his personal experiences of working with the pope and the Curia he has been treated with respect and equality, and his recommendations were generally accepted. All this, of course, could be said of the way bishops often deal with staff people in their chanceries. It does not get at the deeper level of the unique character of the college of bishops, which is Archbishop Quinn's point.

Some Reflections

I close with some brief reflections. Why did these cardinals come out so quickly and strongly against the Archbishop Quinn lecture and the Cardinal Bernardin paper? The list of problems cited in these two papers seems to resonate greatly with the problems sensed by many faithful Catholics. What would the National Federation of Priests Councils, or the Bishops' National Advisory Council (laity, religious, clergy), or pastoral ministers around the country, or diocesan pastoral councils, or parish councils, or the majority of U.S. bishops say about the need to discuss these issues? Are we operating on two levels?

What underlies all this? Are we fearful of leading the flock out of the sheepfold lest they run wild in all directions? Are we fearful of letting people see that the church doesn't always here and now have the final answer on important questions? Do we view our magisterial role with gnostic overtones, as though we have a source of knowledge that others do not have? Does not the church, until the eschaton, always need to know more than it knows? These are questions I can only suggest for further discussion.

Finally, I want to observe that in critiquing the responses of these five cardinals, I do not cite them as isolated cases, nor point to them as the chief offenders. I simply use the window of this public exchange to offer examples of what we all, myself included, do at times when involved in religious discussions.

Checking ourselves on this is important for two reasons. First, in the public forum the critique becomes the story. The media, quite understandably (for they are in the business of selling news), use the template of controversy to attract readership. As a result, the original papers are seen and interpreted by 99 percent of the people through the lens of the criticisms. Hence, the critics have at least as great a responsibility as the original author to be accurate.

The second reason why it is important to learn from this has to do with the level of our discussions at the meetings of the National Conference of Catholic Bishops. Dealing with issues ranging from arguments against inclusive language in the psalms because of their christological typology to legendary discussions of holy days, we have done all of the above and more.

Interestingly enough, we bishops do not do this when we speak on behalf of the conference, give testimony before Congress, or make public statements on social issues. These are done with great care, at the highest level of discourse and with staff assistance. I would rate the level of discussion in those cases much higher—superb. For some reason we often shift down to another level when we deal with church matters. We who have the office of teacher must do better.

Cardinal Bernardin, in his response to the criticisms, said, "I am convinced that a careful reading of the text ought to reassure those who expressed these concerns."

I would add, "and would have prevented a great deal of mis-information."

6

The Wider Church

Introduction

When a doctrine was still under discussion and not clearly determined to be part of Tradition, it was understood that only truth had authority. Recently, however, authority has been used to "establish" truth rather than to add the reality of obligation to a clearly established truth of our Tradition.[1]

Bishop Ken Untener was a theologian rather than a canon lawyer. This was evident in his concern for the relationship between the local church and the wider church in the United States and with the Vatican offices. He was concerned that misunderstandings between local churches and the total church can impact the faith of those in the local church of Saginaw.

Early in his time as bishop, Ken wrote an article (*America*, 1984) on local church and universal church, in which he used a metaphor quoted so often that it ceased to be associated with his name. He said that the church is not a large corporation with headquarters in Rome and "branch offices" around the world. The pope is the bishop of Rome, not the bishop of the dioceses across the world. He noted that "in our own century the trajectory of the exercise of papal power reached its highest point; it will undoubtedly move in another direction, downward from the peak, reaching perhaps the level of papal style of the early centuries."

Bishop Ken was well aware that his mode of viewing the diocese and the Vatican was not widely understood. Yet, he sustained his vision. It was reflected in his communications with Vatican offices, which were articulated as a bishop to fellow bishops rather than as an inferior officer waiting for instructions. He knew that his call was to be a leader, not a manager. That same pattern was reflected in his relationship with the pastors of parishes.

His interventions/contributions at the USCCB were not many, but they were thoughtful. They included the call to discuss the possibilities of ordination for married men, for women in the church, and the implications of *Humanae Vitae* for lay couples.

Need for better conversation at the grass roots, and a possibility for bringing more regional issues of weight to the November meetings, led a group of bishops to propose a different working structure for the NCCB/USCC that would present topics for November meetings coming up from the local regions of the United States, rather than from the top down. Ken proposed the first draft of this restructuring. Another working structure was eventually accepted.

He was involved in Cardinal Dearden's "Call to Action" in Detroit in 1976, and afterward, when issues such as racism, the laity, women, sexuality, divorced Catholics, birth control, and youth were addressed, he continued to be involved. He spoke on many of these issues. Bishop Ken gave priests' and bishops' retreats and conferences across the United States and in Latin America, throughout his time as bishop—saying "no" to three quarters of the requests he received.

The U.S. bishops' pastoral *Economic Justice for All*, published by the NCCB in 1986, also influenced Ken's leadership. He gave and encouraged workshops throughout the diocese and beyond to explain the pastoral. He hoped to sensitize people to the social realities of the poor, who are often invisible to middle-class Catholics. He was concerned about problems the divorced face in the church, those who think about having an abortion, and other issues that affect the poor differently from the way they affect the middle class.

Note

1. *Compass* (May/June 1992): 6–8; the quote is on p. 7.

Local Church and Universal Church

America (October 13, 1984)

Three stories illustrate the way many people view church structure.

1. I gave a talk entitled "The Role of the Catholic Bishop" to an ecumenical group. Using an overhead projector, I pointed out the difference between the church as a worldwide corporation with a central headquarters in Rome and the church as a communion of dioceses. A local newspaper erroneously quoted me as saying: "The Pope is the Pope of Rome, not the Pope of the world."

Catholic readers had a range of reactions: Those familiar with theology figured it was a misquote, average Catholics were confused, and militant conservatives were indignant.

The newspaper was kind enough to publish a correction (a tape of my talk was available), which accurately read: "The Pope is the Bishop of Rome, not the bishop of the world as though the world were all one diocese." Catholic readers had a range of reactions: Those familiar with theology had their puzzle solved, average Catholics remained confused, and militant conservatives remained indignant.

For most Catholics the correct statement was as much of a problem as the incorrect one. It was absolutely orthodox and faithful to our traditions, but it was in conflict with popular Catholic thinking. All of which indicates that popular Catholic thinking on this matter is not entirely orthodox.

2. A first-grade youngster was chatting with me in the vestibule after Mass. He said that he knew who I was and pointed to my picture on the wall. Then to demonstrate the breadth of his knowledge he said, pointing to the pope's picture, "He's your boss

and," pointing to my picture, "you're Father Ed's boss," and pointing to Father Ed's picture, "he's Bonnie's boss." (I later found that Bonnie was the parish secretary.) Rather than try to nuance his ecclesiology, I decided to shake his hand.

Actually, his "picture ecclesiology" was a remarkably accurate explanation of the popular Catholic view of the divine "chain of command": God, Christ, pope, bishop, priest, and laity. The fact that this view is false has not prevented it from taking deep root in popular Catholic thought.

3. I was teaching a two-day workshop on ecclesiology, and I posed this imaginary problem for the group. "Suppose there were a nuclear holocaust and only four Catholic dioceses remained in the whole world: Bombay, Green Bay, Saskatoon, and Manila. Each had its own bishop, the only four bishops left in the world. In terms of church order, what is the first thing you would do?"

They responded: "Elect a pope." They then developed an election process. Using this process, they elected an imaginary priest from Bombay, had him ordained a bishop, and then installed as pope.

I asked what diocese he would have. "None," they responded. "He's in charge of the whole church."

I pointed out that the pope is the bishop of a diocese, who also exercises a special responsibility toward the other dioceses of the world. Since, in my imaginary case, all four dioceses had bishops, what the group should have done was simply elect one of them to fulfill the papal responsibility by taking the role of Peter among the bishops.

The thought had never crossed their minds.

Traditional Popular Ecclesiology

People popularly view the Catholic Church as a corporation with the pope as the chief executive officer, Rome as the headquarters, and bishops as branch managers around the world. Or they see it as a religious empire directed by an absolute sovereign. Traditional ecclesiology is quite different from this popular view, and now that traditional teachings and practices regarding collegiality, subsidiarity, and local church are gradually being reemphasized, the people in the pew are likely to become very confused. We need to communicate a more accurate (and traditional) ecclesiology.

Sometimes this can be achieved simply by taking a different starting point. Our Western theology tends to start with the universal church and then see local churches as concrete realizations of this. Eastern theology, on the other hand, starts with local church as the fundamental reality and then sees the universal church as a reality realized by the communion of local churches. The difference may seem subtle, but it can have a major effect on our thinking.

Yves Congar, OP, also borrowing from Eastern theology, suggested that we use the analogy of the Trinity to understand local church and universal church. Catholics learned in their catechism lessons that each Person of the Trinity is truly distinct from the other and is truly and fully God. In the same way, each distinct local church is truly and fully church. We also learned that the Three Divine Persons, while distinct from and equal to one another, share one and the same divine nature. In the same way, each local church, while distinct and equal as church, participates in one and the same universal church. There is an order within the Trinity, but this does not mean that any Person is less fully God. There is an order within the church, but this does not mean that any local church is less fully church.

Another helpful approach is to examine the titles "vicar of Christ" and "vicar of Peter." People tend to think that the title "vicar of Christ" belongs exclusively to the pope, more or less along the lines of the chain of command outlined by that youngster in the vestibule. Vatican II points out that the term "vicar of Christ" applies to every bishop who leads a diocese. The distinctive title of the pope is "vicar of Peter." The opening prayer of the Mass for a deceased pope reads: "May your servant, our pope, vicar of Peter...." The prayer after communion of the same Mass describes his Petrine role: "You made him the center of unity of your church on earth." There is a significant difference between the pope's relating to the bishops of the world as sole vicar of Christ (and therefore source of all power and authority) and as vicar of Peter (and therefore the center of unity).

The above clarification of titles touches on the heart of the Vatican II teaching on collegiality. People generally tend to think that all apostolic authority resides exclusively in the pope, who then delegates it to other bishops. The truth of the matter is that apostolic authority rests in the entire college of bishops in union with the Holy Father. Neither the pope, nor an individual bishop, nor a group of bishops could claim to possess the fullness of apostolic authority apart from the entire college of bishops. Cardinal Joseph Ratzinger wrote in *The Episcopate and the Primacy*, "A Pope who would excommunicate the entire episcopate could never exist, for a church which had become only Roman would no longer be Catholic. And conversely, a lawful episcopate which would excommunicate the Pope could never exist, since a Catholicity which renounces Rome would no longer be Catholic."

One way to appreciate this teaching is to think of the original apostolic college. What was the source of their apostolic authority? Did it come from Peter, or did it come from the Lord? Did it reside in one of them, or did it reside in the entire body as a college? Clearly, it came from the Lord, and it rested in all of them as a college. Peter had a special unifying role. He was the rock of unity; he was called upon to strengthen his brothers, but he was not the source of their authority. The same is true of the college of bishops today, and of the role of the vicar of Peter.

The Shift toward Centralization

There was a time in the early history of the church when there was only a small number of dioceses, no canon law, no Curia, and very few external structures connecting the Diocese of Rome to the other dioceses. There was internal unity but much external diversity. Each bishop exercised full responsibility for his own diocese, while remaining in communion with the college of bishops, particularly through communion with the bishop of Rome. Almost all the things that today require a dispensation from or clearance from Rome were handled by the local bishop with his priests and ministers.

As the number of dioceses increased (there are approximately 2,350 today), unity became more difficult. The exercise of some responsibilities that belonged to the local bishop was reserved to the bishop of Rome. The reason was clear and simple: There are some things that ought to be done together for the sake of unity.

Over the course of centuries, more and more of these local responsibilities were reserved to the bishop of Rome. This trend toward centralization, which received great impetus in the eleventh century, has continued right up to our own time. It reached its peak just before the Second Vatican Council.

Most people today do not realize this. They have known it only at its peak. What they regard as normal centralization is actually unparalleled in all church history. Having experienced the peak of centralization, recent generations of Catholics quite understandably think of the church as a large corporation with headquarters in Rome and "branch offices" around the world.

The perception of the pope as one who exercises a role that is above the church itself is illustrated by an incident that occurred during the writing of the crucial chapter on collegiality in *Lumen Gentium*, the Constitution on the Church. During the preparation of this chapter, the pope suggested to the theological commission of the council that it insert in the text the phrase that the pope is "answerable to God alone." After considering this, the commission responded that this would be an oversimplification, inasmuch as "the Roman Pontiff is also bound to revelation itself, to the fundamental structure of the church, to the sacraments, to the definitions of earlier councils and other obligations too numerous to mention."

A bishop in an individual diocese does what he thinks is best for that local church. He tries to implement his best pastoral judgment in consultation with others, lay and ordained. The bishop of Rome exercises that kind of leadership for the Diocese of Rome. His leadership of the universal church, however, is somewhat different, for the world is not all one diocese. The bishop of Rome, in relationship to the universal church, is called upon to implement not his own pastoral judgment, but what he believes to be essential and/or important to the unity of the dioceses.

This very important distinction is often misunderstood. The pope, as bishop of the Diocese of Rome, makes certain regulations for that diocese, based on his own pastoral and practical judgment. If the world were all one diocese, then those regulations would automatically apply throughout the world. But such is not the case.

Regulations given to the Diocese of Rome do not automatically apply to the 2,350 dioceses of the world. In 1959, for example, Pope John XXIII decided to convene a council. He also convened a synod for his diocese, which made its own regulations affecting only the Church of Rome. There are two different principles: One has to do with a pastoral judgment about the best way to do things; the other has to do with what is essential and/or important for unity.

When regulations are made for the universal church, they contain an implicit clause: "It is essential and/or important for the unity of the church that...." The principle behind such regulations is not simply pastoral judgment about the best way to do things. That judgment belongs to the local bishop. Rather, the principle is unity.

This concern for and ministry to unity includes many things that go beyond heresy. For example, there is the impact of one local church (or group of churches) on others. The pope also has the important role of calling the bishops together and acting as head of the college when they come together. When necessary, the pope is also the arbiter of differences among bishops. In all of these cases the pope is exercising his role as vicar of Peter, as unifier, not as director of "branch offices" around the world.

This distinction is particularly important when reflecting upon the role of the various curial offices. The impression often exists that they make decisions not on the basis of what is essential and/or important for unity, but rather on the basis of the judgment on how things ought to be done. While that may be a commendable motive, it is not their role. The current discussion about communion under both species on Sundays is a timely example. When an Italian curial official recently was asked about this by a group of American bishops, he replied that the reason for his concern was the fact that communion under both species cannot be administered reverently to a large congregation. It was clear that he was attempting to make a personal decision based on his own pastoral judgment about logistics, rather than on the way such a practice might affect the unity of the church. In doing so, he appeared to be preempting the pastoral and practical judgment of the local bishops. Anyone who has attempted to deal with traffic in Rome can appreciate his practical concern. That, however, is a fairly limited perspective of the possibilities of good order.

A word about church unity would be helpful to our understanding of the Petrine office. The ultimate principle of unity in the church is the Holy Spirit. This belief has sometimes been obscured by statements that could be open to misinterpretation. Pope Pius IX, for example, in rejecting the aims of the Association for the Promotion of the Reunion of Christendom, referred to the papacy as "the beginning, the root and the indefectible source" of unity.

When we affirm the Spirit as our source of unity, possibilities of external diversity widen. Nonetheless, within this diversity our unity must be perceptible. It is more than an abstraction. Thus, in the essentials of faith and sacraments, diversity of expression must not be so great as to make it impossible to perceive our unity in them.

Beyond the essentials of faith and sacraments, there is also the matter of common practices, which, though not absolutely essential to unity, contribute to it in an important way. This is an area of pastoral, prudential judgment, and it is ultimately the responsibility of the Holy Father to make such judgments. It is a distinctive aspect of the Petrine role.

There is a way in which diversity of practice, pushed to an extreme, can be harmful to unity. On the other hand, there is a way in which uniformity of practice, pushed to an extreme, can do the same thing. If the ultimate source of unity is the Holy Spirit, then it must be recognized that uniformity could interfere with the full expression of the Spirit in all people and all cultures and thus prevent us from truly uniting with them. Instead of union, we would have absorption, and absorption is not the kind of communion sought by a church that is "catholic." The Chinese rites controversy in the seventeenth century is an example of how excessive uniformity can actually cause a lack of unity in the spirit.

In this regard one might also keep in mind that at this very moment, the unity of the church is able to sustain such diversity as the Byzantine, Armenian, Chaldean, Antiochene, Alexandrine, and Latin rites, two different codes of canon law, celibate and married priests, leavened and unleavened eucharistic bread—all within the full communion of the Catholic Church.

In his address to the U.S. bishops at Collegeville, Minn., in 1982, Cardinal John Dearden commented on unity and diversity in the church:

This understanding of the local church—and the role of the bishop who presides over it—in no way diminishes the indispensable reality of the universal church, willed as it is by Christ, nor the role of the Holy Father as Peter's successor. What it does is to restore in our thinking the inherent dignity and completeness, in faith and sacrament, of the particular church. The local church is not seen as a fragment or piece of a whole, but as a community of faith having its own integrity even as it relates to the universal church....Parenthetically, this concept of local church related to the "catholica" [universal church] gives us an insight into something that appears new to many Catholics, namely, pluralism among the local churches within the framework of essential unity. When each local church is properly seen as an integral realization of church, then pluralism within unity becomes a sign of strength, not a sign of weakness. Each local church with its uniqueness adds to the richness of the "catholica."

Power in Context

The First Vatican Council (1869–70), apart from the better-known decree on infallibility, described the distinctive role of the pope primarily in terms of jurisdictional power. Because the council was cut short by a war, it never had the opportunity to develop the context of this power, as intended. The pope, the council said, has ordinary and immediate jurisdiction over each and every diocese in the world. Such a statement could easily be misunderstood to mean that the pope rules the church as though it were all one diocese, and that his power absorbs that of the local bishop.

Power in the church, however, must always be situated in its context. For example, Catholics often speak of the "power" of the ordained priest to consecrate bread and wine. To look at this power in itself, apart from its proper context, could lead to much misunderstanding about the role of a priest. For example, if a priest simply wished to accumulate Mass stipends and celebrated ten masses a day, he would not be exercising the role intended. Or to use an example from my seminary days, a priest is certainly not entitled by this power to walk into a bakery and declare over all the bread: "This is my body."

The jurisdictional power of the pope must also be seen in its context. As we have seen, the purpose of this power is the unity of the church, not the absorption of the pastoral and practical judgment of the local bishop.

This misunderstanding is not sheer fantasy, as illustrated by an event that occurred 109 years ago. When he read about the papal powers described in the First Vatican Council, Prince Otto von Bismarck, chancellor of the German Empire, drew some erroneous conclusions. Like many Catholics today, he did not understand the context of these powers, and thus he sent a directive to his diplomatic representatives pointing out that papal jurisdiction as described in Vatican I now absorbed that of the local bishops. Bishops were simply papal functionaries. Governments should therefore bypass the local bishops and deal directly with the pope.

When this statement became public, the German bishops issued a strong statement of their own. Their statement listed eight *errors* in Bismarck's approach:

1. As a result of these conciliar decrees the pope can now take into his own hand the rights of the bishops in each and every diocese and can now substitute his own papal power for that of the residential bishops.

2. Episcopal jurisdiction has been absorbed by papal jurisdiction.

3. The pope no longer exercises, as he did in the past, merely a few determined rights reserved to himself, but now he is the depository of the totality of episcopal rights.

4. He has, in principle, taken the place of each individual bishop.

5. At any time the pope, at his own good pleasure, can in practical affairs take the place of the bishop in his relations with the government.

6. The bishops are now nothing more than his instruments and functionaries with no personal responsibility.

7. The bishops have become, in their relations with their governments, the functionaries of a foreign sovereign.

8. The pope, by virtue of his infallibility, is truly a perfectly absolute sovereign, more absolute than any absolute secular monarch.

The bishops concluded this list by saying:

"All of these statements are without foundation." The German bishops then expanded on the true teaching of the church: "According to this teaching of the Catholic Church, the Pope is Bishop of Rome, not bishop of any other city or diocese, not bishop of Cologne or of Breslau....According to the constant teaching of the Catholic Church...the bishops are not mere instruments of the Pope, nor papal functionaries with no personal responsibility, but rather they have been appointed by the Holy Spirit to take the place of the apostles in order to nurture and rule, as befits good shepherds, the flock committed to them."

These are strong statements. How did Rome react? The response was not long in coming—less than a month. Pius IX said, in words that might surprise some: "Your statement is indeed so clear and sound that, since it leaves nothing to be desired, We ought to content Ourselves by merely giving you Our fullest congratulations."

Nearly ninety years later, *Lumen Gentium* included similar language: "Bishops govern the particular churches entrusted to them as the vicars and ambassadors of Christ....The pastoral office or the habitual care of their sheep is entrusted to them completely. Nor are they to be regarded as vicars of the Roman Pontiff, for they exercise an authority which is proper to them, and are quite correctly called 'prelates,' heads of the people whom they govern." The council, in its official footnote on this passage, cites the above statement by the German bishops and the response of Pope Pius IX.

The Need for Clarification Today

A number of pastoral reasons indicate an urgent need for a clarification of the relationship of the Church of Rome to the other local churches around the world. Among these is the fact that the spirit of Bismarck lives on among some Catholics today. When they have a concern, they bypass the local bishop or even the conference of bishops and go directly to Rome. This practice distorts the nature of the church. It fosters the very model that Bismarck promoted: a model emphatically declared false by the German bishops and by Pope Pius IX.

This practice also tends to communicate to Rome a distorted picture of many local churches. The good news of what is taking place in so many dioceses is twisted into bad news. Horror stories are sent to Rome in deliberately organized campaigns, and they take root before the local bishop has even heard about them. This is not only contrary to proper ecclesiology; it is contrary to the gospel.

Another and more critical reason for clarifying the relationship of the Church of Rome to the other local churches around the world is to prepare the "people in the pew" for changes that have begun to take place. One of the most common complaints during the flurry of changes that took place after Vatican II was that the people were not properly prepared for them. They were given the changes without any prior explanation of the reasons behind them.

Very significant changes are under way in church practice regarding the reality of local churches. Vatican II laid the foundations for these changes, and the new Code of Canon Law has begun to implement them. Local churches are emerging to take their more traditional place in the communion of churches that make up the universal church. There is increasing diversity within unity. Unless Catholics understand the reasons for this, they will become confused, angry, and reactionary. The positive growth of local churches will be perceived as the loss of unity and/or the decay of the papacy. Again, since in our own century the trajectory of the exercise of papal power reached its highest point, it will undoubtedly move in another direction, downward from the peak, reaching perhaps the level of papal style of the early centuries. The less centralized model of the earlier, small church is now made possible in a large church by modern travel and communication.

For those who understand traditional ecclesiology, a trend in this direction will be seen as a sign of health. For others (the vast majority of Catholics), it will be confusing. It will be seen as a threat to the most cherished jewel of Catholicism: the papacy at its peak of power. There will be resistance, charges of heresy, and loyalty tests. Worse than that, the fracas could easily lead to extreme positions: on the one side, those who would want to reclaim the pre–Vatican II model of papacy, and on the other side, those who in reaction to this would want to replace the papacy with a democracy. The first would be a regression; the second runs contrary to the nature of the church.

We learned a lesson about change during the 1960s. Careful explanation is needed so that people understand the reasons for every change. We should take heed from that experience and do this one right.

If a Pope Resigns....

Current church law explicitly provides for the resignation of a pope.

America (March 25, 2000)

Pope John Paul II will celebrate his eightieth birthday on May 18, 2000. This has generated speculation about his possible resignation, which in turn has prompted many Catholics to ask how it is that a pope could no longer be pope.

The purpose of this article is not to discuss whether John Paul II will or should resign, nor is it intended to be a full exposition of the Petrine office. It is simply an opportunity to learn more about the papacy by examining some of the questions that I have heard people ask when the possibility of the pope's resignation comes up.

Could a Pope Resign?

Yes, and some popes have in fact resigned. The number is debated because of historical uncertainties (most cases go back many centuries). One instance of which we are sure is that of Celestine V, who resigned in 1294 after serving less than six months as pope. He was a monk and wanted to live a life of solitude.

Much to the surprise of many people, current church law explicitly provides for the resignation of a pope: "If it should happen that the Roman Pontiff resigns his office, it is required for validity that he make the resignation freely and that it be duly manifested, but not that it be accepted by anyone" (Canon 332.2).

If a Pope Resigns and Another Is Elected, Are There in Effect Two Popes?

No, there are not. It is most helpful here to note that a person is not ordained pope as though this were a fourth category in the sacrament of orders: deacon, priest, bishop, *pope*. Rather, he is *elected* bishop of Rome. (If the person elected by the cardinals were not a bishop, he would be ordained one so that he could be the bishop of Rome.) Canon law puts it this way: "The Roman Pontiff obtains full and supreme power in the Church by means of legitimate election accepted by him, together with episcopal consecration; therefore, one who is already a bishop obtains this same power from the moment he accepts his *election*" (Canon 332.1).

Thus, a person is pope because he has a particular office—bishop of Rome. Contrast this with, say, the Dalai Lama. He is believed by his followers to be the incarnation of a Buddhist deity. In their eyes he is in himself a special person, not a person with a special office. The pope, on the other hand, has this special office because he is bishop of Rome. When he is no longer bishop of Rome, he no longer is pope.

If the Pope Retired, What Would He Be Called?

The title "pope" (from the Greek *pappas*, "father") was a term of affection used of bishops from early times. By the twelfth century, it had come to be understood as particularly appropriate for the bishop of Rome, because his diocese was the center of ecclesial unity. (Hence also the title Holy Father.)

There are no guidelines on what we would call a retired pope. It would seem appropriate to give him an honorary title. We attach *emeritus* to a title we give someone who has the honor but not the power of a previous position (e.g., pastor emeritus). He might appropriately be called pope emeritus.

If the Pope Resigns and Another Is Elected, Do We Have Two Successors of Christ on Earth?

Christ does not have a "successor." He is not retired. His last words in Matthew's Gospel are: "I am with you always, to the end of the age." The Second Vatican Council, speaking of the church in its Dogmatic Constitution on the Church (1964), says, "The Head of this Body is Christ" (no. 7).

The pope is the successor of Peter or, more properly, the vicar of Peter. In many ways the role of the Twelve was unique and did not admit of successors. On the other hand, they were to have successors in their mandate to preach the gospel, make disciples, baptize, and teach all that Jesus had taught them. It is in fulfilling this mandate that bishops are the successors of the apostles, and the pope is the successor to Peter as the leader of the Church of Rome.

In the funeral Mass for a pope, he is referred to as the *vicar* of Peter: "May your servant, [name,] our pope, vicar of Peter, and shepherd of your church, who faithfully administered the mysteries of your forgiveness and love on earth, rejoice with you forever in heaven."

Peter, in addition to being a member of the Twelve, was given by Christ the responsibility to support the unity of the Twelve. He was one of them, but also their leader. He eventually went to Rome, where he was martyred sometime in the 60s. The apostle Paul also spent his last years in Rome and was martyred there at about the same time.

The Church of Rome (we would say Diocese of Rome) enjoyed special regard because it preserved not only the tombs of Peter and Paul but their apostolic tradition as well—all that had been handed on. Other dioceses were committed to teach and live the apostolic tradition, and their unity with the Church of Rome was a sign that they were faithful to this tradition. Rome became the center of the communion of all the churches with one another. Because of the special standing of the Church of Rome, its bishop was recognized as a special witness and minister to the tradition of the apostles and to the unity of the churches. We refer to this distinctive role as the Petrine office.

Isn't It More Accurate to Say that He Is the Vicar of Christ?

The title vicar of Christ has been used by of all bishops since the early centuries. John Paul II, in his 1995 encyclical on ecumenism, *Ut Unum Sint*, uses this title for bishops: "When the Catholic Church affirms that the office of the Bishop of Rome corresponds to the will of Christ, she does not separate this office from the mission entrusted to the whole body of Bishops, who are also 'vicars and ambassadors of Christ.' The Bishop of Rome is a member of the 'College,' and the Bishops are his brothers in the ministry" (no. 95).

A pope who resigned, insofar as he would still be a bishop, would continue to be a vicar of Christ. As we saw above, the designation that is distinctive of the bishop of Rome is "vicar of Peter," a title and role that a pope would no longer have after his resignation.

Would a Retired Pope Still Be Infallible?

Infallibility is a gift given to the church as a whole. It is exercised by the pope when he defines a doctrine to be believed by all the faithful, but it is not a gift given to the pope as a personal quality. It is noteworthy that at the First Vatican Council (1869–70), the title of the section on infallibility was changed from "The Infallibility of the Roman Pontiff" to "The Infallible Magisterium [i.e., teaching authority] of the Roman Pontiff."

The bishop of Rome, because of his office, can give expression to the faith of the church and exercise the infallibility with which the church is endowed. It is helpful to look closely at the key paragraph on this in Vatican II's Dogmatic Constitution on the Church. Much of this paragraph was taken word for word from Vatican I. Note the careful distinctions highlighted here in italics:

> And this infallibility with which the Divine Redeemer willed *His Church to be endowed* in defining doctrine of faith and morals, extends as far as the deposit of Revelation extends....And this is the infallibility which

the Roman Pontiff, the head of the college of bishops, *enjoys in virtue of his office*, when, as the supreme shepherd and teacher of all the faithful, who confirms his brethren in their faith [cf. Luke 22:32], by a definitive act he proclaims a doctrine of faith or morals. And therefore his definitions, of themselves, and not from the consent of the Church, are justly styled irreformable, since they are pronounced with the assistance of the Holy Spirit, promised to him in blessed Peter, and therefore they need no approval of others, nor do they allow an appeal to any other judgment. *For then the Roman Pontiff is not pronouncing judgment as a private person, but as the supreme teacher of the universal Church, in whom the charism of infallibility of the Church itself* is individually present, he is expounding or defending a doctrine of Catholic faith. The infallibility *promised to the Church* resides also in the body of Bishops, when that body exercises the supreme magisterium with the successor of Peter. (no. 25)

Once again, the distinction between the person and the office comes into play. It is because of his relationship to the entire church as bishop of Rome that the pope can exercise the gift of infallibility given to the church. If he resigns from that office, he can no longer act in this way.

He May Be Bishop of Rome, but Isn't the Pope Also Bishop of the Whole Church?

The vicar of Peter has specific churchwide responsibilities because, as bishop of Rome, it is his distinctive role to minister to the unity of the whole church. However, he is not "bishop of the world," as though the world were all one diocese. In 1875, shortly after Vatican I, Prince Otto von Bismarck of the German Empire sent a dispatch to all his diplomatic representatives saying that the council had in effect given to the pope episcopal rights in each diocese and substituted pontifical jurisdiction for that of the bishops.

The German bishops subsequently issued a statement noting that "the pope is bishop of Rome, not bishop of any other city or diocese, not bishop of Cologne or of Breslau...." Pope Pius IX praised the German bishops' statement and expressed his full agreement.

We do not have a pope who, among other things, is the bishop of Rome. We have the bishop of Rome who, because of his election as bishop of Rome has the responsibility of carrying out the Petrine office. It is because of the relationship of the Diocese of Rome to the dioceses of the world that he has a unique status among his brother bishops.

Thus, bishop of Rome is his proper title.

If the Pope Resigned, Could He Appoint His Own Successor?

There are clear procedures for the selection of the bishop of Rome: He is to be elected by the cardinals. Since John Paul II would still be a cardinal, he would be able to join the other cardinals in casting a vote for the next bishop of Rome.

However, if he resigned on or after his eightieth birthday he would no longer be eligible to vote, because only cardinals under eighty can participate in a papal election.

If a Pope Resigns from Being Pope, What Is He?

We have to sort out what is attached to the person, and what is attached to the office. This isn't complicated. We can parallel it to any bishop who resigns as head of a diocese.

In 1984, for example, the Reverend Adam Maida was ordained and installed as bishop of Green Bay. His ordination as a bishop was permanent. His appointment to head the Diocese of Green Bay was not. This ceased in 1990 when he was appointed archbishop of Detroit. (An *arch*bishop, in addition to heading a diocese, also has some responsibilities in reference to the surrounding dioceses.

These dioceses constitute a province, and the archbishop is metropolitan of that province. An example of his responsibilities would be calling and chairing meetings of the diocesan bishops of the province to deal with matters of common concern.)

In 1994, Archbishop Maida was made a cardinal, a personal honor given to him. This gave him certain additional responsibilities, most notably to participate in the election of a pope. The appointment as cardinal, unlike the appointment as metropolitan, did not automatically go with being archbishop of Detroit. It was personal.

If, some years from now, Cardinal Maida resigns as head of the Archdiocese of Detroit, he no longer has the powers specifically associated with that appointment. In other words, he would no longer have the power to govern the Archdiocese of Detroit. And, because his role as metropolitan of the province was linked with being archbishop of Detroit, he would no longer have that role either. He would still be a bishop, however, because of his ordination, and still a cardinal because that was an honor given to him personally.

We can now apply these same principles to the pope. In 1958, Pope John Paul II, then a priest of the Archdiocese of Krakow, was ordained an assistant bishop of Krakow. He was appointed archbishop of Krakow in 1964, and he was created a cardinal in 1967. Then on October 16, 1978, he was elected bishop of Rome.

If he resigns as bishop of Rome, all the responsibilities and powers linked with that office are no longer his. He is, therefore, no longer: vicar of Peter; head of the college of bishops; patriarch of the West, primate (i.e., chief bishop) of the bishops of Italy; metropolitan of the dioceses surrounding Rome, or head of Vatican City-State.

He would remain a bishop and a cardinal.

Where Would a Pope Live After Resigning?

The bishop of Rome is a member of the Conference of Italian Bishops. If he resigns, he continues as a member of that episcopal conference. He may want to stay among them. However, he is free, as any retired bishop is free, to live wherever he wishes.

The Petrine office is a gift of God to the church. The more we understand it properly, the more we appreciate its worth. The Lord assured us: "I still have many things to say to you, but you cannot bear them now. When Spirit of truth comes, he will guide you into all the truth; for he will not speak on his own, but will speak whatever he hears, and he will declare to you the things that are to come. He will glorify me, because he will take what is mine and declare it to you" (John 16:12–15).

This gift of the Spirit has been given to the whole church, and because of this the believing community can be united in one faith. If this unity of faith is to be more than an abstraction, we need the competent exercise of authority in the church. We believe that this has been given to us in the Petrine office, as well as in the whole body of bishops acting together with the pope.

We need the work of theologians, the plurality of various schools of thought, and the sense of the faith that exists in believers around the world. But we have to be able to rise above the restricted outlook of one or the other of these expressions of the faith. We need to learn from one another, but also to know the difference between a particular school of thought and the doctrine of the believing church. The Petrine office is a ministry within the church that enables us to do this.

But it has to be seen in its fullness. Our faith does not rest upon one person, or upon one office in the church that acts alone or with only one part of the church. When we see the Petrine office in its fullness, we rediscover a treasure that is too often obscured and made less believable because it is popularly perceived as isolated, individual, or quasi-magical.

The Petrine office deserves our respect, as does the person who exercises that office. There are some who can so focus on the person of a particular pope with whom they have some disagreement that they become disrespectful of the office. There are others who, in agreement with a particular pope, so focus on the person that they risk future disrespect if his successor is not to their liking.

A clearer understanding of the church's teaching on the nature of the Petrine office enhances it. It has a positive effect, not a negative one. Such an understanding lays the groundwork for a fuller sense and use of collegiality without fear. It also makes the Petrine office more believable for Catholics, and widens the door to greater ecumenical understanding.

In his encyclical *Ut Unum Sint*, Pope John Paul II committed himself "to find a way of exercising the primacy which, while in no way renouncing what is essential to its mission, is nonetheless open to a new situation" (no. 95). It could be that the discussion generated by considering even the possibility of his resignation will itself be that "new situation" that helps all of us to arrive at a restored and refreshed understanding of the Petrine office.

Cardinal Dearden:
A Gentleman of the Church

America (November 26, 1988)

The long line of bishops started down the aisle of the Detroit cathedral. John Dearden's funeral was over. In the midst of this procession, applause began to come forth from the congregation, swelling to a sustained thunderous ovation that sent chills up and down one's spine.

The applauding congregation was a very diverse group of people. Among them were lay people of every kind, the presbyterate of Detroit (hardly a homogeneous group), religious, and a number of priests who had left the active ministry during the cardinal's tenure. Why were they applauding so?

There echoed in my mind the memory of a similar ovation given to this man by an equally diverse group twelve years earlier.

The Call to Action. The year was 1976. To celebrate our nation's bicentennial, the U.S. bishops had planned two major events—a eucharistic congress led by Cardinal John Krol in Philadelphia and a national justice conference entitled a "Call to Action," led by Cardinal John F. Dearden in Detroit. Preparations for the Call to Action included hearings in designated regions and small-group discussions in parishes around the country. From this process there emerged concerns and recommendations from the grass roots on issues such as racism, the laity, women, sexuality, divorced Catholics, birth control, the quality of preaching, and youth.

In October 1976, over 2,000 delegates and observers and 110 bishops met in Detroit to discuss and vote on the recommendations. During these discussions, things were said that seemed shocking to some. (Cardinal Dearden later defended the process by pointing out that lay people had not had the opportunity to speak up on these things for a long time, and so one should not expect them to express all their thoughts and feelings in a calm and orderly fashion.)

Toward the end of the four-day conference, after people had expressed just about every point of view (including protesters waving signs that read "Get rid of the Red Cardinal"), Cardinal Dearden was called upon to address the participants. As he came forward, they rose to their feet in a thunderous ovation that lasted several minutes.

They were applauding him, of course. But they were applauding even more for the church for which he stood.

Vatican II: A Paradigm Shift. Vatican II was not simply part of the ebb and flow of the church's tide as one age follows another. It was more like the sea rising to a new level and breaking through the rocks and cliffs of the shoreline, forming a larger sea with a new configuration, changing the topography. We have not yet been able to chart this sea or fully understand it.

None of the twenty preceding ecumenical councils, from the first in AD 325 to the twentieth in 1869, were like Vatican II. Their length (some lasted only two weeks), their procedures (handled by a small controlling group), their participants (a fraction of the bishops of the world), their purpose (to deal with very specific problems, often disciplinary), and their decrees (usually in the form of condemnatory canons) set them in a different category. They were called to put out fires. Vatican II was called to build one, and to do this it brought together for the first time the bishops of the entire world.

What happened at Vatican II might be compared to the great plates shifting beneath the earth. They don't move fast or far, but when they move the effects are monumental. At Vatican II, the great plates beneath the church shifted in a way that hadn't happened since perhaps the first century. We have experienced some of the vibrations, but we have not yet experienced or understood the full effects of this shift.

Cardinal Dearden understood the shift more than most, and he expressed it in his episcopal leadership. In so doing, he helped us catch a glimpse of a church that has not yet come to be.

The People of God. Through his experience at Vatican II, Cardinal Dearden came to understand at a very profound level that the mystery of the church lives in the entire people of God. That sounds simple enough—we would all get it right on a multiple-choice test. But John Dearden understood the depth of that statement—he had helped to shape the documents that expressed it. He really believed that it was so. And he lived it out.

The mystery of the church lives in the entire people of God. This is a truth easy to say, hard to live—especially if one is in a leadership position. Consider its implications.

The church does not have a written constitution. Rather, it has a living tradition, sustained by the Spirit. As Venerable Bede put it, "The Church gives birth to the Church every day."

If this mystery is not contained in a written constitution, where does one find it? Who "carries" it? Who passes it on from generation to generation?

In years past, we would surely have answered: the hierarchy. They hold it, protect it, and pass it on to the lay people. *The Baltimore Catechism* spoke of the indwelling of the Spirit in the church and then explained this exclusively in terms of the hierarchy teaching, sanctifying, and ruling the faithful.

Vatican II gave a radically different perspective. The mystery of the church lives in the entire people of God.

About a year ago, Cardinal Dearden came to the Diocese of Saginaw and gave a presentation, which was videotaped, on Vatican II. At one point, he spoke of the genesis of the second chapter of the Dogmatic Constitution on the Church *(Lumen Gentium)*, "The People of God." He explained that in the winter of 1963, after going through several drafts, the first three chapters of the Dogmatic Constitution were entitled: (1) "The Mystery of the Church"; (2) "The Hierarchical Structure of the Church"; (3) "The People of God, Especially the Laity." The implication was that the mystery of the church (chapter 1) lived first of all in the hierarchy (chapter 2) and was handed down as from a source to the people of God, understood primarily as the laity (chapter 3). "But then it was decided," Cardinal Dearden explained, "even before we got to the fall session, that there was a basic deficiency in this. We needed to put in a chapter between the first and second to show that the mystery of the church lives in the entire people of God. So we pulled out of the first and third chapters the elements that enabled us to constitute a new second chapter entitled simply 'The People of God.' This represented a major shift. *The structure of the document is almost as significant as its content....*It is very much misunderstood, even to this day."

Then he told the story of a priest who was leading the General Intercessions at Mass. He prayed, "For the Holy Father, the bishops, priests, religious, and the people of God." Cardinal Dearden smiled and said, "The wrong word in there was the 'and.' We are *all* the people of God...the Holy Father, the bishops, the priests, the laity, the entire church."

A Man of the Church. You must understand this about Cardinal Dearden: He was from the top of his head to the soles of his feet a man of the church.

Some wonder how "Iron John" came later to be seen as "Gentle John." They are wrong who suggest that there was some dramatic change in his personality. Cardinal Dearden's personality, temperament, social relationships, spirituality, and way of life stayed basically the same before and after Vatican II. What changed was the church, and this man who lived and breathed the church caught the change and was able to embody it in his ministry.

This was not without considerable effort on his part. The church after Vatican II was not something that naturally fit the personality of Cardinal Dearden. It was the other way around. He fit his personality to the Vatican II church. John Dearden was not a liberal turned loose by the council. He acted out of virtue, not inclination. He knew well what he was doing and knew well the cost. He was able to go against the grain, to accept things that were other than the way he was made, and through it all to be true to himself. He saw his duty, and he did it—gracefully.

A New Style of Church Leadership. The gift of Cardinal Dearden was that when he realized that a thing was true, though clear out of his ken, he was able to take it in. He saw clearly what he saw but knew there was more to be seen. He was open to questions not of his own making. He was humble enough to wonder sometimes if he was right. He was secure enough to go with insights that sometimes made him wonder.

There are some who simply will not listen to a different point of view. They do not have the inner strength or the patience for such things.

There are others who listen but are unable to receive what is said. They have constructed their own world view, and it is complete and inflexible. If you say something that does not fit, they will listen politely and then correct your error.

Then there are some who are able to listen and receive what you say. They do not have a world view so complete and so tight that everything must fit into it or be rejected. They are able to rise to a higher synthesis and broaden their horizons to include things that once seemed outside of them.

Cardinal Dearden was such a person. I never heard him say, "because I said so." He always had reasons, and he wanted to hear yours. He listened and took in what you said, and if it rang true, he could accept it. Actually, he was more a listener than an oracle. Because of this, he became a symbol of a new model of the church.

During his years as president of the newly formed National Council of Catholic Bishops (NCCB), there were some, myself included, who thought he should use the power of this position to exercise more influence through statements and speeches on various issues. On one occasion when we were pressing him to do so, he said, "You have to remember…I am president of the bishops' conference, not czar. I don't have something all that important to say on everything. It's better to have something to say than to have to say something."

Another time some of us wanted him to form a committee to deal with a particular issue. He was willing but reminded us, "Don't ever ask for people's advice unless you are really open to take seriously what they have to say." He wasn't suggesting that committees should always have the final say. He was simply pointing out that one had to enter such a process with an open mind, which, as I recall, was the farthest thing from our minds at the time. This was a subtle reminder that the Spirit works through the people of God, that church leaders should not use committees to bolster their own preordained conclusions.

At the 1987 NCCB meeting, the assembled bishops were engaged in a long and intense discussion about the statement to be issued on the Hunthausen case. A statement had been drafted by the executive committee, and many bishops rose to remind us that the committee put hours and hours into this…it was a very complicated and delicate matter…and we should trust their wisdom. Others rose to object to various aspects of the statement and the debate went on…and on.

Toward the end of a long afternoon Cardinal Dearden raised his hand. He stood and turned, not to the head table, but to the body of bishops and said, "I, as you, appreciate the hard work of the executive committee, but I would be careful about putting too much emphasis on this. Remember, they work on behalf of the entire body, and at this moment we have the entire body gathered together. It is the wisdom of the entire body, not of the executive committee, that is important here."

It was the same theme—the Spirit works in the entire people of God. Cardinal Dearden believed this whether it had to do with the executive committee of the NCCB in relation to the entire body, or whether it had to do with the hierarchy in relation to the laity.

This is a truth easy to say, hard to live. It is food for thought whether you are a pastor or a director of religious education, a bishop or a parish liturgy commission member, head of a parish council or chancellor of a diocese, pope or pastoral associate, curial cardinal or head of the parish carnival, musician or monsignor.

Advice for the Future. At the end of Cardinal Dearden's talk in Saginaw on Vatican II, as the question-and-answer session was winding down, I asked if he would have any advice for us "younger folks" in the church who might get discouraged now and then because of certain things we see happening today. His response I have transcribed from the videotape:

> We have to realize what the church is. It is not simply a human institution that has one policy in one administration, and a different policy in another. It is more than a human institution. It is something that comes to us through Christ, and the action of the Spirit, accomplishing his will in his time and in his way.
>
> We must be conscious of the action of the Spirit not here and there, but at all times. I speak as one who was present for what I would call dramatic moments in the manifestation of the Spirit, particularly in the council.

You could almost feel the Spirit moving us in a particular direction.

When you are conscious of that, then the church isn't just something you judge by human standards or procedures. It is something of God, in spite of its human imperfections. I know and you know that it is never going to achieve the fullness of its perfection on earth. We have to accept the imperfections. We are, after all, pilgrims on a journey, and pilgrims get dirty. The road is a dusty one. But we should not let this cause us to lose sight of the more profound reality of what the church is—the instrument of God that he has given us to bring us closer to him, and to bring all people closer to him.

It is this that gives me hope, and confidence, and love for the church. A love of the church ought to be a basic part of our lives. But you can love it only if you understand it, and you can understand it only through faith. The first chapter of *Lumen Gentium* on the mystery of the church—the one that is so often passed over—is profound. It presents to us God's design for his creatures, and it talks of how this design is to be realized— imperfectly, but realized nonetheless. This is the underlying reality of the church. And in God's own way, and in God's own time, it will come.

Bishop Kenneth Untener:
An Appreciation

Archbishop John R. Quinn

At Bishop Untener's funeral, I was reminiscing about Ken with Cardinal Maida, who had come from Detroit. The Cardinal said, "He really was our brother." Often I think of his visits to California and how he would arrive from the airport in the early evening, and through the old beveled glass of the front door I could see the darkened outline of a man carrying a knapsack on his back. When I opened the door, there he stood with his smile and friendly greeting. It was the visit of a brother, someone familiar, who was at home even in a distant place, someone who belonged, a member of the family.

This spontaneous, amiable warmth belonged to a man who did his doctoral studies on the eminent French theologian Yves Congar. Like Ken, I have always loved Congar. Congar's knowledge was vast but his thought lucid. Ken, too, was always lucid, orderly in his thought, and, like Congar, Ken was marked by a fierce love for the Church one and Catholic and a love for truth.

His own great talent enabled him to teach and write and speak thoughtfully and effectively on issues of current interest in the Church. Like Congar, Ken was sometimes misrepresented, but a striking quality was that this never made him bitter or hostile to those who criticized him. He was never closed to argument or disagreement. He weighed it carefully without rancor and accepted it graciously.

During his visits with me, we concelebrated Mass each day. His unaffected and simple demeanor and his way of praying the liturgy made it evident that this was a man of firm faith, a man who prayed and for whom God was indeed a living God. This enabled him to live with courage and magnanimity, with charity toward all, and in the larger perspective of Providence.

This book enables his voice to speak his witness of charity, clarity, and faith once more. His deepest goal was service to the Church in the conviction of John's Gospel that the real goal of faith is life: "I have come that you may have life." Surely those who may find fault with one or other position taken in this book will feel challenged to emulate the charity and goodness of heart, the faith and perseverance of a humble bishop who never forgot that he was a disciple.